BAUER WORLD PRESS

Bauer World Press gladly makes available an array of literary treasures hailing from around the globe.

In each accessible volume, Bauer World Press upholds its dedication to erudition by furnishing only the most authentic and original texts.

Unwavering commitment to research and accuracy spans the breadth of our works, often augmented with commentary and context.

Our Works

ALL QUIET ON THE WESTERN FRONT

THE ART OF BEING RIGHT
38 Ways to Win an Argument

THE ART OF MONEY GETTING
or, Golden Rules for Making Money

COMMON SENSE

FROM SILENCE TO STATESMAN
Essays & Writings of Benjamin Franklin

THE HARDY BOYS
Tower Treasure

THE LIFE OF CHARLEMAGNE
Vita Karoli Magni

THE TRUMPETER OF KRAKOW

BAUER WORLD PRESS

From Silence to Statesman

Essays & Writings of
Benjamin Franklin

Written by
Benjamin Franklin

Introduction by
Ingall Nocturne

BAUER WORLD PRESS

Bauer World Press is a division of The Bauer Company™.
Bauer World Press furthers the Company's objective of excellence in historical research, education, and knowledge by publishing digital and paperback content worldwide.

First Published as a Bauer World Press Paperback 2024

info@bauerworldpress.com

Paperback ISBN: 979-8-9920278-0-8
Hardcover ISBN: 979-8-9920278-2-2

Published in the United States of America by Bauer World Press

CONTENTS

Part III

Part IV

Part V

Part VI

Part VII

Part VIII

Introduction

If this is your initial exposure to the writings of Benjamin Franklin, I must inform you that you are opening a door which may not easily close. Diligent in his industry, Franklin's craft as a printer afforded him an outlet for the distillation and distribution of his accumulated wisdom. Operating as a seasoned engineer of writing mechanics, there exists in Franklin's work a thoughtful structure accompanying what is received by the reader as the appearance of fluid prose.

It was reading Charlie Munger, formerly the Vice Chairman of Berkshire Hathaway, where I grew intrigued about Franklin beyond common knowledge. Charlie seemed to reference Franklin every chance he could get when there was occasion for worldly wisdom. When journalist Becky Quick asked Charlie his thoughts on Franklin in an interview just months before his passing, Charlie had this to say: "He started in absolute poverty. He was almost entirely self-educated. To rise from that kind of a starting position, and become the best inventor in his country, the best scientist in his country, the best writer in his country, the best diplomat in his country—he was a very unusual person." I soon found Franklin's reach extended to other eminent personalities such as Warren Buffett, Elon Musk, Jamie Dimon, and Bill Ackman.

Acting on Charlie's advice, I purchased a copy of *The Autobiography*. You'll be pleased to know that I shall refrain from boring you with the details regarding the immediate effects this book had on me; however, I ask you allow this brief thought: The impact of Franklin's work on the life of this individual has since been immeasurable. The value of *The Autobiography, Poor Richard*, and the contents herein of *From Silence to Statesman*, have been markedly generous in equipping my personage with invaluable knowledge, felicity, and solace. Perhaps it will do the same for you.

Upon reading the *Autobiography* or perusing *Poor Richard,* one might observe Franklin's proclivity toward dense and memorable bon mots. As a result his essays, penetrative as they are creative, are often overlooked. This is a shame, as Franklin's more comprehensive papers pack the same punch as their shorter counterparts. In the years since, a great deal of Franklin's work has been incorrectly reprinted, inaccurately ascribed, and in many cases—lost. Nor did Franklin make the task of accounting for his work particularly straightforward. He assumed identities such as Silence Dogood, The Busy-Body, Americanus, Arator, and a smattering of acronymic pseudonyms. Thanks to the efforts of historians, as well as Franklin's own family and acquaintances, namely his grandson, William Temple Franklin; we possess today a plenitude of works positively identified as being written by Franklin.

This book will bring together those works under one roof; original diction and punctuation maintained in their inaugural form. Denying the temptation to embark upon analysis of these papers, I default to a simple question: Were one to read a comprehensive film-review prior to viewing, can one expect to absorb the same novel experience as the impartial viewer? Any attempt at analysis here will certainly fall short, or worse, spoil the joys of a new read; a pleasure which I myself enjoyed, and shan't deny that pleasure to others.

Franklin's work could command a lifetime of study, fortunately there are those who have taken up the challenge. For the greatest insight into Franklin's life there is no book I could recommend more than Carl van Doren's 1939 Pulitzer Prize winning biography, *Benjamin Franklin.* For a thoughtfully composed selection of Poor Richard's greatest quotes, I would recommend the Peter Pauper Press version of *Poor Richard's Al-*

manack. Regarding full-editions of *Poor Richard's Almanack*, Bauer World Press will be publishing all *Almanack's* (1732-1758) as a sequential volume to this book in the upcoming year. If no such volume surfaces, presume us broke or perished.

In the arrangement of this text, it appeared initially suitable to topically categorise Franklin's writings. The problem that arose had to do with Franklin's polymathy. Even if one were to arrange Franklin's works by overarching themes of Philosophy, Science, Politics, Industry, Self-Improvement, et cetera; there is too much gradation in subject matter to definitively pigeonhole neat labels. Worse yet, ascribing such labels risks detracting from the nuance of the essays themselves. Alternatively, by arranging this work in order of chronological publication, the focus shifts to Franklin's development as a pansophic writer. Observe how his clarity and order of thought develop from the early letters of "Silence Dogood" up through more urgent critiques as in "Plain Truth." Observe the ways in which irreverence, satire, morality, and Socratic enquiry fortify his positions, epigrammatically appealing to a common logic that few are able to articulate with comparable brevity.

For those unfamiliar with Franklin's writing, the Silence Dogood Letters are a prime initiation into his burgeoning style. Writing under his own name in 1722 at a mere sixteen years-of-age, Franklin was denied publication in his brother's newspaper, *The New-England Courant*. Despite for making up in ability what he lacked in age, an escalating feud between Benjamin and the elder James meant that Franklin's likelihood of authorship grew increasingly bleak. In order to circumvent this, Franklin took up a habit that would continue throughout his life—publishing his work under pseudonymous personas.

The character of Silence Dogood was a middle-aged widow. She was virtuous, patriotic, and opinionated; expressing it all with a keen wit. Her commentary concerned a breadth of subjects most often having to do with, and critiquing, life in the Colonies. Franklin knew that an adolescent was unlikely to be taken seriously by the general public, an observation he touches on in the opening lines of the First Letter. But Silence Dogood? She possessed the benefit of years, living through the throes of fortune and misfortune; now humbly offering her findings to the general public over a series of Fourteen Letters.

The strain between Benjamin and his brother James continued. After Franklin anonymously published the Silence Dogood Letters, he determined it was time to carve his own way.

Upon running away from his native Boston to Philadelphia at the age of seventeen, Franklin sought work as a printer. As anyone working in Franklin's trade knew, the biggest name in town was Andrew Bradford. Not only was Bradford a printer and newspaper publisher, he was also Postmaster. This allowed him to distribute his newspapers throughout Pennsylvania essentially free of competition.

When Franklin attempted to land a job with the affluent printer, Bradford informed him no openings were available; however, he would introduce Franklin to a rival printer (of little consequence), Samuel Keimer. The London-born Keimer was mercurial, choleric, and worked with an old printing-press using worn out typefaces. Franklin, having come to Philadelphia without a pence in his pocket, begrudgingly took the job with Keimer. Once it came to light that Keimer's eventual plans for a newspaper were no more than a ruse to retain Franklin's employ, he quit. Enticed by a series of empty-promises by the excitable and unreliable Sir William Keith, Franklin found himself working as a printer in London for the next eighteen months.

After returning to Philadelphia, Franklin and another of Keimer's employees, Hugh Meredith, established a partnership creating their own printing press. The problem, however, was that they faced a great competitive disadvantage. Despite Keimer's business being poorly managed and accumulating debt, he was well-connected in Philadelphia. Even worse, Andrew Bradford had grown to become largest printer in Pennsylvania, receiving preferment as the official printer to the Pennsylvania Government.

Franklin knew they would have to work like never before to make a name for themselves; however, Meredith proved to not share the same ambitious qualities. In order to drum up business, Franklin found himself doubling-down on his connections within the Junto, an intellectual-social-club he'd founded years before. It was here an opportunity arose.

For three years, Keimer had been composing a publication of the *Folio History of the Quakers* by William Sewel for the local Quaker community. Joseph Breitnal, a Junto member, secured from the Quakers a portion of the Sewel publication to be printed by Franklin.

Franklin toiled through sleepless nights, pushing out page-after-page of the *Folio*, completing the contract in an astonishing forty days. "This industry, visible to our neighbours; began to give us character and credit-" said Franklin. This local credibility was crucial, as Franklin was planning his most ambitious move yet—the launch of a newspaper.

Upon hearing his ex-employee planned to enter the newspaper business, Keimer, notwithstanding his mounting debt, rushed to establish *The Pennsylvania Gazette*. Franklin possessed not the means nor the distribution to launch his newspaper in competition with Keimer. After Bradford's successful *American Weekly Mercury*, there was hardly room for a second newspaper in Philadelphia, let alone a third.

So what did Franklin do? Instead of fighting the tide, he went with it. While it may appear counterintuitive, Franklin responded to Keimer's launch by writing an anonymous series of letters for Bradford's *Mercury* newspaper titled the Busy-Body. Indeed, while this may have increased the readership of the *Mercury*, it achieved Franklin's ultimate goal, detracting readers from Keimer.

Similar to the Dogood Letters, the Busy-Body is straightforward and humourous. It was an opportunity for Franklin to express his position on ethics, values, and urge the general public toward the useful pursuit of knowledge. It was a commentary on life in Philadelphia, which Franklin believed readers would find reassuring and relatable. Lastly, it took subtle digs at Keimer. Even if readers weren't aware to whom the Busy-Body specifically referred, Franklin's penmanship was unmistakable to his former employer.

Keimer's poor management and risky gambles compounded. He began evading his debtors and planned to flee Philadelphia for the sunny shores of Barbados. So, what was to become of the *The Pennsylvania Gazette*? Keimer had no choice but to find a buyer for his fledgling newspaper. Fortunately, a buyer stepped forward—Benjamin Franklin.

Ladies and Gentlemen, From Silence to Statesman

Ingall Nocturne

From Silence to Statesman

Essays & Writings of
Benjamin Franklin

Part I

2 APRIL, 1722 - 1726

Silence Dogood No. 1

Silence Dogood No. 2

Silence Dogood No. 3

Silence Dogood No. 4

Silence Dogood No. 6

Silence Dogood No. 8

Silence Dogood No. 12

Silence Dogood No. 14

On Titles of Honor

Plan for Attaining Moral Perfection

Silence Dogood, No. 1

2 April, 1722

To the Author of the *New-England Courant.*

Sir,

It may not be improper in the first place to inform your Readers, that I intend once a Fortnight to present them, by the Help of this Paper, with a short Epistle, which I presume will add somewhat to their Entertainment.

And since it is observed, that the Generality of People, now a days, are unwilling either to commend or dispraise what they read, until they are in some measure informed who or what the Author of it is, whether he be *poor* or *rich, old* or *young*, a *Schollar* or a *Leather Apron Man*, &c. and give their Opinion of the Performance, according to the Knowledge which they have of the Author's Circumstances, it may not be amiss to begin with a short Account of my past Life and present Condition, that the Reader may not be at a Loss to judge whether or not my Lucubrations are worth his reading.

At the time of my Birth, my Parents were on Ship-board in their Way from London to N. England. My Entrance into this troublesome World was attended with the Death of my Father, a Misfortune, which tho' I was not then capable of knowing, I shall never be able to forget; for as he, poor Man, stood upon the Deck rejoycing at my Birth, a merciless Wave entred the Ship, and in one Moment carry'd him beyond Reprieve. Thus, was the *first Day* which I saw, the *last* that was seen by my Father; and thus was my disconsolate Mother at once made both a *Parent* and a *Widow.*

When we arrived at Boston (which was not long after) I was put to Nurse in a Country Place, at a small Distance from the Town, where I went to School, and past my Infancy and Childhood in Vanity and Idleness, until I was bound out Apprentice, that I might no longer be a Charge to my Indigent Mother, who was put to hard Shifts for a Living.

My Master was a Country Minister, a pious good-natur'd young Man, and a Batchelor: He labour'd with all his Might to instil vertuous and godly Principles into my tender Soul, well knowing that it was the most suitable Time to make deep and lasting Impressions on the Mind, while it was yet untainted with Vice, free and unbiass'd. He endeavour'd that I might be instructed in all that Knowledge and Learning which is necessary for our Sex, and deny'd me no Accomplishment that could possibly be attained in a Country Place; such as all Sorts of Needle-Work, Writing, Arithmetick, &c. and observing that I took a more than ordinary Delight in reading ingenious Books, he gave me the free Use of his Library, which tho' it was but small, yet it was well chose, to inform the Understanding rightly, and enable the Mind to frame great and noble Ideas.

Before I had liv'd quite two Years with this Reverend Gentleman, my indulgent Mother departed this Life, leaving me as it were by my self, having no Relation on Earth within my Knowledge.

I will not abuse your Patience with a tedious Recital of all the frivolous Accidents of my Life, that happened from this Time until I arrived to Years of Discretion, only inform you that I liv'd a chearful Country Life, spending my leisure Time either in some innocent Diversion with the neighbouring Females, or in some shady Retirement, with the best of Company, *Books*. Thus I past away the Time with a Mixture of Profit and Pleasure, having no affliction but what was imaginary, and created in my own Fancy; as nothing is more common with us Women, than to be grieving for nothing, when we have nothing else to grieve for.

As I would not engross too much of your Paper at once, I will defer the Remainder of my Story until my next Letter; in the mean time desiring your Readers to exercise their Patience, and bear with my Humours now and then, because I shall trouble them but seldom. I am not insensible of the Impossibility of pleasing all, but I would not willingly displease any; and for those who will take Offence where none is intended, they are beneath the Notice of Your Humble Servant,

Silence Dogood

Silence Dogood, No. 2

16 April, 1722

To the Author of the *New-England Courant.*

Sir,

Histories of Lives are seldom entertaining, unless they contain something either admirable or exemplar: And since there is little or nothing of this Nature in my own Adventures, I will not tire your Readers with tedious Particulars of no Consequence, but will briefly, and in as few Words as possible, relate the most material Occurrences of my Life, and according to my Promise, confine all to this Letter.

My Reverend Master who had hitherto remained a Batchelor, (after much Meditation on the Eighteenth verse of the Second Chapter of Genesis,) took up a Resolution to marry; and having made several unsuccessful fruitless Attempts on the more topping Sort of our Sex, and being tir'd with making troublesome Journeys and Visits to no Purpose, he began unexpectedly to cast a loving Eye upon Me, whom he had brought up cleverly to his Hand.

There is certainly scarce any Part of a Man's Life in which he appears more silly and ridiculous, than when he makes his first Onset in Courtship. The aukward Manner in which my Master first discover'd his Intentions, made me, in spite of my Reverence to his Person, burst out into an unmannerly Laughter: However, having ask'd his Pardon, and with much ado compos'd my Countenance, I promis'd him I would take his Proposal into serious Consideration, and speedily give him an Answer.

As he had been a great Benefactor (and in a Manner a Father to me) I could not well deny his Request, when I once perceived he was in earnest. Whether it was Love, or Gratitude, or Pride, or all Three that made me consent, I know not; but it is certain, he found it no hard Matter, by the Help of his Rhetorick, to conquer my Heart, and perswade me to marry him.

This unexpected Match was very astonishing to all the Country round about, and served to furnish them with Discourse for a long Time after; some approving it, others disliking it, as they were led by their various Fancies and Inclinations.

We lived happily together in the Heighth of conjugal Love and mutual Endearments, for near Seven Years, in which Time we added Two likely Girls and a Boy to the Family of the Dogoods: But alas! When my Sun was in its meridian Altitude, inexorable unrelenting Death, as if he had envy'd my Happiness and Tranquility, and resolv'd to make me entirely miserable by the Loss of so good an Husband, hastened his Flight to the Heavenly World, by a sudden unexpected Departure from this.

I have now remained in a State of Widowhood for several Years, but it is a State I never much admir'd, and I am apt to fancy that I could be easily perswaded to marry again, provided I was sure of a good-humour'd, sober, agreeable Companion: But one, even with these few good Qualities, being hard to find, I have lately relinquish'd all Thoughts of that Nature.

At present I pass away my leisure Hours in Conversation, either with my honest Neighbour Rusticus and his Family, or with the ingenious Minister of our Town, who now lodges at my House, and by whose Assistance I intend now and then to beautify my Writings with a Sentence or two in the learned Languages, which will not only be fashionable, and pleasing to those who do not understand it, but will likewise be very ornamental.

I shall conclude this with my own Character, which (one would think) I should be best able to give. *Know then*, That I am an Enemy to Vice, and a Friend to Vertue. I am one of an extensive Charity, and a great Forgiver of *private* Injuries: A hearty Lover of the Clergy and all good Men, and a mortal Enemy to arbitrary Government and unlimited Power. I am naturally very jealous for the Rights and Liberties of my Country; and the least appearance of an Incroachment on those invaluable Priviledges, is apt to make my Blood boil exceedingly. I have likewise a natural Inclination to observe and reprove the Faults of others, at which I have an excellent Faculty. I speak this by Way of Warning to all such whose Offences shall come under my Cognizance, for I never intend to wrap my Talent in a Napkin. To be brief; I am courteous and affable, good humour'd (unless I am first provok'd,) and handsome, and sometimes witty, but always, Sir, Your Friend and Humble Servant,

SILENCE DOGOOD

Silence Dogood, No. 3

30 April, 1722

To the Author of the *New-England Courant.*

Sir,

It is undoubtedly the Duty of all Persons to serve the Country they live in, according to their Abilities; yet I sincerely acknowledge, that I have hitherto been very deficient in this Particular; whether it was for want of Will or Opportunity, I will not at present stand to determine: Let it suffice, that I now take up a Resolution, to do for the future all that *lies in my Way* for the Service of my Countrymen.

I have from my Youth been indefatigably studious to gain and treasure up in my Mind all useful and desireable Knowledge, especially such as tends to improve the Mind, and enlarge the Understanding: And as I have found it very beneficial to me, I am not without Hopes, that communicating my small Stock in this Manner, by Peace-meal to the Publick, may be at least in some Measure useful.

I am very sensible that it is impossible for me, or indeed any *one* Writer to please *all* Readers at once. Various Persons have different Sentiments; and that which is pleasant and delightful to one, gives another a Disgust. He that would (in this Way of Writing) please all, is under a Necessity to make his Themes almost as numerous as his Letters. He must one while be merry and diverting, then more solid and serious; one while sharp and satyrical, then (to mollify that) be sober and religious; at one Time let the Subject be Politicks, then let the next Theme be Love: Thus will every one, one Time or other find some thing agreeable to his own Fancy, and in his Turn be delighted.

According to this Method I intend to proceed, bestowing now and then a few gentle Reproofs on those who deserve them, not forgetting at the same time to applaud those whose Actions merit Commendation. And here I must not forget to invite the ingenious Part of your Readers, particularly those of my own Sex to enter into a Correspondence with me, assuring them, that their Condescension in this Particular shall be received as a Favour, and accordingly acknowledged.

I think I have now finish'd the Foundation, and I intend in my next to begin to raise the Building. Having nothing more to write at present, I must make the usual excuse in such Cases, of *being in haste*, assuring you that I speak from my Heart when I call my self, The most humble and obedient of all the Servants your Merits have acquir'd,

Silence Dogood

Silence Dogood, No. 4

14 May, 1722

An sum etiam nunc vel Graecè loqui vel Latinè docendus?[1] Cicero.

To the Author of the *New-England Courant.*

Sir,

Discoursing the other Day at Dinner with my Reverend Boarder, formerly mention'd, (whom for Distinction sake we will call by the Name of Clericus,) concerning the Education of Children, I ask'd his Advice about my young Son William, whether or no I had best bestow upon him Academical Learning, or (as our Phrase is) *bring him up at our College:* He perswaded me to do it by all Means, using many weighty Arguments with me, and answering all the Objections that I could form against it; telling me withal, that he did not doubt but that the Lad would take his Learning very well, and not idle away his Time as too many there now-a-days do. These Words of Clericus gave me a Curiosity to inquire a little more strictly into the present Circumstances of that famous Seminary of Learning; but the Information which he gave me, was neither pleasant, nor such as I expected.

As soon as Dinner was over, I took a solitary Walk into my Orchard, still ruminating on Clericus's Discourse with much Consideration, until I came to my usual Place of Retirement under the *Great Apple-Tree;* where having seated my self, and carelessly laid my Head on a verdant Bank, I fell

---

1. *Must I still be taught either to speak Greek or Latin?*

by Degrees into a soft and undisturbed Slumber. My waking Thoughts remained with me in my Sleep, and before I awak'd again, I dreamt the following DREAM.

I fancy'd I was travelling over pleasant and delightful Fields and Meadows, and thro' many small Country Towns and Villages; and as I pass'd along, all Places resounded with the Fame of the Temple of LEARNING: Every Peasant, who had wherewithal, was preparing to send one of his Children at least to this famous Place; and in this Case most of them consulted their own Purses instead of their Childrens Capacities: So that I observed, a great many, yea, the most part of those who were travelling thither, were little better than Dunces and Blockheads. Alas! alas!

At length I entred upon a spacious Plain, in the Midst of which was erected a large and stately Edifice: It was to this that a great Company of Youths from all Parts of the Country were going; so stepping in among the Crowd, I passed on with them, and presently arrived at the Gate.

The Passage was kept by two sturdy Porters named *Riches* and *Poverty*, and the latter obstinately refused to give Entrance to any who had not first gain'd the Favour of the former; so that I observed, many who came even to the very Gate, were obliged to travel back again as ignorant as they came, for want of this necessary Qualification. However, as a Spectator I gain'd Admittance, and with the rest entred directly into the Temple.

In the Middle of the great Hall stood a stately and magnificent Throne, which was ascended to by two high and difficult Steps. On the Top of it sat LEARNING in awful State; she was apparelled wholly in Black, and surrounded almost on every Side with innumerable Volumes in all Languages. She seem'd very busily employ'd in writing something on half a Sheet of Paper, and upon Enquiry, I understood she was preparing a Paper, call'd, *The New-England Courant*. On her Right Hand sat *English*, with a pleasant smiling Countenance, and handsomely attir'd; and on her left were seated several *Antique Figures* with their Faces vail'd. I was considerably puzzl'd to guess who they were, until one informed me, (who stood beside me,) that those Figures on her left Hand were *Latin, Greek, Hebrew*, &c. and that they were very much reserv'd, and seldom or never unvail'd their Faces here, and then to few or none, tho' most of those who have in this Place acquir'd so much Learning as to distinguish them from *English*, pretended to an intimate Acquaintance with them. I then enquir'd of him, what could be the Reason why they continued vail'd, in this Place especially: He pointed to the Foot of the Throne, where I saw *Idleness*, attended with *Ignorance*, and these (he informed me) were they, who first vail'd them, and still kept them so.

Now I observed, that the whole Tribe who entred into the Temple with me, began to climb the Throne; but the Work proving troublesome and difficult to most of them, they withdrew their Hands from the Plow, and contented themselves to sit at the Foot, with Madam *Idleness* and her Maid *Ignorance*, until those who were assisted by Diligence and a docible Temper, had well nigh got up the first Step: But the Time drawing nigh in which they could no way avoid ascending, they were fain to crave the Assistance of those who had got up before them, and who, for the Reward perhaps of a *Pint of Milk*, or a *Piece of Plumb-Cake*, lent the Lubbers a helping Hand, and sat them in the Eye of the World, upon a Level with themselves.

The other Step being in the same Manner ascended, and the usual Ceremonies at an End, every Beetle-Scull seem'd well satisfy'd with his own Portion of Learning, tho' perhaps he was *e'en just* as ignorant as ever. And now the Time of their Departure being come, they march'd out of Doors to make Room for another Company, who waited for Entrance: And I, having seen all that was to be seen, quitted the Hall likewise, and went to make my Observations on those who were just gone out before me.

Some I perceiv'd took to Merchandizing, others to Travelling, some to one Thing, some to another, and some to Nothing; and many of them from henceforth, for want of Patrimony, liv'd as poor as Church Mice, being unable to dig, and asham'd to beg, and to live by their Wits it was impossible. But the most Part of the Crowd went along a large beaten Path, which led to a Temple at the further End of the Plain, call'd, *The Temple of Theology*.

The Business of those who were employ'd in this Temple being laborious and painful, I wonder'd exceedingly to see so many go towards it; but while I was pondering this Matter in my Mind, I spy'd *Pecunia* behind a Curtain, beckoning to them with her Hand, which Sight immediately satisfy'd me for whose Sake it was, that a great Part of them (I will not say all) travel'd that Road. In this Temple I saw nothing worth mentioning, except the ambitious and fraudulent Contrivances of Plagius, who (notwithstanding he had been severely reprehended for such Practices before) was diligently transcribing some eloquent Paragraphs out of Tillotson's *Works*, &c., to embellish his own.

Now I bethought my self in my Sleep, that it was Time to be at Home, and as I fancy'd I was travelling back thither, I reflected in my Mind on the extream Folly of those Parents, who, blind to their Childrens Dulness, and insensible of the Solidity of their Skulls, because they think their Purses can afford it, will needs send them to the Temple of Learning, where, for want of a suitable Genius, they learn little more than how to carry themselves handsomely, and enter a Room genteely, (which might as well be acquir'd at a Dancing-School,) and from whence they return, after Abundance of Trouble and Charge, as great Blockheads as ever, only more proud and self-conceited.

While I was in the midst of these unpleasant Reflections, Clericus (who with a Book in his Hand was walking under the Trees) accidentally awak'd me; to him I related my Dream with all its Particulars, and he, without much Study, presently interpreted it, assuring me, *That it was a lively Representation of* HARVARD COLLEGE, *Etcetera*. I remain, Sir, Your Humble Servant,

SILENCE DOGOOD

Silence Dogood, No. 6

11 June, 1722

Quem Dies videt veniens Superbum,
Hunc Dies vidit fugiens jacentem.[1] Seneca.

To the Author of the *New-England Courant.*

Sir,

Among the many reigning Vices of the Town which may at any Time come under my Consideration and Reprehension, there is none which I am more inclin'd to expose than that of *Pride*. It is acknowledg'd by all to be a Vice the most hateful to God and Man. Even those who nourish it in themselves, hate to see it in others. The proud Man aspires after Nothing less than an unlimited Superiority over his Fellow-Creatures. He has made himself a King in *Soliloquy;* fancies himself conquering the World; and the Inhabitants thereof consulting on proper Methods to acknowledge his Merit. I speak it to my Shame, I my self was a Queen from the Fourteenth to the Eighteenth Year of my Age, and govern'd the World all the Time of my being govern'd by my Master. But this speculative Pride may be the Subject of another Letter: I shall at present confine my Thoughts to what we call *Pride of Apparel*. This Sort of Pride has been growing upon us ever since we parted with our Homespun Cloaths for *Fourteen Penny Stuffs*, &c. And the *Pride of Apparel* has begot and nourish'd in us a *Pride of Heart*,

1. Whom the Day sees coming proudly, This Day sees fleeing, lying low.

which portends the Ruin of Church and State. *Pride goeth before Destruction, and a haughty Spirit before a Fall:* And I remember my late Reverend Husband would often say upon this Text, That a Fall was the *natural Consequence*, as well as *Punishment* of Pride. Daily Experience is sufficient to evince the Truth of this Observation. Persons of small Fortune under the Dominion of this Vice, seldom consider their Inability to maintain themselves in it, but strive to imitate their Superiors in Estate, or Equals in Folly, until one Misfortune comes upon the Neck of another, and every Step they take is a Step backwards. By striving to appear rich they become really poor, and deprive themselves of that Pity and Charity which is due to the humble poor Man, who is made so more immediately by Providence.

This Pride of Apparel will appear the more foolish, if we consider, that those airy Mortals, who have no other Way of making themselves considerable but by gorgeous Apparel, draw after them Crowds of Imitators, who hate each other while they endeavour after a Similitude of Manners. They destroy by Example, and envy one another's Destruction.

I cannot dismiss this Subject without some Observations on a particular Fashion now reigning among my own Sex, the most immodest and inconvenient of any the Art of Woman has invented, namely, that of *Hoop-Petticoats*. By these they are incommoded in their General and Particular Calling, and therefore they cannot answer the Ends of either necessary or ornamental Apparel. These monstrous topsy-turvy *Mortar-Pieces*, are neither fit for the Church, the Hall, or the Kitchen; and if a Number of them were well mounted on Noddles-Island, they would look more like Engines of War for bombarding the Town, than Ornaments of the Fair Sex. An honest Neighbour of mine, happening to be in Town some time since on a publick Day, inform'd me, that he saw four Gentlewomen with their Hoops half mounted in a Balcony, as they withdrew to the Wall, to the great Terror of the Militia, who (he thinks) might attribute their irregular Volleys to the formidable Appearance of the Ladies Petticoats.

I assure you, Sir, I have but little Hopes of perswading my Sex, by this Letter, utterly to relinquish the extravagant Foolery, and Indication of

Immodesty, in this monstrous Garb of their's; but I would at least desire them to lessen the Circumference of their Hoops, and leave it with them to consider, Whether they, who pay no Rates or Taxes, ought to take up more Room in the King's High-Way, than the Men, who yearly contribute to the Support of the Government. I am, Sir, Your Humble Servant,

SILENCE DOGOOD

Silence Dogood, No. 8

9 July, 1722

To the Author of the *New-England Courant.*

Sir,

I prefer the following Abstract from the London Journal to any Thing of my own, and therefore shall present it to your Readers this week without any further Preface.

"Without Freedom of Thought, there can be no such Thing as Wisdom; and no such Thing as publick Liberty, without Freedom of Speech; which is the Right of every Man, as far as by it, he does not hurt or controul the Right of another: And this is the only Check it ought to suffer, and the only Bounds it ought to know.

"This sacred Privilege is so essential to free Governments, that the Security of Property, and the Freedom of Speech always go together; and in those wretched Countries where a Man cannot call his Tongue his own, he can scarce call any Thing else his own. Whoever would overthrow the Liberty of a Nation, must begin by subduing the Freeness of Speech; a *Thing* terrible to Publick Traytors.

"This Secret was so well known to the Court of King Charles the First, that his wicked Ministry procured a Proclamation, to forbid the People to talk of Parliaments, which those Traytors had laid aside. To assert the undoubted Right of the Subject, and defend his Majesty's legal Prerogative, was called Disaffection, and punished as Sedition. Nay, People were forbid to talk of Religion in their Families: For the Priests had combined with the Ministers to cook up Tyranny, and suppress Truth and the Law, while the late King James, when Duke of York, went avowedly to Mass, Men were fined, imprisoned and undone, for saying he was a Papist: And that King Charles the Second might live more securely a Papist, there was an Act of Parliament made, declaring it Treason to say that he was one.

"That Men ought to speak well of *their Governours* is true, while *their Governours* deserve to be well spoken of; but to do publick Mischief, without hearing of it, is only the Prerogative and Felicity of Tyranny: A free People will be shewing that they are *so*, by their Freedom of Speech.

"The Administration of Government, is nothing else but the Attendance of the *Trustees of the People* upon the Interest and Affairs of the People: And as it is the Part and Business of the People, for whose Sake alone all publick Matters are, or ought to be transacted, to see whether they be well or ill transacted; so it is the Interest, and ought to be the Ambition, of all honest Magistrates, to have their Deeds openly examined, and publickly scann'd: Only the *wicked Governours* of Men dread what is said of them; *Audivit Tiberius probra queis lacerabitur, atque* perculsus est[1] . The publick Censure was true, else he had not felt it bitter.

"Freedom of Speech is ever the Symptom, as well as the Effect of a good Government. In old Rome, all was left to the Judgment and Pleasure of the People, who examined the publick Proceedings with such Discretion, and censured those who administred them with such Equity and Mildness, that in the space of Three Hundred Years, not five publick Ministers suffered unjustly. Indeed whenever the *Commons* proceeded to Violence, the great Ones had been the Agressors.

"*Guilt* only dreads Liberty of Speech, which drags it out of its lurking Holes, and exposes its Deformity and Horrour to Daylight. Horatius, Valerius, Cincinnatus, and other vertuous and undesigning Magistrates of the Roman Commonwealth, had nothing to fear from Liberty

1. *Tiberius heard the insults with which he was being torn apart, and he was struck with fear.*

of Speech. *Their virtuous* Administration, the more it was examin'd, the more it brightned and gain'd by Enquiry. When Valerius in particular, was accused upon some slight grounds of affecting the Diadem; he, who was the first Minister of Rome, does not accuse the People for examining his Conduct, but approved his Innocence in a Speech to them; and gave such Satisfaction to them, and gained such Popularity to himself, that they gave him a new Name; *inde cognomenfactum Publicolae est*[2]*;* to denote that he was their Favourite and their Friend. *Latae deinde leges—Ante omnes de provocatione*[3] ADVERSUS MAGISTRATUS AD POPULUM[4], Livii, lib. 2. Cap. 8.

"But Things afterwards took another Turn. Rome, with the Loss of its Liberty, lost also its Freedom of Speech; then Mens Words began to be feared and watched; and then first began the *poysonous Race of Informers*, banished indeed under the righteous Administration of Titus, Narva, Trajan, Aurelius, &c. but encouraged and enriched under the *vile Ministry* of Sejanus, Tigillinus, Pallas, and Cleander: *Queri libet, quod in secreta nostra non inquirant principes, nisi quos Odimus*[5], says Pliny to Trajan.

"The best Princes have ever encouraged and promoted Freedom of Speech; they know that upright Measures would defend themselves, and that all upright Men would defend them. Tacitus, speaking of the Reign of some of the Princes above mention'd, says with Extasy, *Rara Temporum*

---

2. *From this, the name Publicola was made.*

3. *Subsequently, laws were passed—Above all, concerning the right of appeal.*

4. *Against the Magistrate to the People*

5. *It is permissible to complain because our leaders do not inquire into our secrets, except those we hate.*

felicitate, ubi sentire quae velis, & quae sentias dicere licet: A blessed Time when you might think what you would, and speak what you thought.

"I doubt not but old Spencer and his Son, who were the *Chief Ministers* and *Betrayers* of Edward the Second, would have been very glad to have stopped the Mouths of all the honest Men in England. They dreaded to be called *Traytors*, because they were *Traytors*. And I dare say, Queen Elizabeth's Walsingham, who deserved no Reproaches, feared none. Misrepresentation of publick Measures is easily overthrown, by representing publick Measures truly; when they are honest, they ought to be publickly known, that they may be publickly commended; but if they are knavish or pernicious, they ought to be publickly exposed, in order to be publickly detested." Yours, &c.,

SILENCE DOGOOD

Silence Dogood, No. 10

13 August, 1722

Optimè societas hominum servabitur.[1] Cic.

To the Author of the *New-England Courant.*

Sir,

Discoursing lately with an intimate Friend of mine of the lamentable Condition of Widows, he put into my Hands a Book, wherein the ingenious Author proposes (I think) a certain Method for their Relief. I have often thought of some such Project for their Benefit my self, and intended to communicate my Thoughts to the Publick; but to prefer my own Proposals to what follows, would be rather an Argument of Vanity in me than Good Will to the many Hundreds of my Fellow-Sufferers now in New-England.

"We have (says he) abundance of Women, who have been Bred well, and Liv'd well, Ruin'd in a few Years, and perhaps, left Young, with a House full of Children, and nothing to Support them; which falls generally upon the Wives of the Inferior Clergy, or of Shopkeepers and Artificers.

"They marry Wives with perhaps £300 to £1000 Portion, and can settle no Jointure upon them; either they are Extravagant and Idle, and Waste it, or Trade decays, or Losses, or a Thousand Contingences happen to bring a Tradesman to Poverty, and he Breaks; the Poor Young Woman, it may be,

1. *The society of men will be best preserved.*

has Three or Four Children, and is driven to a thousand shifts, while he lies in the Mint or Fryars under the *Dilemma* of a Statute of Bankrupt; but if he Dies, then she is absolutely Undone, unless she has Friends to go to.

"Suppose an Office to be Erected, to be call'd *An Office of Ensurance for Widows*, upon the following Conditions;

"Two thousand Women, or their Husbands for them, Enter their Names into a Register to be kept for that purpose, with the Names, Age, and Trade of their Husbands, with the Place of their abode, Paying at the Time of their Entring 5*s.* down with 1*s.* 4*d.* *per* Quarter, which is to the setting up and support of an Office with Clerks, and all proper Officers for the same; *for there is no maintaining such without Charge;* they receive every one of them a Certificate, Seal'd by the Secretary of the Office, and Sign'd by the Governors, for the Articles hereafter mentioned.

"If any one of the Women becomes a Widow, at any Time after Six Months from the Date of her Subscription, upon due Notice given, and Claim made at the Office in form, as shall be directed, she shall receive within Six Months after such Claim made, the Sum of £500 in Money, without any Deductions, saving some small Fees to the Officers, which the Trustees must settle, that they may be known.

"In Consideration of this, every Woman so Subscribing, Obliges her self to Pay as often as any Member of the Society becomes a Widow, the due Proportion or Share allotted to her to Pay, towards the £500 for the said Widow, provided her Share does not exceed the Sum of 5*s.*

"No Seamen or Soldiers Wives to be accepted into such a Proposal as this, on the Account before mention'd, because the Contingences of their Lives are not equal to others, unless they will admit this general Exception, supposing they do not Die out of the Kingdom.

"It might also be an Exception, That if the Widow, that Claim'd, had really, *bona fide*, left her by her Husband to her own use, clear of all Debts and Legacies, £2000 she shou'd have no Claim; the Intent being to Aid the Poor, not add to the Rich. But there lies a great many Objections against such an Article: As

"1. It may tempt some to forswear themselves.

"2. People will Order their Wills so as to defraud the Exception.

"One Exception must be made; and that is, Either very unequal Matches, as when a Woman of Nineteen Marries an old Man of Seventy; or Women who have infirm Husbands, I mean known and publickly so. To remedy which, Two things are to be done.

"1. The Office must have moving Officers without doors, who shall inform themselves of such matters, and if any such Circumstances appear, the Office should have 14 days time to return their Money, and declare their Subscriptions Void.

"2. No Woman whose Husband had any visible Distemper, should claim under a Year after her Subscription.

"One grand Objection against this Proposal, is, How you will oblige People to pay either their Subscription, or their Quarteridge.

"To this I answer, *By no Compulsion* (tho' that might be perform'd too) but altogether voluntary; only with this Argument to move it, that if they do not continue their Payments, they lose the Benefit of their past Contributions.

"I know it lies as a fair Objection against such a Project as this, That the number of Claims are so uncertain, That no Body knows what they engage in, when they Subscribe, for so many may die Annually out of Two Thousand, as may perhaps make my Payment £20 or 25 *per Ann.*, and if a Woman happen to Pay that for Twenty Years, though she receives the £500 at last she is a great Loser; but if she dies before her Husband, she has lessened his Estate considerably, and brought a great Loss upon him.

"*First*, I say to this, That I wou'd have such a Proposal as this be so fair and easy, that if any Person who had Subscrib'd found the Payments too high, and the Claims fall too often, it shou'd be at their Liberty at any Time, upon Notice given, to be released and stand Oblig'd no longer; and if so, *Volenti non fit Injuria;* every one knows best what their own Circumstances will bear.

"In the next Place, because Death is a Contingency, no Man can directly Calculate, and all that Subscribe must take the Hazard; yet that a Prejudice against this Notion may not be built on wrong Grounds, let's examine a little the Probable hazard, and see how many shall die Annually out of 2000 Subscribers, accounting by the common proportion of Burials, to the number of the Living.

"Sir William Petty in his *Political Arithmetick*, by a very Ingenious Calculation, brings the Account of Burials in London, to be 1 in 40 Annually, and proves it by all the proper Rules of proportion'd Computation; and I'le take my Scheme from thence. If then One in Forty of all the People in England should Die, that supposes Fifty to Die every Year out of our Two Thousand Subscribers; and for a Woman to Contribute 5*s.* to every one, would certainly be to agree to Pay £12 10*s. per Ann.* upon her Husband's Life, to receive £500 when he Di'd, and lose it if she Di'd first; and yet this wou'd not be a hazard beyond reason too great for the Gain.

"But I shall offer some Reasons to prove this to be impossible in our Case; First, Sir William Petty allows the City of London to contain about a Million of People, and our Yearly Bill of Mortality never yet amounted to 25000 in the most Sickly Years we have had, Plague Years excepted, sometimes but to 20000, which is but One in Fifty: Now it is to be consider'd here, that Children and Ancient People make up, one time with another, at least one third of our Bills of Mortality; and our *Assurances* lies upon none but the Midling Age of the People, which is the only age wherein Life is any thing steady; and if that be allow'd, there cannot Die by his Computation, above One in Eighty of such People, every Year; but because I would be sure to leave Room for Casualty, I'le allow one in Fifty shall Die out of our Number Subscrib'd.

"Secondly, It must be allow'd, that our Payments falling due only on the Death of Husbands, this One in Fifty must not be reckoned upon the Two thousand; for 'tis to be suppos'd at least as many Women shall die as Men, and then there is nothing to Pay; so that One in Fifty upon One Thousand, is the most that I can suppose shall claim the Contribution in a Year, which is Twenty Claims a Year at 5*s.* each, and is £5 *per Ann.* and if a Woman pays this for Twenty Year, and claims at last, she is Gainer enough, and no extraordinary Loser if she never claims at all: And I verily believe any Office might undertake to demand at all Adventures not above £6 *per Ann.* and secure the Subscriber £500 in case she come to claim as a Widow."

I would leave this to the Consideration of all who are concern'd for their own or their Neighbour's Temporal Happiness; and I am humbly of Opinion, that the Country is ripe for many such *Friendly Societies*, whereby every Man might help another, without any Disservice to himself. We have many charitable Gentlemen who Yearly give liberally to the Poor, and where can they better bestow their Charity than on those who become so by Providence, and for ought they know on themselves. But above all, the Clergy have the most need of coming into some such Project as this. They as well as poor Men (according to the Proverb) generally abound in Children; and how many Clergymen in the Country are forc'd to labour in their Fields, to keep themselves in a Condition above Want? How then shall they be able to leave any thing to their forsaken, dejected, and almost forgotten Wives and Children. For my own Part, I have nothing left to live on, but Contentment and a few Cows; and tho' I cannot expect to be reliev'd by this Project, yet it would be no small Satisfaction to me to see it put in Practice for the Benefit of others. I am, Sir, &c.

Silence Dogood

Silence Dogood, No. 12

10 September, 1722

Quod est in cordi sobrii, est in ore ebrii.[1]

To the Author of the *New-England Courant.*

Sir,

It is no unprofitable tho' unpleasant Pursuit, diligently to inspect and consider the Manners and Conversation of Men, who, insensible of the greatest Enjoyments of humane Life, abandon themselves to Vice from a false Notion of *Pleasure* and *good Fellowship*. A true and natural Representation of any Enormity, is often the best Argument against it and Means of removing it, when the most severe Reprehensions alone, are found ineffectual.

I would in this letter improve the little Observation I have made on the Vice of *Drunkeness*, the better to reclaim the *good Fellows* who usually pay the Devotions of the Evening to Bacchus.

I doubt not but *moderate Drinking* has been improv'd for the Diffusion of Knowledge among the ingenious Part of Mankind, who want the Talent of a ready Utterance, in order to discover the Conceptions of their Minds in an entertaining and intelligible Manner. 'Tis true, drinking does not *improve* our Faculties, but it enables us to *use* them; and therefore I conclude, that much Study and Experience, and a little Liquor, are of

1. *What is in the heart of a sober man is in the mouth of a drunkard.*

absolute Necessity for some Tempers, in order to make them accomplish'd Orators. Dic. Ponder discovers an excellent Judgment when he is inspir'd with a Glass or two of *Claret*, but he passes for a Fool among those of small Observation, who never saw him the better for Drink. And here it will not be improper to observe, That the moderate Use of Liquor, and a well plac'd and well regulated Anger, often produce this same Effect; and some who cannot ordinarily talk but in broken Sentences and false Grammar, do in the Heat of Passion express themselves with as much Eloquence as Warmth. Hence it is that my own Sex are generally the most eloquent, because the most passionate. "It has been said in the Praise of some Men, (says an ingenious Author,) that they could talk whole Hours together upon any thing; but it must be owned to the Honour of the other Sex, that there are many among them who can talk whole Hours together upon Nothing. I have known a Woman branch out into a long extempore Dissertation on the Edging of a Petticoat, and chide her Servant for breaking a China Cup, in all the Figures of Rhetorick."

But after all it must be consider'd, that no Pleasure can give Satisfaction or prove advantageous to a *reasonable Mind*, which is not attended with the *Restraints of Reason*. Enjoyment is not to be found by Excess in any sensual Gratification; but on the contrary, the immoderate Cravings of the Voluptuary, are always succeeded with Loathing and a palled Appetite. What Pleasure can the Drunkard have in the Reflection, that, while in his Cups, he retain'd only the Shape of a Man, and acted the Part of a Beast; or that from reasonable Discourse a few Minutes before, he descended to Impertinence and Nonsense?

I cannot pretend to account for the different Effects of Liquor on Persons of different Dispositions, who are guilty of Excess in the Use of it. 'Tis strange to see Men of a regular Conversation become rakish and profane when intoxicated with Drink, and yet more surprizing to observe, that some who appear to be the most profligate Wretches when sober, become mighty religious in their Cups, and will then, and at no other Time address their Maker, but when they are destitute of Reason, and actually affronting him. Some shrink in the Wetting, and others swell to such an unusual Bulk in their Imaginations, that they can in an Instant understand all Arts and Sciences, by the liberal Education of a little vivifying *Punch*, or a sufficient Quantity of other exhilerating Liquor.

And as the Effects of Liquor are various, so are the Characters given to its Devourers. It argues some Shame in the Drunkards themselves, in that they have invented numberless Words and Phrases to cover their Folly, whose proper Significations are harmless, or have no Signification at all. They are seldom known to be *drunk*, tho' they are very often *boozey, cogey, tipsey, fox'd, merry, mellow, fuddl'd, groatable, Confoundedly cut, See two Moons*, are *Among the Philistines, In a very good Humour, See the Sun*, or, *The Sun has shone upon them;* they *Clip the King's English*, are *Almost froze, Feavourish, In their Altitudes, Pretty well enter'd*, &c. In short, every Day produces some new Word or Phrase which might be added to the Vocabulary of the *Tiplers:* But I have chose to mention these few, because if at any Time a Man of Sobriety and Temperance happens to *cut himself confoundedly*, or is *almost froze*, or *feavourish*, or accidentally *sees the Sun*, &c. he may escape the Imputation of being *drunk*, when his Misfortune comes to be related. I am Sir, Your Humble Servant,

Silence Dogood

Silence Dogood, No. 14

8 October, 1722

Earum causarum quantum quaeque valeat, videamus.[1] Cicero.

To the Author of the *New-England Courant.*

Sir,

It often happens, that the most zealous Advocates for any Cause find themselves disappointed in the first Appearance of Success in the Propagation of their Opinion; and the Disappointment appears unavoidable, when their easy Proselytes too suddenly start into Extreams, and are immediately fill'd with Arguments to invalidate their former Practice. This creates a Suspicion in the more considerate Part of Mankind, that those who are thus *given to Change*, neither *fear God*, nor *honour the King*. In Matters of Religion, he that alters his Opinion on a *religious Account*, must certainly go thro' much Reading, hear many Arguments on both Sides, and undergo many Struggles in his Conscience, before he can come to a full Resolution: Secular Interest will indeed make quick Work with an immoral Man, especially if, notwithstanding the Alteration of his Opinion, he can with any Appearance of Credit retain his Immorality. But, by this Turn of Thought I would not be suspected of Uncharitableness to those Clergymen at Connecticut, who have lately embrac'd the Establish'd Religion of our Nation, some of whom I hear made their Professions with a Serious-

---

1. *Let us see how much each of these causes is worth.*

ness becoming their Order: However, since they have deny'd the Validity of *Ordination* by the Hands of *Presbyters*, and consequently their Power of Administring the *Sacraments*, &c. we may justly expect a suitable Manifestation of their Repentance for invading the *Priests* Office, and living so long in a Corah-like Rebellion. All I would endeavour to shew is, That an indiscreet Zeal for spreading an Opinion, hurts the Cause of the Zealot. There are too many blind Zealots among every Denomination of Christians; and he that propagates the Gospel among *Rakes* and *Beaus* without reforming them in their Morals, is every whit as ridiculous and impolitick as a Statesman who makes Tools of Ideots and Tale-Bearers.

Much to my present Purpose are the Words of two Ingenious Authors of the Church of England, tho' in all Probability they were tainted with Whiggish Principles; and with these I shall conclude this Letter.

"I would (says one) have every zealous Man examine his Heart thoroughly, and, I believe, he will often find that what he calls a Zeal for his Religion, is either Pride, Interest or Ill-nature. A Man who differs from another in Opinion sets himself above him in his own Judgment, and in several Particulars pretends to be the wiser Person. This is a great Provocation to the Proud Man, and gives a keen Edge to what he calls his Zeal. And that this is the Case very often, we may observe from the Behaviour of some of the most Zealous for Orthodoxy, who have often great Friendships and Intimacies with vicious immoral Men, provided they do but agree with them in the same Scheme of Belief. The Reason is, because the vicious Believer gives the Precedency to the virtuous Man, and allows the good Christian to be the worthier Person, at the same Time that he cannot come up to his Perfections. This we find exemplified in that trite Passage which we see quoted in almost every System of Ethicks, tho' upon another Occasion;

— Video meliore proboque

Deteriora sequor[2] —

On the contrary, it is certain if our Zeal were true and genuine, we should be much more angry with a Sinner than a Heretick, since there are several Cases which may excuse the latter before his great Judge, but none which can excuse the former."

"I have (says another) found by Experience, that it is impossible to talk distinctly without defining the Words of which we make use. There is not a Term in our Language which wants Explanation so much as the Word *Church*. One would think when People utter it, they should have in their Minds Ideas of Virtue and Religion; but that important Monosyllable drags all the other Words in the Language after it, and it is made use of to express both Praise and Blame, according to the Character of him who speaks it. By this means it happens, that no one knows what his Neighbour means when he says such a one is for or against the Church. It has happen'd that he who is seen every Day at Church, has not been counted in the Eye of the World a Churchman; and he who is very zealous to oblige every one to frequent it but himself, has been a very good Son of the Church. This Praepossession is the best Handle imaginable for Politicians to make use of, for managing the Loves and Hatreds of Mankind to the Purposes to which they would lead them. But this is not a Thing for Fools to meddle with, for they only bring Disesteem upon those whom they attempt to serve, when they unskilfully pronounce Terms of Art. I have observed great Evils arise from this Practice, and not only the Cause of Piety, but also the secular Interest of Clergymen, has extreamly suffered by the general unexplained Signification of the Word *Church*." I am, Sir, Your Humble Servant.

SILENCE DOGOOD

---

2. *I see and approve of the better course, but I follow the worse.*

On Titles of Honor

18 February, 1723

Mero meridie si dixerit illi tenebras esse, credit.[1]

There is nothing in which Mankind reproach themselves more than in their Diversity of Opinions. Every Man sets himself above another in his own Opinion, and there are not two Men in the World whose Sentiments are alike in every thing. Hence it comes to pass, that the same Passages in the Holy Scriptures or the Works of the Learned, are wrested to the meaning of two opposite Parties, of contrary Opinions, as if the Passages they recite were like our Master Janus, looking *two ways at once*, or like Lawyers, who with equal Force of Argument, can plead either for the *Plaintiff* or *Defendant.*

The most absurd and ridiculous Opinions, are sometimes spread by the least colour of Argument: But if they stop at the first Broachers, *they* have still the Pleasure of being wiser (in their own Conceits) than the rest of the World, and can with the greatest Confidence pass a Sentence of Condemnation upon the Reason of all Mankind, who dissent from the peculiar Whims of their troubled Brains.

We were easily led into these Reflections at the last Meeting of our Club, when one of the Company read to us some Passages from a zealous Author against *Hatt-Honour, Titular Respects*, &c. which we will communicate to

1. *If he says it is dark to him at high noon, he is believed.*

the Reader for the Diversion of this Week, if he is dispos'd to be merry with the Folly of his Fellow-Creature.

"*Honour*, Friend, *says he*, properly ascends, and not descends; yet the Hat, when the Head is uncover'd, *descends*, and therefore there can be no Honour in it. Besides, Honour was from the *Beginning*, but Hats are an Invention of a *late Time*, and consequently true Honour standeth not therein.

"In old Time it was no disrespect for Men and Women to be call'd by their own Names: Adam, was never called *Master* Adam; we never read of Noah *Esquire*, Lot *Knight* and *Baronet*, nor the *Right Honourable* Abraham, *Viscount Mesopotamia, Baron of Carran;* no, no, they were plain Men, honest Country Grasiers, that took Care of their Families and their Flocks. Moses was a great Prophet, and Aaron a Priest of the Lord; but we never read of the *Reverend* Moses, nor the *Right Reverend Father in God*, Aaron, by Divine Providence, *Lord Arch-Bishop of Israel:* Thou never sawest *Madam* Rebecca in the Bible, my *Lady* Rachel, nor Mary, tho' a Princess of the Blood after the Death of Joseph, call'd the *Princess Dowager of Nazareth;* no, plain Rebecca, Rachel, Mary, or the *Widow* Mary, or the like: It was no Incivility then to mention their naked Names as they were expressed."

If common civility, and a generous Deportment among Mankind, be not put out of Countenance by the profound Reasoning of this Author, we hope they will continue to treat one another handsomely to the end of the World. We will not pretend an Answer to these Arguments against *modern Decency* and *Titles of Honour;* yet one of our Club will undertake to prove, that tho' Abraham was not styl'd *Right Honourable*, yet he had the Title of *Lord* given him by his Wife Sarah, which he thinks entitles her to the Honour of *My Lady* Sarah; and Rachel being married into the same Family, he concludes she may deserve the Title of *My Lady* Rachel. But this is but the Opinion of one Man; it was never put to Vote in the Society.

P.S. At the last Meeting of our Club, it was unanimously agreed, That all Letters to be inserted in this Paper, should come directed to old Janus; whereof our Correspondents are to take Notice, and conform themselves accordingly.

Plan for Attaining Moral Perfection

1726

(Editor's Note: An Excerpt from The Autobiography)

It was about this time I conceived the bold and arduous project of arriving at moral perfection. I wish'd to live without committing any fault at any time; I would conquer all that either natural inclination, custom, or company might lead me into. As I knew, or thought I knew, what was right and wrong, I did not see why I might not always do the one and avoid the other. But I soon found I had undertaken a task of more difficulty than I had imagined. While my care was employ'd in guarding against one fault, I was often surprised by another; habit took the advantage of inattention; inclination was sometimes too strong for reason. I concluded, at length, that the mere speculative conviction that it was our interest to be completely virtuous, was not sufficient to prevent our slipping; and that the contrary habits must be broken, and good ones acquired and established, before we can have any dependence on a steady, uniform rectitude of conduct. For this purpose I therefore contrived the following method.

In the various enumerations of the moral virtues I had met with in my reading, I found the catalogue more or less numerous, as different writers included more or fewer ideas under the same name. Temperance, for example, was by some confined to eating and drinking, while by others it was extended to mean the moderating every other pleasure, appetite, inclination, or passion, bodily or mental, even to our avarice and ambition. I propos'd to myself, for the sake of clearness, to use rather more names, with fewer ideas annex'd to each, than a few names with more ideas; and I included under thirteen names of virtues all that at that time occurr'd to me as necessary or desirable, and annexed to each a short precept, which fully express'd the extent I gave to its meaning.

These names of virtues, with their precepts, were:

1. Temperance

Eat not to dullness; drink not to elevation.

2. Silence.

Speak not but what may benefit others or yourself; avoid trifling conversation.

3. Order.

Let all your things have their places; let each part of your business have its time.

4. Resolution.

Resolve to perform what you ought; perform without fail what you resolve.

5. Frugality.

Make no expense but to do good to others or yourself; *i. e.*, waste nothing.

6. Industry.

Lose no time; be always employ'd in something useful; cut off all unnecessary actions.

7. Sincerity.

Use no hurtful deceit; think innocently and justly; and, if you speak, speak accordingly.

8. Justice.

Wrong none by doing injuries, or omitting the benefits that are your duty.

9. Moderation.

Avoid extreams; forbear resenting injuries so much as you think they deserve.

10. Cleanliness.

Tolerate no uncleanliness in body, cloaths, or habitation.

11. Tranquillity.

Be not disturbed at trifles, or at accidents common or unavoidable.

12. Chastity.

Rarely use venery but for Health or Offspring; Never to Dulness, Weakness, or the Injury of your own or another's Peace or Reputation.

13. Humility.

Imitate Jesus and Socrates.

My intention being to acquire the *habitude* of all these virtues, I judg'd it would be well not to distract my attention by attempting the whole at once, but to fix it on one of them at a time; and, when I should be master of that, then to proceed to another, and so on, till I should have gone thro' the thirteen; and, as the previous acquisition of some might facilitate the acquisition of certain others, I arrang'd them with that view, as they stand above. Temperance first, as it tends to procure that coolness and clearness of head, which is so necessary where constant vigilance was to be kept up, and guard maintained against the unremitting attraction of ancient habits, and the force of perpetual temptations. This being acquir'd and establish'd, Silence would be more easy; and my desire being to gain knowledge at the same time that I improv'd in virtue, and considering that in conversation it was obtain'd rather by the use of the ears than of the tongue, and therefore wishing to break a habit I was getting into of prattling, punning, and joking, which only made me acceptable to trifling company, I gave *Silence* the second place. This and the next, *Order*, I expected would allow me more time for attending to my project and my studies. *Resolution*, once become habitual, would keep me firm in my endeavours to obtain all the subsequent virtues; *Frugality* and Industry freeing me from my remaining debt, and producing affluence and independence, would make more easy the practice of Sincerity and Justice, &c.&c. Conceiving then, that, agreeably to the advice of Pythagoras in his Golden Verses, daily examination would be necessary, I contrived the following method for conducting that examination.

I made a little book, in which I allotted a page for each of the virtues. I rul'd each page with red ink, so as to have seven columns, one for each day of the week, marking each column with a letter for the day. I cross'd these columns with thirteen red lines, marking the beginning of each line with the first letter of one of the virtues, on which line, and in its proper column, I might mark, by a little black spot, every fault I found upon examination to have been committed respecting that virtue upon that day.

I determined to give a week's strict attention to each of the virtues successively. Thus, in the first week, my great guard was to avoid every the least offense against *Temperance*, leaving the other virtues to their ordinary chance, only marking every evening the faults of the day. Thus, if in the first week I could keep my first line, marked T, clear of spots, I suppos'd the habit of that virtue so much strengthen'd, and its opposite weaken'd, that I might venture extending my attention to include the next, and for the following week keep both lines clear of spots. Proceeding thus to the last, I could go thro' a course compleat in thirteen weeks, and four courses in a year. And like him who, having a garden to weed, does not attempt to eradicate all the bad herbs at once, which would exceed his reach and his strength, but works on one of the beds at a time, and, having accomplish'd the first, proceeds to a second, so I should have, I hoped, the encouraging pleasure of seeing on my pages the progress I made in virtue, by clearing successively my lines of their spots, till in the end, by a number of courses, I should be happy in viewing a clean book, after a thirteen weeks' daily examination.

Part II

4 FEBRUARY – 27 MARCH, 1729

The Busy-Body No. 1

The Busy-Body No. 2

The Busy-Body No. 3

The Busy-Body No. 4

The Busy-Body No. 8

The Busy-Body, No. 1

4 February, 1729

Mr. Andrew Bradford,

I design this to acquaint you, that I, who have long been one of your *Courteous Readers*, have lately entertain'd some Thoughts of setting up for an Author my Self; not out of the least Vanity, I assure you, or Desire of showing my Parts, but purely for the Good of my Country.

I have often observ'd with Concern, that your *Mercury* is not always equally entertaining. The Delay of Ships expected in, and want of fresh Advices from Europe, make it frequently very Dull; and I find the Freezing of our River has the same Effect on News as on Trade. With more Concern have I continually observ'd the growing Vices and Follies of my Country-folk. And tho' Reformation is properly the concern of every Man; that is, *Every one ought to mend One;* yet 'tis too true in this Case, that *what is every Body's Business is no Body's Business*, and the Business is done accordingly. I, therefore, upon mature Deliberation, think fit to take *no Body's Business* wholly into my own Hands; and, out of Zeal for the Publick Good, design to erect my Self into a Kind of *Censor Morum;* proposing with your Allowance, to make Use of the *Weekly Mercury* as a Vehicle in which my Remonstrances shall be convey'd to the World.

I am sensible I have, in this Particular, undertaken a very unthankful Office, and expect little besides my Labour for my Pains. Nay, 'tis probable I may displease a great Number of your Readers, who will not very well like to pay 10*s.* a Year for being told of their Faults. But as most People delight in Censure when they themselves are not the Objects of it, if any are offended at my publickly exposing their private Vices, I promise they shall have the Satisfaction, in a very little Time, of seeing their good Friends and Neighbours in the same Circumstances.

However, let the Fair Sex be assur'd, that I shall always treat them and their Affairs with the utmost *Decency* and Respect. I intend now and then to dedicate a Chapter wholly to their Service; and if my Lectures any Way contribute to the Embellishment of their Minds, and Brightning of their Understandings, without offending their *Modesty*, I doubt not of having their Favour and Encouragement.

'Tis certain, that no Country in the World produces naturally finer Spirits than ours, Men of Genius for every kind of Science, and capable of acquiring to Perfection every Qualification that is in Esteem among Mankind. But as few here have the Advantage of good Books, for want of which, good Conversation is still more scarce, it would doubtless have been very acceptable to your Readers, if, instead of an old out-of-date Article from Muscovy or Hungary, you had entertained them with some well-chosen Extract from a good Author. This I shall sometimes do, *when I happen to have nothing of my own to say that I think of more Consequence*. Sometimes, I propose to deliver Lectures of Morality or Philosophy, and (because I am naturally enclin'd to be meddling with Things that don't concern me) perhaps I may sometimes talk Politicks. And if I can by any means furnish out a Weekly Entertainment for the Publick, that will give a rational Diversion, and at the same Time be instructive to the Readers, I shall think my Leisure Hours well employ'd: And if you publish this I hereby invite all ingenious Gentlemen and others, (that approve of such an Undertaking) to my Assistance and Correspondence.

'Tis like by this Time you have a Curiosity to be acquainted with my Name and Character. As I do not aim at publick Praise I design to remain concealed; and there are such Numbers of our Family and Relations at this Time in the Country, that tho' I've sign'd my Name at full Length, I am not under the least Apprehension of being distinguish'd and discover'd by it. My Character indeed I would favour you with, but that I am cautious of praising my Self, lest I should be told *my Trumpeter's dead:*And I cannot find in my Heart, at present, to say any Thing to my own Disadvantage.

It is very common with Authors in their first Performances to talk to their Readers thus, *If this meets with a* SUITABLE *Reception;* Or, *If this should meet with*due *Encouragement, I shall hereafter publish*, *&c.* This only manifests the Value they put on their own Writings, since they think to frighten the Publick into their Applause, by threatning, that unless you approve what they have already wrote, they intend never to write again; when perhaps, it mayn't be a Pin Matter whether they ever do or no. As I have not observ'd the Criticks to be more favourable on this Account, I shall always avoid saying any Thing of the Kind; and conclude with telling you, that if you send me a Bottle of Ink and a Quire of Paper by the Bearer, you may depend on hearing further from Sir, Your most humble Servant

THE BUSY BODY

The Busy-Body, No. 2

11 February, 1729

All Fools have still an Itching to deride;
And fain would be upon the laughing Side. Pope.

Monsieur Rochefocaut tells us somewhere in his Memoirs, that the Prince of Conde delighted much in Ridicule; and us'd frequently to shut himself up for Half a Day together in his Chamber with a Gentleman that was his Favourite, purposely to divert himself with examining what was the Foible or ridiculous side of every Noted Person in the Court. That Gentleman said afterwards in some Company, that he thought nothing was more ridiculous in any Body, than this same Humour in the Prince; and I am somewhat inclin'd to be of his Opinion. The General Tendency there is among us to this Embellishment, (which I fear has too often been grossly imposed upon my loving Countrymen instead of Wit) and the Applause it meets with from a rising Generation, fill me with fearful Apprehensions for the future Reputation of my Country: A young Man of Modesty (which is the most certain Indication of large Capacities) is hereby discourag'd from attempting to make any Figure in Life: His Apprehensions of being outlaugh'd, will force him to continue in a restless Obscurity, without having an Opportunity of knowing his own Merit himself, or discovering it to the World, rather than venture to expose himself in a Place where a Pun or a Sneer shall pass for Wit, Noise for Reason, and the Strength of the Argument be judg'd by that of the Lungs. Among these witty Gentlemen let us take a View of Ridentius: What a contemptible Figure does he make with his Train of paultry Admirers? This Wight shall give himself an Hours Diversion with the Cock of a Man's Hat, the Heels of his Shoes, an unguarded Expression in his Discourse, or even some Personal Defect; and the Height of his low Ambition is to put some One of the Company to the Blush, who perhaps must pay an equal Share of the Reckoning with himself. If such a Fellow makes Laughing the sole End and Purpose of his Life, if it is necessary to his Constitution, or if he has a great Desire of growing suddenly fat, let him treat; let him give publick Notice where any dull stupid Rogues may get a Quart of Four-penny for being laugh'd at; but 'tis barbarously unhandsome, when Friends meet for the Benefit of Conversation, and a proper Relaxation from Business, that one should be the *Butt* of the Company, and Four Men made merry at the Cost of the Fifth.

How different from this Character is that of the good-natur'd gay Eugenius? who never spoke yet but with a Design to divert and please; and who was never yet baulk'd in his Intention. Eugenius takes more Delight in applying the Wit of his Friends, than in being admir'd himself: And if any one of the Company is so unfortunate as to be touch'd a little too nearly, he will make Use of some ingenious Artifice to turn the Edge of Ridicule another Way, chusing rather to make even himself a publick Jest, than be at the Pain of seeing his Friend in Confusion.

Among the Tribe of Laughers I reckon the *pretty Gentlemen* that write *Satyrs*, and carry them about in their Pockets, reading them themselves in all Company they happen into; taking an Advantage of the ill Taste of the Town, to make themselves famous for a Pack of paultry low Nonsence, for which they deserve to be kick'd, rather than admir'd, by all who have the least Tincture of Politeness. These I take to be the most incorrigible of all my Readers; nay I expect they will be squibbing at the Busy-Body himself: However the only Favour he begs of them is this; that if they cannot controul their over-bearing Itch of *Scribbling*, let him be attack'd in downright BITING LYRICKS; for there is no *Satyr* he Dreads half so much as an Attempt towards a Panegyrick.

The Busy-Body, No. 3

18 February, 1729

Non vultus instantis Tyranni
Mente quatit solida—neque Auster
Dux inquieti turbidus Adriae,
Nec fulminantis magna Jovis manus.[1] Hor.

It is said that the Persians in their ancient Constitution, had publick Schools in which Virtue was taught as a Liberal Art or Science; and it is certainly of more Consequence to a Man that he has learnt to govern his Passions; in spite of Temptation to be just in his Dealings, to be Temperate in his Pleasures, to support himself with Fortitude under his Misfortunes, to behave with Prudence in all Affairs and in every Circumstance of Life; I say, it is of much more real Advantage to him to be thus qualified, than to be a Master of all the Arts and Sciences in the World beside.

Virtue alone is sufficient to make a Man Great, Glorious and Happy. He that is acquainted with Cato, as I am, cannot help thinking as I do now, and will acknowledge he deserves the Name without being honour'd by it. Cato is a Man whom Fortune has plac'd in the most obscure Part of the Country. His Circumstances are such as only put him above Necessity, without affording him many Superfluities; Yet who is greater than Cato? I

---

1. *Not the face of the threatening Tyrant / Shakes my steadfast mind—nor the South Wind / The turbulent leader of the restless Adriatic, / Nor the great hand of thundering Jupiter.*

happened but the other Day to be at a House in Town, where among others were met Men of the most Note in this Place: Cato had Business with some of them, and knock'd at the Door. The most trifling Actions of a Man, in my Opinion, as well as the smallest Features and Lineaments of the Face, give a nice Observer some Notion of his Mind. Methought he rapp'd in such a peculiar Manner, as seem'd of itself to express, there was One who deserv'd as well as desir'd Admission. He appear'd in the plainest Country Garb; his Great Coat was coarse and looked old and thread-bare; his Linnen was homespun; his Beard perhaps of Seven Days Growth, his Shoes thick and heavy, and every Part of his Dress corresponding. Why was this Man receiv'd with such concurring Respect from every Person in the Room, even from those who had never known him or seen him before? It was not an exquisite Form of Person, or Grandeur of Dress that struck us with Admiration. I believe long Habits of Virtue have a sensible Effect on the Countenance: There was something in the Air of his Face that manifested the true Greatness of his Mind; which likewise appear'd in all he said, and in every Part of his Behaviour, obliging us to regard him with a Kind of Veneration. His Aspect is sweetned with Humanity and Benevolence, and at the same Time emboldned with Resolution, equally free from a diffident Bashfulness and an unbecoming Assurance. The Consciousness of his own innate Worth and unshaken Integrity renders him calm and undaunted in the Presence of the most Great and Powerful, and upon the most extraordinary Occasions. His strict Justice and known Impartiality make him the Arbitrator and Decider of all Differences that arise for many Miles around him, without putting his Neighbours to the Charge, Perplexity and Uncertainty of Law-Suits. He always speaks the Thing he means, which he is never afraid or asham'd to do, because he knows he always means well; and therefore is never oblig'd to blush and feel the Confusion of finding himself detected in the Meanness of a Falshood. He never contrives Ill against his Neighbour, and therefore is never seen with a lowring suspicious Aspect. A mixture of Innocence and Wisdom makes him ever seriously chearful. His generous Hospitality to Strangers according to his Ability, his Goodness, his Charity, his Courage in the Cause of the Oppressed, his Fidelity in Friendship, his Humility, his Honesty and Sincerity, his Moderation and his Loyalty to the Government, his Piety, his Temperance, his Love to Mankind, his Magnanimity, his Publick-spiritedness, and in fine, his *Consummate Virtue*, make him justly deserve to be esteem'd the Glory of his Country.

——The Brave do never shun the Light,
Just are their Thoughts and open are their Tempers;
Freely without Disguise they love and hate;
Still are they found in the fair Face of Day,
And Heaven and Men are Judges of their Actions. Rowe.

Who would not rather chuse, if it were in his Choice, to merit the above Character, than be the richest, the most learned, or the most powerful Man in the Province without it?

Almost every Man has a strong natural Desire of being valu'd and esteem'd by the rest of his Species; but I am concern'd and griev'd to see how few fall into the Right and only infallible Method of becoming so. That laudable Ambition is too commonly misapply'd and often ill employ'd. Some to make themselves considerable pursue Learning, others grasp at Wealth, some aim at being thought witty, and others are only careful to make the most of an handsome Person; But what is Wit, or Wealth, or Form, or Learning when compar'd with Virtue? 'Tis true, we love the handsome, we applaud the Learned, and we fear the Rich and Powerful; but we even Worship and adore the Virtuous. Nor is it strange; since Men of Virtue, are so rare, so very rare to be found. If we were as industrious to become Good, as to make ourselves Great, we should become really Great by being Good, and the Number of valuable Men would be much increased; but it is a Grand Mistake to think of being Great without Goodness; and I pronounce it as certain, *that there was never yet a truly Great Man that was not at the same Time truly Virtuous.*

O Cretico! Thou sowre Philosopher! Thou cunning States-man! Thou art crafty, but far from being Wise. When wilt thou be esteem'd, regarded and belov'd like Cato? When wilt thou, among thy Creatures meet with that unfeign'd Respect and warm Goodwill that all Men have for him? Wilt thou never understand that the cringing, mean, submissive Deportment of thy Dependants, is (like the Worship paid by Indians to the Devil) rather thro' Fear of the Harm thou may'st do to them, than out of Gratitude for the Favours they have receiv'd of thee? Thou art not wholly void of Virtue; there are many good Things in thee, and many good Actions reported of thee. Be advised by thy Friend: Neglect those musty Authors; let them be cover'd with Dust, and moulder on their proper Shelves; and do thou apply thy self to a Study much more profitable, The Knowledge of Mankind, and of thy Self.

This is to give Notice that the BUSY-BODY *strictly forbids all Persons, from this Time forward, of what Age, Sex, Rank, Quality, Degree or Denomination soever, on any Pretence to enquire who is the Author of this Paper, on Pain of his Displeasure, (his own near and Dear Relations only excepted).*

'Tis to be observ'd that if any bad Characters happen to be drawn in the Course of these Papers, they mean no particular Person, if they are not particularly apply'd.

Likewise that the Author is no Partyman, but a general Meddler.

N.B. *Cretico lives in a neighbouring Province.*

The Busy-Body, No. 4

25 February, 1729

Nequid nimis.[1]

In my first Paper I invited the Learned and the Ingenious to join with me in this Undertaking; and I now repeat that Invitation. I would have such Gentlemen take this Opportunity, (by trying their Talent in Writing) of diverting themselves and their Friends, and improving the Taste of the Town. And because I would encourage all Wit of our own Growth and Produce, I hereby promise, that whoever shall send me a little Essay on some moral or other Subject, that is fit for publick View in this Manner (and not basely borrow'd from any other Author) I shall receive it with Candour, and take Care to place it to the best Advantage. It will be hard if we cannot muster up in the whole Country, a sufficient Stock of Sense to supply the *Busy-Body*at least for a Twelvemonth. For my own Part, I have already profess'd that I have the Good of my Country wholly at Heart in this Design, without the least sinister View; my chief Purpose being to inculcate the noble Principles of Virtue, and depreciate Vice of every kind. But as I know the Mob hate Instruction, and the Generality would never read beyond the first Line of my Lectures, if they were usually fill'd with nothing but wholesome Precepts and Advice; I must therefore sometimes humour them in their own Way. There are a Set of Great Names in the Province, who are the common Objects of Popular Dislike. If I can now

1. *Moderation in all things.*

and then overcome my Reluctance, and prevail with my self to Satyrize a little, one of these Gentlemen, the Expectation of meeting with such a Gratification, will induce many to read me through, who would otherwise proceed immediately to the Foreign News. As I am very well assured that the greatest Men among us have a sincere Love for their Country, notwithstanding its Ingratitude, and the Insinuations of the Envious and Malicious to the contrary, so I doubt not but they will chearfully tolerate me in the Liberty I design to take for the End above mentioned.

As yet I have but few Correspondents, tho' they begin now to increase. The following Letter, left for me at the Printers, is one of the first I have receiv'd, which I regard the more for that it comes from one of the Fair Sex, and because I have my self oftentimes suffer'd under the Grievance therein complain'd of.

To the Busy-Body.

"Sir,

"You having set your self up for a *Censurer Morum* (as I think you call it) which is said to mean a *Reformer of Manners*, I know no Person more proper to be apply'd to for Redress in all the Grievances we suffer from *Want of Manners* in some People. You must know I am a single Woman, and keep a Shop in this Town for a Livelyhood. There is a certain Neighbour of mine, who is really agreeable Company enough, and with whom I have had an Intimacy of some Time standing; But of late she makes her Visits so excessively often, and stays so very long every Visit, that I am tir'd out of all Patience. I have no Manner of Time at all to my self; and you, who seem to be a wise Man, must needs be sensible that every Person has little Secrets and Privacies that are not proper to be expos'd even to the nearest Friend. Now I cannot do the least Thing in the World, but she must know all about it; and it is a Wonder I have found an Opportunity to write you this Letter. My Misfortune is, that I respect her very well, and know not how to disoblige her so much as to tell her I should be glad to have less of her Company; for if I should once hint such a Thing, I am afraid she would resent it so as never to darken my Door again. But, alas, Sir, I have not yet told you half my Afflictions. She has two Children that are just big enough to run about and do pretty Mischief: These are continually along with Mamma, either in my Room or Shop, if I have never so many Customers or People with me about Business. Sometimes they pull the Goods off my low Shelves down to the Ground, and perhaps where one of them has just been making Water; My Friend takes up the Stuff, and cries, *Eh! thou little wicked mischievous Rogue! — But however, it has done no great Damage; 'tis only wet a little;* and so puts it up upon the Shelf again. Sometimes they get to my Cask of Nails behind the Counter, and divert themselves, to my great Vexation, with mixing my Ten-penny and Eight-penny and Four-penny together. I Endeavour to conceal my Uneasiness as much as possible, and with a grave Look go to Sorting them out. She cries, *Don't thee trouble thy self, Neighbour: Let them play a little; I'll put all to rights my self before I go.* But Things are never so put to rights but that I find a great deal of Work to do after they are gone. Thus, Sir, I have all the Trouble and Pesterment of Children, without the Pleasure of — calling them my own; and they are now so us'd to being here that they will be content no where else. If she would have been so kind as to have moderated her Visits to ten times a Day, and stay'd but half an hour at a Time, I should have been contented, and I believe never have given you this Trouble: But this very Morning they have so tormented me that I could bear no longer; For while the Mother was asking me twenty impertinent Questions, the youngest got to my Nails, and with great Delight rattled them by handfuls all over the Floor; and the other at the same Time made such a terrible Din upon my Counter with a Hammer, that I grew half distracted. I was just then about to make my self a new Suit of Pinners, but in the Fret and Confusion I cut it quite out of all Manner of Shape, and utterly spoil'd a Piece of the first Muslin. Pray, Sir, tell me what I shall do. And talk a little against such unreasonable Visiting in your next Paper: Tho' I would not have her affronted with me for a great Deal, for sincerely I love her and her Children as well I think, as a Neighbour can, and she buys a great many Things in a Year at my Shop. But I would beg her to consider that she uses me unmercifully; Tho' I believe it is only for want of Thought. But I have twenty Things more to tell you besides all this; There is a handsome Gentleman that has a Mind (I don't question) to make love to me, but he can't get the least Opportunity to —: O dear, here she comes again; I must conclude Yours, &c.

PATIENCE"

Indeed, 'tis well enough, as it happens, that *she is come*, to shorten this Complaint which I think is full long enough already, and probably would otherwise have been as long again. However, I must confess I cannot help pitying my Correspondent's Case, and in her Behalf exhort the Visitor to remember and consider the Words of the Wise Man, *Withdraw thy Foot from the House of thy Neighbour least he grow weary of thee, and so hate thee*. It is, I believe, a nice thing and very difficult, to regulate our Visits in such a Manner, as never to give Offence by coming too seldom, or too often, or departing too abruptly, or staying too long. However, in my Opinion, it is safest for most People, in a general way, who are unwilling to disoblige, to visit seldom, and tarry but a little while in a Place; notwithstanding pressing invitations, which are many times insincere. And tho' more of your Company should be really desir'd; yet in this Case, too much Reservedness is a Fault more easily excus'd than the Contrary.

Men are subjected to various Inconveniences meerly through lack of a small Share of Courage, which is a Quality very necessary in the common Occurences of Life, as well as in a Battle. How many Impertinences do we daily suffer with great Uneasiness, because we have not Courage enough to discover our Dislike? And why may not a Man use the Boldness and Freedom of telling his Friends that their long Visits sometimes incommode him? On this Occasion, it may be entertaining to some of my Readers, if I acquaint them with the Turkish Manner of entertaining Visitors, which I have from an Author of unquestionable Veracity; who assures us, that even the Turks are not so ignorant of Civility, and the Arts of Endearment, but that they can practice them with as much Exactness as any other Nation, whenever they have a Mind to shew themselves obliging.

"When you visit a Person of Quality, (says he) and have talk'd over your Business, or the Complements, or whatever Concern brought you thither, he makes a Sign to have Things serv'd in for the Entertainment, which is generally, a little Sweetmeat, a Dish of Sherbet, and another of Coffee; all which are immediately brought in by the Servants, and tender'd to all the Guests in Order, with the greatest Care and Awfulness imaginable. At last comes the finishing Part of your Entertainment, which is, Perfuming the Beards of the Company; a Ceremony which is perform'd in this Manner. They have for the Purpose a small Silver Chaffing-Dish, cover'd with a Lid full of Holes, and fixed upon a handsome Plate. In this they put some fresh Coals, and upon them a piece of *Lignum Aloes*, and shutting it up, the Smoak immediately ascends with a grateful Odour thro' the Holes of the Cover. This Smoak is held under every one's Chin, and offer'd as it were a Sacrifice to his Beard. The bristly Idol soon receives the Reverence done to it, and so greedily takes in and incorporates the gummy Steam, that it retains the Savour of it, and may serve for a Nosegay a good while after.

"This Ceremony may perhaps seem ridiculous at first hearing; but it passes among the Turks for an high Gratification. And I will say this in its Vindication, that it's Design is very wise and useful. For it is understood to give a civil Dismission to the Visitants; intimating to them, that the Master of the House has Business to do, or some other Avocation, that permits them to go away as soon as they please; and the sooner after this Ceremony the better. By this Means you may, at any Time, without Offence, deliver your self from being detain'd from your Affairs by tedious and unseasonable Visits; and from being constrain'd to use that Piece of Hypocrisy so common in the World, of pressing those to stay longer with you, whom perhaps in your Heart you wish a great Way off for having troubled you so long already."

Thus far my Author. For my own Part, I have taken such a Fancy to this Turkish Custom, that for the future I shall put something like it in Practice. I have provided a Bottle of right French Brandy for the Men, and Citron-Water for the Ladies. After I have treated with a Dram, and presented a Pinch of my best Snuff, I expect all Company will retire, and leave me to pursue my Studies for the Good of the Publick.

Advertisement.

I give Notice that I am now actually compiling, and design to publish in a short Time, the true History of the Rise, Growth and Progress of the renowned Tiff-Club. All Persons who are acquainted with any Facts, Circumstances, Characters, Transactions, &c. which will be requisite to the Perfecting and Embellishment of the said Work, are desired to communicate the same to the Author, and direct their Letters to be left with the Printer hereof.

The Letter sign'd *Would-be-something* is come to hand.

The Busy-Body, No. 8

27 March, 1729

——Quid non mortalia Pectora cogis
Auri sacra Fames![1] Virgil.

One of the greatest Pleasures an Author can have is certainly the Hearing his Works applauded. The hiding from the World our Names while we publish our Thoughts, is so absolutely necessary to this Self-Gratification, that I hope my Well-wishers will congratulate me on my Escape from the many diligent, but fruitless Enquiries that have of late been made after me. Every Man will own, That an Author, as such, ought to be try'd by the Merit of his Productions only; but Pride, Party, and Prejudice at this Time run so very high, that Experience shews we form our Notions of a Piece by the Character of the Author. Nay there are some very humble Politicians in and about this City, who will ask on which Side the Writer is, before they presume to give their Opinion of the Thing wrote. This ungenerous Way of Proceeding I was well aware of before I publish'd my first Speculation; and therefore concealed my Name. And I appeal to the more generous Part of the World, if I have since I appear'd in the Character of the Busy-Body given an Instance of my siding with any Party more than another, in the unhappy Divisions of my Country; and I have above all, this Satisfaction in my Self, That neither Affection, Aversion or Interest,

---

1. *"To what do you not drive mortal hearts, accursed hunger for gold!?"* Aeneid (Book III, Line 56)

have byass'd me to use any Partiality towards any Man, or Sett of Men; but whatsoever I find nonsensically ridiculous, or immorally dishonest, I have, and shall continue openly to attack with the Freedom of an honest Man, and a Lover of my Country.

I profess I can hardly contain my Self, or preserve the Gravity and Dignity that should attend the *Censorial-Office*, when I hear the odd and unaccountable Expositions that are put upon some of my Works, thro' the malicious Ignorance of some, and the vain Pride of more than ordinary Penetration in others; one Instance of which many of my Readers are acquainted with. A certain Gentleman has taken a great Deal of Pains to write a key to the Letter in my *No.* 4. wherein he has ingeniously converted a gentle Satyr upon tedious and impertinent Visitants into a Libel on some in the Government: This I mention only as a Specimen of the Taste of the Gentlemen, I am forsooth, bound to please in my Speculations, not that I suppose my Impartiality will ever be called in Question upon that Account. Injustices of this Nature I could complain of in many Instancies; but I am at present diverted by the Reception of a Letter, which tho' it regards me only in my Private Capacity, as an Adept, yet I venture to publish it for the Entertainment of my Readers.

"To Censor Morum, Esq; Busy-Body General of the Province of Pennsylvania, and the Counties of Newcastle, Kent, and Sussex, upon Delaware.

"Honourable Sir,

"I judge by your Lucubrations, that you are not only a Lover of Truth and Equity, but a Man of Parts and Learning, and a Master of Science; as such I honour you. Know then, *Most profound Sir*, that I have from my Youth up, been a very indefatigable Student in, and Admirer of that Divine Science, *Astrology*. I have read over Scot, Albertus Magnus, and Cornelius Agrippa above 300 Times; and was in hopes by my Knowledge and Industry, to gain enough to have recompenced me for my Money expended, and Time lost in the Pursuit of this Learning. You cannot be ignorant, Sir, (for your intimate *Second sighted* Correspondent knows all Things) that there are large Sums of Money hidden under Ground in divers

Places about this Town, and in many Parts of the Country; But alas, Sir, Notwithstanding I have used all the Means laid down in the *immortal Authors* beforementioned, and when they fail'd, the ingenious Mr. P—d—l with his *Mercurial Wand* and *Magnet*, I have still fail'd in my Purpose. This therefore I send to Propose and desire an Acquaintance with you, and I do not doubt, notwithstanding my repeated Ill-Fortune, but we may be exceedingly serviceable to each other in our Discoveries; and that if we use our united Endeavours, the Time will come when the Busy-Body, his *Second-sighted Correspondent*, and *your very humble Servant*, will be Three of the richest Men in the Province: And then, Sir, what may not we do? *A Word to the Wise is sufficient.* I conclude with all demonstrable Respect, Yours, and Urania's Votary,

TITAN PLEIADES."

In the Evening after I had received this Letter, I made a Visit to my *Second-sighted* Friend, and communicated to him the Proposal. When he had read it, he assur'd me, that to his certain Knowledge there is not at this Time so much as one Ounce of Silver or Gold hid under Ground in any Part of this Province, For that the late and present Scarcity of Money had obliged those who were living, and knew where they had formerly hid any, to take it up, and use it in their own necessary Affairs: And as to all the Rest which was buried by Pyrates and others in old Times, who were never like to come for it, he himself had long since dug it all up and applied it to charitable Uses, And this he desired me to publish for general Good. For, as he acquainted me, There are among us great Numbers of honest Artificers and labouring People, who fed with a vain Hope of growing suddenly rich, neglect their Business, almost to the ruining of themselves and Families, and voluntarily endure abundance of Fatigue in a fruitless Search after Imaginary hidden Treasure. They wander thro' the Woods and Bushes by Day, to discover the Marks and Signs; at Midnight they repair to the hopeful Spot with Spades and Pickaxes; full of Expectation they labour violently, trembling at the same Time in every Joint, thro' Fear of certain malicious Demons who are said to haunt and guard such Places. At length a mighty hole is dug, and perhaps several Cartloads of Earth thrown out, but alas, no Cag or Iron Pot is found! no Seaman's Chest cram'd with Spanish Pistoles, or weighty Pieces of Eight! Then they conclude, that thro' some Mistake in the Procedure, some rash Word spoke, or some Rule of Art neglected, the Guardian Spirit had Power to sink it deeper into the Earth and convey it out of their Reach. Yet when a Man is once thus infatuated, he is so far from being discouraged by ill Success, that he is rather animated to double his Industry, and will try again and again in a Hundred Different Places, in Hopes at last of meeting with some lucky Hit, that shall at once Sufficiently reward him for all his Expence of Time and Labour.

This odd Humour of Digging for Money thro' a Belief that much has been hid by Pirates formerly frequenting the River, has for several Years been mighty prevalent among us; insomuch that you can hardly walk half a Mile out of Town on any Side, without observing several Pits dug with that Design, and perhaps some lately opened. Men, otherwise of very good Sense, have been drawn into this Practice thro' an over weening Desire of sudden Wealth, and an easy Credulity of what they so earnestly wish'd might be true. While the rational and almost certain Methods of acquiring Riches by Industry and Frugality are neglected or forgotten. There seems to be some peculiar Charm in the conceit of *finding* Money; and if the Sands of Schuylkil were so much mixed with small Grains of Gold, that a Man might in a Day's Time with Care and Application get together to the Value of half a Crown, I make no Question but we should find several People employ'd there, that can with Ease earn Five Shillings a Day at their proper Trades.

Many are the idle Stories told of the private Success of some People, by which others are encouraged to proceed; and the Astrologers, with whom the Country swarms at this Time, are either in the Belief of these things themselves, or find their Advantage in persuading others to believe them; for they are often consulted about the critical Times for Digging, the Methods of laying the Spirit, and the like Whimseys, which renders them very necessary to and very much caress'd by the poor deluded *Money-hunters.*

There is certainly something very bewitching in the Pursuit after Mines of Gold and Silver, and other valuable Metals; And many have been ruined by it. A Sea Captain of my Acquaintance used to blame the English for envying Spain their Mines of Silver; and too much despising or overlooking the Advantages of their own Industry and Manufactures. For my Part, says he, I esteem the Banks of Newfoundland to be a more valuable Possession than the Mountains of Potosi; and when I have been there on the Fishing Account, have look'd upon every Cod pull'd up into the Vessel as a certain Quantity of Silver Ore, which required only carrying to the next Spanish Port to be coin'd into Pieces of Eight; not to mention the *National Profit* of fitting out and Employing such a Number of Ships and Seamen. Let honest Peter Buckrum, who has long without Success been a Searcher after hidden Money, reflect on this, and be reclaimed from that unaccountable Folly. Let him consider that every Stitch he takes when he is on his Shop-board, is picking up part of a Grain of Gold that will in a few Days Time amount to a Pistole; And let Faber think the same of every Nail he drives, or every Stroke with his Plain. Such Thoughts may make them industrious, and of consequence in Time they may be Wealthy. But how absurd is it to neglect a certain Profit for such a ridiculous Whimsey: To spend whole Days at the George, in company with an idle Pretender to Astrology, contriving Schemes to discover what was never hidden, and forgetful how carelessly Business is managed at Home in their Absence: To leave their Wives and a warm Bed at Midnight (no matter if it rain, hail, snow or blow a Hurricane, provided that be the critical Hour) and fatigue themselves with the Violent Exercise of Digging for what they shall never find, and perhaps getting a Cold that may cost their Lives, or at least disordering themselves so as to be fit for no Business beside for some Days after. Surely this is nothing less than the most egregious Folly and Madness.

I shall conclude with the Words of my discreet Friend Agricola, of Chester-County, when he gave his Son a Good Plantation, *My Son*, says he, *I give thee now a Valuable Parcel of Land; I assure thee I have found a considerable Quantity of Gold by Digging there; Thee mayst do the same. But thee must carefully observe this. Never to dig more than Plow-deep.*

Part III

3 APRIL, 1729 – 13 JANUARY, 1737

The Nature and Necessity of a Paper-Currency

Doctrine to be Preached

Miscellaneous Observations

Proposals and Queries to be Asked the Junto

On Literary Style

On Protection of Towns from Fire

A Man of Sense

Self-Denial Not the Essence of Virtue

The Drinker's Dictionary

The Nature and Necessity of a Paper-Currency

3 April, 1729

A Modest Enquiry, &c.

There is no Science, the Study of which is more useful and commendable than the Knowledge of the true Interest of one's Country; and perhaps there is no Kind of Learning more abstruse and intricate, more difficult to acquire in any Degree of Perfection than This, and therefore none more generally neglected. Hence it is, that we every Day find Men in Conversation contending warmly on some Point in Politicks, which, altho' it may nearly concern them both, neither of them understand any more than they do each other.

Thus much by way of Apology for this present *Enquiry into the Nature and Necessity of a Paper Currency.* And if any Thing I shall say, may be a Means of fixing a Subject that is now the chief Concern of my Countrymen, in a clearer Light, I shall have the Satisfaction of thinking my Time and Pains well employed.

To proceed, then,

There is a certain proportionate Quantity of Money requisite to carry on the Trade of a Country freely and currently; More than which would be of no Advantage in Trade, and Less, if much less, exceedingly detrimental to it.

This leads us to the following general Considerations.

First, *A great Want of Money in any Trading Country, occasions Interest to be at a very high Rate.* And here it may be observed, that it is impossible by any Laws to restrain Men from giving and receiving exorbitant Interest, where Money is suitably scarce: For he that wants Money will find out

Ways to give 10 *per Cent.* when he cannot have it for less, altho' the Law forbids to take more than 6 *per Cent.* Now the Interest of Money being high is prejudicial to a Country several Ways: It makes Land bear a low Price, because few Men will lay out their Money in Land, when they can make a much greater Profit by lending it out upon Interest: And much less will Men be inclined to venture their Money at Sea, when they can, without Risque or Hazard, have a great and certain Profit by keeping it at home; thus Trade is discouraged. And if in two Neighbouring Countries the Traders of one, by Reason of a greater Plenty of Money, can borrow it to trade with at a lower Rate than the Traders of the other, they will infallibly have the Advantage, and get the greatest Part of that Trade into their own Hands; For he that trades with Money he hath borrowed at 8 or 10 *per Cent.* cannot hold Market with him that borrows his Money at 6 or 4. — On the contrary, *A plentiful Currency will occasion Interest to be low:* And this will be an Inducement to many to lay out their Money in Lands, rather than put it out to Use, by which means Land will begin to rise in Value and bear a better Price: And at the same Time it will tend to enliven Trade exceedingly, because People will find more Profit in employing their Money that Way than in Usury; and many that understand Business very well, but have not a Stock sufficient of their own, will be encouraged to borrow Money to trade with, when they can have it at moderate Interest.

Secondly, *Want of Money in a Country reduces the Price of that Part of its Produce which is used in Trade:* Because Trade being discouraged by it as above, there is a much less Demand for that Produce. And this is another Reason why Land in such a Case will be low, especially where the Staple Commodity of the Country is the immediate Produce of the Land, because that Produce being low, fewer People find an Advantage in Husbandry, or the Improvement of Land. — On the contrary, *A Plentiful Currency will occasion the Trading Produce to bear a good Price:* Because Trade being encouraged and advanced by it, there will be a much greater Demand for that Produce; which will be a great Encouragement of Husbandry and Tillage, and consequently make Land more valuable, for that many People would apply themselves to Husbandry, who probably might otherwise have sought some more profitable Employment.

As we have already experienced how much the Increase of our Currency by what Paper Money has been made, has encouraged our Trade; particularly to instance only in one Article, *Ship-Building;* it may not be amiss to observe under this Head, what a great Advantage it must be to us as a Trading Country, that has Workmen and all the Materials proper for that Business within itself, to have *Ship-Building* as much as possible advanced: For every Ship that is built here for the English Merchants, gains the Province her clear Value in Gold and Silver, which must otherwise have been sent Home for Returns in her Stead; and likewise, every Ship built in and belonging to the Province, not only saves the Province her first Cost, but all the Freight, Wages and Provisions she ever makes or requires as long as she lasts; provided Care is taken to make This her *Pay Port*, and that she always takes Provisions with her for the whole Voyage, which may easily be done. And how considerable an Article this is yearly in our Favour, every one, the least acquainted with mercantile Affairs, must needs be sensible; for if we could not Build our selves, we must either purchase so many Vessels as we want from other Countries, or else Hire them to carry our Produce to Market, which would be more expensive than Purchasing; and on many other Accounts exceedingly to our Loss. Now as Trade in general will decline where there is not a plentiful Currency, so *Ship-Building* must certainly of Consequence decline where Trade is declining.

Thirdly, *Want of Money in a Country discourages Labouring and Handicrafts Men (which are the chief Strength and Support of a People) from coming to settle in it, and induces many that were settled to leave the Country, and seek Entertainment and Employment in other Places, where they can be better paid.* For what can be more disheartning to an industrious labouring Man, than this, that after he hath earned his Bread with the Sweat of his Brows, he must spend as much Time, and have near as much Fatigue in getting it, as he had to earn it. *And nothing makes more bad Paymasters than a general Scarcity of Money.* And here again is a Third Reason for Land's bearing a low Price in such a Country, because Land always increases in Value in Proportion with the Increase of the People settling on it, there being so many more Buyers; and its Value will infallibly be diminished, if the Number of its Inhabitants diminish. — On the contrary, *A Plentiful Currency will encourage great Numbers of Labouring and Handicrafts Men to come and Settle in the Country*, by the same Reason that a Want of it will discourage and drive them out. Now the more Inhabitants, the greater Demand for Land (as is said above) upon which it must necessarily rise in Value, and bear a better Price. The same may be said of the Value of House-Rent, which will be advanced for the same Reasons; and by the Increase of Trade and Riches People will be enabled to pay greater Rents. Now the Value of House-Rent rising, and Interest becoming low, many that in a Scarcity of Money practised Usury, will probably be more inclined to Building; which will likewise sensibly enliven Business in any Place; it being an Advantage not only to *Brickmakers, Bricklayers, Masons, Carpenters, Joiners, Glaziers*, and several other Trades immediately employ'd by Building, but likewise to *Farmers, Brewers, Bakers, Taylors, Shoemakers, Shop-keepers*, and in short to every one that they lay their Money out with.

Fourthly, *Want of Money in such a Country as ours, occasions a greater Consumption of English and European Goods, in Proportion to the Number of the People, than there would otherwise be.* Because Merchants and Traders, by whom abundance of Artificers and labouring Men are employed, finding their other Affairs require what Money they can get into their hands, oblige those who work for them to take one half, or perhaps two thirds Goods in Pay. By this Means a greater Quantity of Goods are disposed of, and to a greater Value; because Working Men and their Families are thereby induced to be more profuse and extravagant in fine Apparel and the like, than they would be if they were obliged to pay ready Money for such Things after they had earn'd and received it, or if such Goods were not imposed upon them, of which they can make no other Use: For such People cannot send the Goods they are paid with to a Foreign Market, without losing considerably by having them sold for less than they stand 'em in here;

neither can they easily dispose of them at Home, because their Neighbours are generally supplied in the same Manner; But how unreasonable would it be, if some of those very Men who *have been a Means* of thus forcing People into unnecessary Expence, should be the first and most earnest in accusing them of *Pride and Prodigality*. Now tho' this extraordinary Consumption of Foreign Commodities may be a Profit to particular Men, yet the Country in general grows poorer by it apace. — On the contrary, As *A plentiful Currency will occasion a less Consumption of European Goods, in Proportion to the Number of the People*, so it will be a means of making the Balance of our Trade more equal than it now is, if it does not give it in our Favour; because our own Produce will be encouraged at the same Time. And it is to be observed, that tho' less Foreign Commodities are consumed in Proportion to the Number of People, yet this will be no Disadvantage to the Merchant, because the Number of People increasing, will occasion an increasing Demand of more Foreign Goods in the Whole.

Thus we have seen some of the many heavy Disadvantages a Country (especially such a Country as ours) must labour under, when it has not a sufficient Stock of running Cash to manage its Trade currently. And we have likewise seen some of the Advantages which accrue from having Money sufficient, or a Plentiful Currency.

The foregoing Paragraphs being well considered, we shall naturally be led to draw the following Conclusions with Regard to what Persons will probably be for or against Emitting a large Additional Sum of Paper Bills in this Province.

1. Since Men will always be powerfully influenced in their Opinions and Actions by what appears to be their particular Interest: Therefore all those, who wanting Courage to venture in Trade, now practise Lending Money on Security for exorbitant Interest, which in a Scarcity of Money will be done notwithstanding the Law, I say all such will probably be against a large Addition to our present Stock of Paper-Money; because a plentiful Currency will lower Interest, and make it common to lend on less Security.

2. All those who are Possessors of large Sums of Money, and are disposed to purchase Land, which is attended with a great and sure Advantage in a growing Country as this is; I say, the Interest of all such Men will encline them to oppose a large Addition to our Money. Because their Wealth is now continually increasing by the large Interest they receive, which will enable them (if they can keep Land from rising) to purchase More some time hence than they can at present; and in the mean time all Trade being discouraged, not only those who borrow of them, but the Common People in general will be impoverished, and consequently obliged to sell More Land for less Money than they will do at present. And yet, after such Men are possessed of as much Land as they can purchase, it will then be their Interest to have Money made Plentiful, because that will immediately make Land rise in Value in *their* Hands. Now it ought not to be wonder'd at, if People from the Knowledge of a Man's Interest do sometimes make a true Guess at his Designs; for, *Interest*, they say, *will not Lie*.

3. Lawyers, and others concerned in Court Business, will probably many of them be against a plentiful Currency; because People in that Case will have less Occasion to run in Debt, and conesquently less Occasion to go to Law and Sue one another for their Debts. Tho' I know some even among these Gentlemen, that regard the Publick Good before their own apparent private Interest.

4. All those who are any way Dependants on such Persons as are above mentioned, whether as holding Offices, as Tenants, or as Debtors, must at least *appear* to be against a large Addition; because if they do not, they must sensibly feel their present Interest hurt. And besides these, there are, doubtless, many well-meaning Gentlemen and Others, who, without any immediate private Interest of their own in View, are against making such an Addition, thro' an Opinion they may have of the Honesty and sound Judgment of some of their Friends that oppose it,(perhaps for the Ends aforesaid) without having given it any thorough Consideration themselves. And thus it is no Wonder if there is a *powerful* Party on that Side.

On the other Hand, Those who are Lovers of Trade, and delight to see Manufactures encouraged, will be for having a large Addition to our Currency: For they very well know, that People will have little Heart to advance Money in Trade, when what they can get is scarce sufficient to purchase Necessaries, and supply their Families with Provision. Much less will they lay it out in advancing new Manufactures; nor is it possible new Manufactures should turn to any Account, where there is not Money to pay the Workmen, who are discouraged by being paid in Goods, because it is a great Disadvantage to them.

Again, Those who are truly for the Proprietor's Interest (and have no separate Views of their own that are predominant) will be heartily for a large Addition: Because, as I have shewn above, Plenty of Money will for several Reasons make Land rise in Value exceedingly: And I appeal to those immediately concerned for the Proprietor in the Sale of his Lands, whether Land has not risen very much since the first Emission of what Paper Currency we now have, and even by its Means. Now we all know the Proprietary has great Quantities to sell.

And since a Plentiful Currency will be so great a Cause of advancing this Province in Trade and Riches, and increasing the Number of its People; which, tho' it will not sensibly lessen the Inhabitants of Great Britain, will occasion a much greater Vent and Demand for their Commodities here; and allowing that the Crown is the more powerful for its Subjects increasing in Wealth and Number, I cannot think it the Interest of England to oppose us in making as great a Sum of Paper Money here, as we, who are the best Judges of our own Necessities, find convenient. And if I were not sensible that the Gentlemen of Trade in England, to whom we have already parted with our Silver and Gold, are misinformed of our Circumstances, and therefore endeavour to have our Currency stinted to what it now is, I should think the Government at Home had some Reasons for discouraging and impoverishing this Province, which we are not acquainted with.

It remains now that we enquire, *Whether a large Addition to our Paper Currency will not make it sink in Value very much;* And here it will be requisite that we first form just Notions of the Nature and Value of Money in general.

As Providence has so ordered it, that not only different Countries, but even different Parts of the same Country, have their peculiar most suitable Productions; and likewise that different Men have Genius's adapted to Variety of different Arts and Manufactures, Therefore *Commerce*, or the Exchange of one Commodity or Manufacture for another, is highly convenient and beneficial to Mankind. As for Instance, *A* may be skilful in the Art of making Cloth, and *B* understand the raising of Corn; *A* wants Corn, and *B* Cloth; upon which they make an Exchange with each other for as much as each has Occasion, to the mutual Advantage and Satisfaction of both.

But as it would be very tedious, if there were no other Way of general Dealing, but by an immediate Exchange of Commodities; because a Man that had Corn to dispose of, and wanted Cloth for it, might perhaps in his Search for a Chapman to deal with, meet with twenty People that had Cloth to dispose of, but wanted no Corn; and with twenty others that wanted his Corn, but had no Cloth to suit him with. To remedy such Inconveniences, and facilitate Exchange, Men have invented Money, properly called a *Medium of Exchange*, because through or by its Means Labour is exchanged for Labour, or one Commodity for another. And whatever particular Thing Men have agreed to make this Medium of, whether Gold, Silver, Copper, or Tobacco; it is, to those who possess it (if they want any Thing) that very Thing which they want, because it will immediately procure it for them. It is Cloth to him that wants Cloth, and Corn to those that want Corn; and so of all other Necessaries, it *is* whatsoever it will procure. Thus he who had Corn to dispose of, and wanted to purchase Cloth with it, might sell his Corn for its Value in this general Medium, to one who wanted Corn but had no Cloth; and with this Medium he might purchase Cloth of him that wanted no Corn, but perhaps some other

Thing, as Iron it may be, which this Medium will immediately procure, and so he may be said to have exchanged his Cloth for Iron; and thus the general Exchange is soon performed, to the Satisfaction of all Parties, with abundance of Facility.

For many Ages, those Parts of the World which are engaged in Commerce, have fixed upon Gold and Silver as the chief and most proper Materials for this Medium; they being in themselves valuable Metals for their Fineness, Beauty, and Scarcity. By these, particularly by Silver, it has been usual to value all Things else: But as Silver it self is of no certain permanent Value, being worth more or less according to its Scarcity or Plenty, therefore it seems requisite to fix upon Something else, more proper to be made a *Measure of Values*, and this I take to be *Labour*.

By Labour may the Value of Silver be measured as well as other Things. As, Suppose one Man employed to raise Corn, while another is digging and refining Silver; at the Year's End, or at any other Period of Time, the compleat Produce of Corn, and that of Silver, are the natural Price of each other; and if one be twenty Bushels, and the other twenty Ounces, then an Ounce of that Silver is worth the Labour of raising a Bushel of that Corn. Now if by the Discovery of some nearer, more easy or plentiful Mines, a Man may get Forty Ounces of Silver as easily as formerly he did Twenty, and the same Labour is still required to raise Twenty Bushels of Corn, then Two Ounces of Silver will be worth no more than the same Labour of raising One Bushel of Corn, and that Bushel of Corn will be as cheap at two Ounces, as it was before at one; *cæteris paribus*[1].

Thus the Riches of a Country are to be valued by the Quantity of Labour its Inhabitants are able to purchase, and not by the Quantity of Silver and Gold they possess; which will purchase more or less Labour, and therefore is more or less valuable, as is said before, according to its Scarcity or Plenty. As those Metals have grown much more plentiful in Europe

1. *All other things being equal.*

since the Discovery of America, so they have sunk in Value exceedingly; for, to instance in England, formerly one Penny of Silver was worth a Days Labour, but now it is hardly worth the sixth Part of a Days Labour; because not less than Six-pence will purchase the Labour of a Man for a Day in any Part of that Kingdom; which is wholly to be attributed to the much greater Plenty of Money now in England than formerly. And yet perhaps England is in Effect no richer now than at that Time; because as much Labour might be purchas'd, or Work got done of almost any kind, for £100 then, as will now require or is now worth £600.

In the next Place let us consider the Nature of *Banks* emitting *Bills of Credit*, as they are at this Time used in Hamburgh, Amsterdam, London and Venice.

Those Places being Seats of vast Trade, and the Payment of great Sums being for that Reason frequent, *Bills of Credit* are found very convenient in Business; because a great Sum is more easily counted in Them, lighter in Carriage, concealed in less Room, and therefore safer in Travelling or Laying up, and on many other Accounts they are very much valued. The Banks are the general Cashiers of all Gentlemen, Merchants and great Traders in and about those Cities; there they deposite their Money, and may take out Bills to the Value, for which they can be certain to have Money again at the Bank at any Time: This gives the Bills a Credit; so that in England they are never less valuable than Money, and in Venice and Amsterdam they are generally worth more. And the Bankers always reserving Money in hand to answer more than the common Run of Demands (and some People constantly putting in while others are taking out) are able besides to lend large Sums, on good Security, to the Government or others, for a reasonable Interest, by which they are paid for their Care and Trouble; and the Money which otherwise would have lain dead in their Hands, is made to circulate again thereby among the People: And thus the Running Cash of the Nation is as it were doubled; for all great Payments being made in Bills, Money in lower Trade becomes much more plentiful: And this is an exceeding great Advantage to a Trading Country, that is not over-stock'd with Gold and Silver.

As those who take Bills out of the Banks in Europe, put in Money for Security; so here, and in some of the neighbouring Provinces, we engage our Land. Which of these Methods will most effectually secure the Bills from actually sinking in Value, comes next to be considered.

Trade in general being nothing else but the Exchange of Labour for Labour, the Value of all Things is, as I have said before, most justly measured by Labour. Now suppose I put my Money into a Bank, and take out a Bill for the Value; if this Bill at the Time of my receiving it, would purchase me the Labour of one hundred Men for twenty Days; but some time after will only purchase the Labour of the same Number of Men for fifteen Days; it is plain the Bill has sunk in Value one fourth Part. Now Silver and Gold being of no permanent Value; and as this Bill is founded on Money, and therefore to be esteemed as such, it may be that the Occasion of this Fall is the increasing Plenty of Gold and Silver, by which Money is one fourth Part less valuable than before, and therefore one fourth more is given of it for the same Quantity of Labour; and if Land is not become more plentiful by some proportionate Decrease of the People, one fourth Part more of Money is given for the same Quantity of Land, whereby it appears that it would have been more profitable to me to have laid that Money out in Land which I put into the Bank, than to place it there and take a Bill for it. And it is certain that the Value of Money has been continually sinking in England for several Ages past, because it has been continually increasing in Quantity. But if Bills could be taken out of a Bank in Europe on a Land Security, it is probable the Value of such Bills would be more certain and steady, because the Number of Inhabitants continue to be near the same in those Countries from Age to Age.

For as Bills issued upon Money Security are Money, so Bills issued upon Land, are in Effect *Coined Land*.

Therefore (to apply the Above to our own Circumstances) If Land in this Province was falling, or any way likely to fall, it would behove the Legislature most carefully to contrive how to prevent the Bills issued upon Land from falling with it. But as our People increase exceedingly, and will be further increased, as I have before shewn, by the Help of a large Addition to our Currency; and as Land in consequence is continually rising, So, in case no Bills are emitted but what are upon Land Security, the Money-Acts in every Part punctually enforced and executed, the Payments of Principal and Interest being duly and strictly required, and the Principal *bona fide* sunk according to Law, it is absolutely impossible such Bills should ever sink below their first Value, or below the Value of the Land on which they are founded. In short, there is so little Danger of their sinking, that they would certainly rise as the Land rises, if they were not emitted in a proper Manner for preventing it; That is, by providing in the Act *That Payment may be made, either in those Bills, or in any other Bills made current by any Act of the Legislature of this Province;* and that the Interest, as it is received, may be again emitted in Discharge of Publick Debts; whereby circulating it returns again into the Hands of the Borrowers, and becomes Part of their future Payments; and thus as it is likely there will not be any Difficulty for want of Bills to pay the Office, they are hereby kept from rising above their first Value: For else, supposing there should be emitted upon mortgaged Land its full present Value in Bills; as in the Banks in Europe the full Value of the Money deposited is given out in Bills; and supposing the Office would take nothing but the same Sum in those Bills in Discharge of the Land; as in the Banks aforesaid, the same Sum in their Bills must be brought in, in order to receive out the Money: In such Case the Bills would most surely rise in Value as the Land rises; as certainly as the Bank Bills founded on Money would fall if that Money was falling. Thus if I were to mortgage to a Loan-Office, or Bank, a Parcel of Land now valued at £100 in Silver, and receive for it the like Sum in Bills, to be paid in again at the Expiration of a certain Term of Years; before which, my Land rising in Value, becomes worth £150 in Silver: 'Tis plain, that if I have not these Bills in Possession, and the Office will take nothing but these Bills, or else what it is now become worth in Silver, in Discharge of my Land; I say it appears plain, that those Bills will now be worth £150 in Silver to the Possessor; and if I can purchase them for less, in order to redeem my Land, I shall by so much be a Gainer.

I need not say any Thing to convince the Judicious that our Bills have not yet sunk, tho' there is and has been some Difference between them and Silver; because it is evident that that Difference is occasioned by the Scarcity of the latter, which is now become a Merchandize, rising and falling, like other Commodities, as there is a greater or less Demand for it, or as it is more or less Plenty.

Yet farther, in order to make a true Estimate of the Value of Money, we must distinguish between Money as it is Bullion, which is Merchandize, and as by being coin'd it is made a Currency: For its Value as a Merchandize, and its Value as a Currency, are two distinct Things; and each may possibly rise and fall in some Degree independent of the other. Thus if the Quantity of Bullion increases in a Country, it will proportionably decrease in Value; but if at the same Time the Quantity of current Coin should decrease, (supposing Payments may not be made in Bullion) what Coin there is will rise in Value as a Currency, i.e. People will give more Labour in Manufactures for a certain Sum of ready Money.

In the same Manner must we consider a *Paper Currency* founded on Land; as it is Land, and as it is a Currency:

Money as Bullion, or as Land, is valuable by so much Labour as it costs to procure that Bullion or Land.

Money, as a Currency, has an Additional Value by so much Time and Labour as it saves in the Exchange of Commodities.

If, as a Currency, it saves one Fourth Part of the Time and Labour of a Country; it has, on that Account, one Fourth added to its original Value.

When there is no Money in a Country, all Commerce must be by Exchange. Now if it takes one fourth Part of the Time and Labour of a Country, to exchange or get their Commodities exchanged; then, in computing their Value, that Labour of Exchanging must be added to the Labour of manufacturing those Commodities: But if that Time or Labour is saved by introducing Money sufficient, then the additional Value on Account of the Labour of Exchanging may be abated, and Things sold for only the Value of the Labour in making them; because the People may now in the same Time make one Fourth more in Quantity of Manufactures than they could before.

From these Considerations it may be gathered, that in all the Degrees between having no Money in a Country, and Money sufficient for the Trade, it will rise and fall in Value as a Currency, in Proportion to the Decrease or Increase of its Quantity: And if there may be at some Time more than enough, the Overplus will have no Effect towards making the Currency, as a Currency, of less Value than when there was but enough; because such Overplus will not be used in Trade, but be some other way disposed of.

If we enquire, *How much* per Cent. *Interest ought to be required upon the Loan of these Bills;* we must consider what is the Natural Standard of Usury: And this appears to be, where the Security is undoubted, at least the Rent of so much Land as the Money lent will buy: For it cannot be expected that any Man will lend his Money for less than it would fetch him in as Rent if he laid it out in Land, which is the most secure Property in the World. But if the Security is casual, then a kind of Ensurance must be enterwoven with the simple natural Interest, which may advance the Usury very conscionably to any height below the Principal it self. Now among us, if the Value of Land is twenty Years Purchase, Five *per Cent.* is the just Rate of Interest for Money lent on undoubted Security. Yet if Money grows scarce in a Country, it becomes more difficult for People to make punctual Payments of what they borrow, Money being hard to be raised; likewise Trade being discouraged, and Business impeded for want of a Currency, abundance of People must be in declining Circumstances, and by these Means Security is more precarious than where Money is plenty. On such Accounts it is no wonder if People ask a greater Interest for their Money than the natural Interest; and what is above is to be look'd upon as a kind of *Præmium* for the Ensurance of those Uncertainties, as they are greater or less. Thus we always see, that where Money is scarce, Interest is high, and low where it is plenty. Now it is certainly the Advantage of a Country to make Interest as low as possible, as I have already shewn; and this can be done no other way than by making Money plentiful. And since, in Emitting Paper Money among us, the Office has the best of Security, the Titles to the Land being all skilfully and strictly examined and ascertained; and as it is only permitting the People by Law to coin their own Land, which costs the Government nothing, the Interest being more than enough to pay the Charges of Printing, Officers Fees, &c. I cannot see any good Reason why Four *per Cent.* to the Loan-Office should not be thought fully sufficient. As a low Interest may incline more to take Money out, it will become more plentiful in Trade; and this may bring down the common Usury, in which Security is more dubious, to the Pitch it is determined at by Law.

If it should be objected, *That Emitting It at so low an Interest, and on such easy Terms, will occasion more to be taken out than the Trade of the Country really requires:* It may be answered, That, as has already been shewn, there can never be so much of it emitted as to make it fall below the Land it is founded on; because no Man in his Senses will mortgage his Estate for what is of no more Value to him than That he has mortgaged, especially if the Possession of what he receives is more precarious than of what he mortgages, as that of Paper Money is when compared to Land: And if it should ever become so plenty by indiscreet Persons continuing to take out a large Overplus, above what is necessary in Trade, so as to make People imagine it would become by that Means of less Value than their mortgaged Lands, they would immediately of Course begin to pay it in again to the Office to redeem their Land, and continue to do so till there was no more left in Trade than was absolutely necessary. And thus the Proportion would find it self, (tho' there were a Million too much in the Office to be let out) without giving any one the Trouble of Calculation.

It may perhaps be objected to what I have written concerning the Advantages of a large Addition to our Currency, *That if the People of this Province increase, and Husbandry is more followed, we shall overstock the Markets with our Produce of Flower*, &c. To this it may be answered, that we can never have too many People (nor too much Money) For when one Branch of Trade or Business is overstocked with Hands, there are the more to spare to be employed in another. So if raising Wheat proves dull, more may (if there is Money to support and carry on new Manufactures) proceed to the raising and manufacturing of *Hemp, Silk, Iron*, and many other Things the Country is very capable of, for which we only want People to work, and Money to pay them with.

Upon the Whole it may be observed, That it is the highest Interest of a Trading Country in general to make Money plentiful; and that it can be a Disadvantage to none that have honest Designs. It cannot hurt even the Usurers, tho' it should sink what they receive as Interest; because they will be proportionably more secure in what they lend; or they will have an Opportunity of employing their Money to greater Advantage, to themselves as well as to the Country. Neither can it hurt those Merchants who have great Sums out-standing in Debts in the Country, and seem on that Account to have the most plausible Reason to fear it; *to wit*, because a large Addition being made to our Currency, will increase the Demand of our Exporting Produce, and by that Means raise the Price of it, so that they will not be able to purchase so much Bread or Flower with £100 when they shall receive it after such an Addition, as they now can, and may if there is no Addition: I say it cannot hurt even such, because they will get in their Debts just in exact Proportion so much the easier and sooner as the Money becomes plentier; and therefore, considering the Interest and Trouble saved, they will not be Losers; because it only sinks in Value as a Currency, proportionally as it becomes more plenty. It cannot hurt the Interest of Great Britain, as has been shewn; and it will greatly advance the Interest of the Proprietor. It will be an Advantage to every industrious Tradesman, &c. because his Business will be carried on more freely, and Trade be universally enlivened by it. And as more Business in all Manufactures will be done, by so much as the Labour and Time spent in Exchange is saved, the Country in general will grow so much the richer.

It is nothing to the Purpose to object the wretched Fall of the Bills in New-England and South-Carolina, unless it might be made evident that their Currency was emitted with the same Prudence, and on such good Security as ours is; and it certainly was not.

As this Essay is wrote and published in Haste, and the Subject in it self intricate, I hope I shall be censured with Candour, if, for want of Time carefully to revise what I have written, in some Places I should appear to have express'd my self too obscurely, and in others am liable to Objections I did not foresee. I sincerely desire to be acquainted with the Truth, and on that Account shall think my self obliged to any one, who will take the Pains to shew me, or the Publick, where I am mistaken in my Conclusions, And as we all know there are among us several Gentlemen of acute Parts and profound Learning, who are very much against any Addition to our Money, it were to be wished that they would favour the Country with their Sentiments on this Head in Print; which, supported with Truth and good Reasoning, may probably be very convincing. And this is to be desired the rather, because many People knowing the Abilities of those Gentlemen to manage a good Cause, are apt to construe their Silence in This, as an Argument of a bad One. Had any Thing of that Kind ever yet appeared, perhaps I should not have given the Publick this Trouble: But as those ingenious Gentlemen have not yet (and I doubt never will) think it worth their Concern to enlighten the Minds of their erring Countrymen in this Particular, I think it would be highly commendable in every one of us, more fully to bend our Minds to the Study of *What is the true Interest of* PENNSYLVANIA; whereby we may be enabled, not only to reason pertinently with one another; but, if Occasion requires, to transmit Home such clear Representations, as must inevitably convince our Superiors of the Reasonableness and Integrity of our Designs.

Philadelphia, April 3. 1729.

B. B.

Doctrine to be Preached

1731

Doct. to be prea[che]d

That there is one God Father of the Universe.

That he [is] infinitely good, Powerful and wise.

That he is omnipresent.

That he ought to be worshipped, by Adoration Prayer and Thanksgiving both in publick and private.

That he loves such of his Creatures as love and do good to others: and will reward them either in this World or hereafter.

That Men's Minds do not die with their Bodies, but are made more happy or miserable after this Life according to their Actions.

That Virtuous Men ought to league together to strengthen the Interest of Virtue, in the World: and so strengthen themselves in Virtue.

That Knowledge and Learning is to be cultivated, and Ignnorance dissipated.

That none but the Virtuous are wise.

That Man's Perfection is in Virtue. [*Remainder lost*]

Miscellaneous Observations

1732

The great Secret of succeeding in Conversation, is, To admire little, to hear much; allways to distrust our own Reason, and sometimes that of our Friends; never to pretend to Wit, but to make that of others appear as much as possibly we can: to hearken to what is said, and to answer to the purpose.

Ut jam nunc dicat jam nunc debentia dici.[1]

—

In vain are musty Morals taught in Schools
By rigid Teachers, and as rigid Rules,
Where Virtue with a Frowning Aspect Stands,
And frights the pupil with her rough Commands.
But Woman — —
Charming Woman can true Converts make,
We love the Precepts for the Teacher's Sake;
Virtue in them appears so bright and gay
We hear with Transport, and with Pride obey.

—

You may first write a Letter that may carry good Sense, to your Friend, but let the Lines be wide asunder: Then between these Lines write your Secret Letter with Gall Water only, wherein the Galls have been infused but

1. *"Let him now say what ought to be said now."* Horace, *Ars Poetica*

a little while. Dissolve Copperas in fair Water, dip a pensil in the Water and moisten the Paper in the Interlining.

Pennyworth of Spirit of Vitriol in a Thumb-bottle [and] half as much Spring Water—Write—Fire.

—

I am about Courting a Girl I have had but little Acquaintance with; how shall I come to a Knowledge of her Fawlts? and whether she has the Virtues I imagine she has?

Answ. Commend her among her Female Acquaintance.

—

If a sound Body and a sound Mind, which is as much as to say Health and Virtue are to be preferred before all other Considerations; Ought not Men in choosing of a Business either for themselves or Children to refuse such as are unwholesome for the Body; and such as make a Man too dependent, too much oblig'd to please others, and too much subjected to their Humours in order to be recommended and get a Livelihood.

Proposals and Queries to be Asked the Junto

1732

Proposals

That P S[1] and A N[2] be immediately invited into the Junto.

That all New Members be qualified by the 4 qualifications and all the old ones take it.

That these Queries [be] copied at the beginning of a Book [and] be read distinctly each Meeting [with] a Pause between each while one might fill and drink a Glass of Wine.

That if they cannot all be gone thro' in one Night we begin the next where we left off, only such as particularly regard the Junto to be read every Night.

That it be not hereafter the Duty of any Member to bring Queries but left to his Discretion.

That an old Declamation be without fail read every Night when there is no New One.

That Mr. Brientnals Poem on the Junto be read once a Month, and hum'd in Consort, by as many as can hum it.

---

1. Philip Syng, Silversmith. Crafted the Syng Inkstand used to sign the Declaration of Independence and the United States Constitution.

2. Anthony Nichols, Blacksmith. Constructed fire engines and other equipment in Philadelphia.

That once a Month in Spring, Summer and Fall the Junto meet of a Sunday in the Afternoon in some proper Place cross the River for Bodily Exercise.

That in the aforesaid Book be kept Minutes thus

Fryday June 30. 1732.

Present ABCDEF &c.

1. HP read this Maxim viz. or this Experiment viz or &c.

5. Lately arriv'd one —— of such a Profession or such a Science &c.

7. XY grew rich by this Means &c.

That these Minutes be read once a Year at the Anniversary.

That all Fines due be immediately paid in, and that penal Laws for Queries and Declamations [be] abolish'd only he who is absent above ten Times in the Year, to pay 10*s.* towards the Anniversary Entertainment.

That the Secretary for keeping the Minutes be allow'd one Shilling per Night, to be paid out of the Money already in his Hands.

That after the Queries are begun reading, all Discourse foreign to them shall be deem'd impertinent.

When any thing from Reading an Author is mention'd, if it excead (*incomplete*) lines and the Junto require it; The Person shall bring the Passage, or an Extract from [*written above*: Abstract of] it, in Writing, the next Night, if he has it not [with] him.

When the Books of the Library come: Every Member shall undertake some Author, that he may not be without Observations to communicate.

—

Queries to be ask'd the Junto

Whence comes the Dew that stands on the Outside of a Tankard that has cold Water in it in the Summer Time?

Does the Importation of Servants increase or advance the Wealth of our Country?

Would not an Office of Insurance for Servants be of Service, and what Methods are proper for the erecting such an Office?

Qu. Whence does it proceed, that the Proselytes to any Sect or Persuasion generally appear more zealous than those who are bred up in it?

Answ. I Suppose that People *bred* in different Persuasions are nearly zealous alike. He that changes his Party is either sincere, or not sincere; that is he either does it for the sake of the Opinions merely, or with a View of Interest. If he is sincere and has no View of Interest; and considers before he declares himself, how much Ill will he shall have from those he leaves, and that those he is about to go among will be apt to suspect his Sincerity: if he is not really zealous he will not declare; and therefore must be zealous if he does declare. If he is not sincere, He is oblig'd at least to put on an Appearance of great Zeal, to convince the better, his New Friends that he is heartily in earnest, for his old ones he knows dislike him. And as few Acts of Zeal will be more taken Notice of than such as are done against the Party he has left, he is inclin'd to injure or malign them, because he knows they contemn and despise him. Hence one Renegade is (as the Proverb says) worse than 10 Turks.

—

Qu. Can a Man arrive at Perfection in this Life as some Believe; or is it impossible as others believe?

A. Perhaps they differ in the meaning of the Word Perfection.

I suppose the Perfection of any Thing to be only the greatest the Nature of that Thing is capable of;

different Things have different Degrees of Perfection; and the same thing at different Times.

Thus an Horse is more perfect than an Oyster yet the Oyster may be a perfect Oyster as well as the Horse a perfect Horse.

And an Egg is not so perfect as a Chicken, nor a Chicken as a Hen; for the Hen has more Strength than the Chicken, and the C[hicken] more Life than the Egg: Yet it may be a perfect Egg, Chicken and Hen.

If they mean, a Man cannot in this Life be so perfect as an Angel, it is [*written above:* may be] true; for an Angel by being incorporeal is allow'd some Perfections we are at present incapable of, and less liable to some Imperfections that we are liable to.

If they mean a Man is not capable of being so perfect here as he is capable of being in Heaven, that may be true likewise. But that a Man is not capable of being so perfect here, as he is capable of being here; is not Sense; it is as if I should say, a Chicken in the State of a Chicken is not capable of being so perfect as a Chicken is capable of being in that State. In the above Sense if there may be a perfect Oyster, a perfect Horse, a perfect Ship, why not a perfect Man? that is as perfect as his present Nature and Circumstances admit?

—

Quest. Wherein consists the Happiness of a rational Creature?

Ans. In having a Sound Mind and a healthy Body, a Sufficiency of the Necessaries and Conveniencies of Life, together with the Favour of God, and the Love of Mankind.

Qu. What do you mean by a sound Mind?

A. A Faculty of reasoning justly and truly in searching after [and] discovering such Truths as relate to my Happiness. Which Faculty is the Gift of God, capable of being improv'd by Experience and Instruction, into Wisdom.

Q. What is Wisdom?

A. The Knowledge of what will be best for us on all Occasions and of the best Ways of attaining it.

Q. Is any Man wise at all Times, and in all Things?

A. No; but some are much more frequently wise than others.

Q. What do you mean by the Necessaries of Life?

A. Having wholesome Food and Drink wherewith to satisfie Hunger and Thirst, Cloathing and a Place of Habitation fit to secure against the inclemencies of the Weather.

Q. What do you mean by the Conveniencies of Life?

A. Such a Plenty [*uncompleted*]

—

And if in the Conduct of your Affairs you have been deceived by others, or have committed any Error your self, it will be a Discretion in you to observe and note the same, and the Defailance, with the Means or Expedient to repair it.

No Man truly wise but who hath been deceived.

Let all your observations be committed to writing every Night before you go to Sleep.

—

Query, Whether it is worth a Rational Man's While to forego the Pleasure arising from the present Luxury of the Age in Eating and Drinking and artful Cookery, studying to gratify the Appetite for the Sake of enjoying healthy Old Age, a Sound Mind and a Sound Body, which are the Advantages reasonably to be expected from a more simple and temperate Diet.

Whether those Meats and Drinks are not the best, that contain nothing in their natural Tastes, nor have any Thing added by Art so pleasing as to induce us to Eat or Drink when we are not athirst or Hungry or after Thirst and Hunger are satisfied; Water for Instance for Drink and Bread or the Like for Meat?

What is the [*written above:* is there any] Difference between Knowledge and Prudence?

If there is any, which of the two is most Eligible?

Is it justifiable to put private Men to Death for the Sake of publick Safety or Tranquility, who have committed no Crime?

As in the Case of the Plague to stop Infection, or as in the Case of the Welshmen here Executed.

—

Whether Men ought to be denominated Good or ill Men from their Actions or their Inclinations?

If the Sovereign Power attempts to deprive a Subject of his Right, (or which is the same Thing, of what he thinks his Right) is it justifiable in him to resist if he is able?

What general Conduct of Life is most suitable for Men in such Circumstances as most of the Members of the Junto are; Or, of the many Schemes of Living which are in our Power to pursue, which will be most probably conducive to our Happiness.

Which is best to make a Friend of, a wise and good Man that is poor; or a Rich Man that is neither wise nor good? Which of the two is the greatest Loss to a Country, if they both die?

Which of the two is happiest in Life?

Does it not in a general Way require great Study and intense Application for a Poor Man to become rich and Powerful, if he would do it, without the Forfeiture of his Honesty?

Does it not require as much Pains, Study and Application to become truly Wise and strictly Good and Virtuous as to become rich?

Can a Man of common Capacity pursue both Views with Success at the same Time?

If not, which of the two is it best for him to make his whole Application to?

On Literary Style

2 August, 1733

To the Printer of the *Gazette.*

There are few Men, of Capacity for making any considerable Figure in Life, who have not frequent Occasion to communicate their Thoughts to others in *Writing;* if not sometimes publickly as Authors, yet continually in the Management of their private Affairs, both of Business and Friendship: and since, when ill-express'd, the most proper Sentiments and justest Reasoning lose much of their native Force and Beauty, it seems to me that there is scarce any Accomplishment more necessary to a Man of Sense, than that of *Writing well* in his Mother Tongue: But as most other polite Acquirements, make a greater Appearance in a Man's Character, this however useful, is generally neglected or forgotten.

I believe there is no better Means of learning to write well, than this of attempting to entertain the Publick now and then in one of your Papers. When the Writer conceals himself, he has the Advantage of hearing the Censure both of Friends and Enemies, express'd with more Impartiality. And since, in some degree, it concerns the Credit of the Province, that such Things as are printed be performed tolerably well, mutual Improvement seems to be the Duty of all Lovers of Writing: I shall therefore frankly communicate the Observations I have made or collected on this Subje[sym]ct, and request those of others in Return.

I have thought in general, that whoever would write so as not to displease good Judges, should have particular Regard to these three Things, viz. That his Performance be *smooth, clear*, and *short:* For the contrary Qualities are apt to offend, either the Ear, the Understanding, or the Patience.

'Tis an Observation of Dr. Swift, that modern Writers injure the Smoothness of our Tongue, by omitting Vowels wherever it is possible, and joining the harshest Consonants together with only an Apostrophe between; thus for *judged*, in it self not the smoothest of Words, they say *judg'd;* for *disturbed, disturb'd*, &c. It may be added to this, says another, that by changing *eth* into *s*, they have shortned one Syllable in a multitude of Words, and have thereby encreased, not only the *Hissing*, too offensive before, but also the great Number of Monosyllables, of which, without great Difficulty, a smooth Sentence cannot be composed. The Smoothness of a Period is also often Hurt by Parentheses, and therefore the best Writers endeavour to avoid them.

To write *clearly*, not only the most expressive, but the plainest Words should be chosen. In this, as well as in every other Particular requisite to Clearness, Dr. Tillotson is an excellent Example. The Fondness of some Writers for such Words as carry with them an Air of Learning, renders them unintelligible to more than half their Countrymen. If a Man would that his Writings have an Effect on the Generality of Readers, he had better imitate that Gentleman, who would use no Word in his Works that was not well understood by his Cook-maid.

A too frequent Use of Phrases ought likewise to be avoided by him that would write clearly. They trouble the Language, not only rendring it extreamly difficult to Foreigners, but make the Meaning obscure to a great number of English Readers. Phrases, like learned Words, are seldom used without Affectation; when, with all true Judges, the simplest Stile is the most beautiful.

But supposing the most proper Words and Expressions chosen, the Performance may yet be weak and obscure, if it has not *Method*. If a Writer would *persuade*, he should proceed gradually from Things already allow'd, to those from which Assent is yet with-held, and make their Connection manifest. If he would *inform*, he must advance regularly from Things known to things unknown, distin[sym]ly without Confusion, and the lower he begins the better. It is a common Fault in Writers, to allow their Readers too much Knowledge: They begin with that which should be the Middle, and skipping backwards and forwards, 'tis impossible for any one but he who is perfect in the Subject before, to understand their Work, and such an one has no Occasion to read it. Perhaps a Habit of using good Method, cannot be better acquired, than by learning a little Geometry or Algebra.

Amplification, or the Art of saying Little in Much, should only be allowed to Speakers. If they preach, a Discourse of considerable Length is expected from them, upon every Subject they undertake, and perhaps they are not stock'd with naked Thoughts sufficient to furnish it out. If they plead in the Courts, it is of Use to speak abundance, tho' they reason little; for the Ignorant in a Jury, can scarcely believe it possible that a Man can talk so much and so long without being in the Right. Let them have the Liberty then, of repeating the same Sentences in other Words; let them put an Adjective to every Substantive, and double every Substantive with a Synonima; for this is more agreeable than hauking, spitting, taking Snuff, or any other Means of concealing Hesitation. Let them multiply Definitions, Comparisons, Similitudes and Examples. Permit them to make a Detail of Causes and Effects, enumerate all the Consequences, and express one Half by Metaphor and Circumlocution: Nay, allow the Preacher to to tell us whatever a Thing is negatively, before he begins to tell us what it is affirmatively; and suffer him to divide and subdivide as far as *Two and fiftiethly*. All this is not intolerable while it is not written. But when a Discourse is to be bound down upon Paper, and subjected to the calm leisurely Examination of nice Judgment, every Thing that is needless gives Offence; and therefore all should be retrenched, that does not directly conduce to the End design'd. Had this been always done, many large and tiresome Folio's would have shrunk into Pamphlets, and many a Pamphlet into a single Period. However, tho' a multitude of Words obscure the Sense, and 'tis necessary to abridge a verbose Author in order to understand him;

yet a Writer should take especial Care on the other Hand, that his Brevity doth not hurt his Perspicuity.

After all, if the Author does not intend his Piece for general Reading, he must exactly suit his Stile and Manner to the particular Taste of those he proposes for his Readers. Every one observes, the different Ways of Writing and Expression used by the different Sects of Religion; and can readily enough pronounce, that it is improper to use some of these Stiles in common, or to use the common Stile, when we address some of these Sects in particular.

To conclude, I shall venture to lay it down as a Maxim, *That no Piece can properly be called good, and well written, which is void of any Tendency to benefit the Reader, either by improving his Virtue or his Knowledge.* This Principle every Writer would do well to have in View, whenever he undertakes to write. All Performances done for meer Ostentation of Parts, are really contemptible; and withal far more subject to the Severity of Criticism, than those more meanly written, wherein the Author appears to have aimed at the Good of others. For when 'tis visible to every one, that a Man writes to show his Wit only, all his Expressions are sifted, and his Sense examined, in the nicest and most ill-natur'd manner; and every one is glad of an Opportunity to mortify him. But, what a vast Destruction would there be of Books, if they were to be saved or condemned on a Tryal by this Rule!

Besides, Pieces meerly humorous, are of all Sorts the hardest to succeed in. If they are not natural, they are stark naught; and there can be no real Humour in an Affectation of Humour.

Perhaps it may be said, that an ill Man is able to write an ill Thing well; that is, having an ill Design, and considering who are to be his Readers, he may use the properest Stile and Arguments to attain his Point. In this Sense, that is best wrote, which is best adapted to the Purpose of the Writer.

I am apprehensive, dear Readers, lest in this Piece, I should be guilty of every Fault I condemn, and deficient in every Thing I recommend; so much easier it is to offer Rules than to practise them. I am sure, however, of this, that I am Your very sincere Friend and Servant.

On Protection of Towns from Fire

4 February, 1735

Mr. Franklin,

Being old and lame of my Hands, and thereby uncapable of assisting my Fellow Citizens, when their Houses are on Fire; I must beg them to take in good Part the following Hints on the Subject of Fires.

In the first Place, as *an Ounce of Prevention is worth a Pound of Cure*, I would advise 'em to take Care how they suffer living Brands-ends, or Coals in a full Shovel, to be carried out of one Room into another, or up or down Stairs, unless in a Warmingpan shut; for Scraps of Fire may fall into Chinks, and make no Appearance till Midnight; when your Stairs being in Flames, you may be forced, (as I once was) to leap out of your Windows, and hazard your Necks to avoid being over-roasted.

And now we talk of Prevention, where would be the Damage, if, to the Act for preventing Fires, by regulating Bakehouses and Coopers Shops, a Clause were added to regulate all other Houses in the particulars of too shallow Hearths, and the detestable Practice of putting wooden Mouldings on each side the Fire Place, which being commonly of Heart-of-Pine and full of Turpentine, stand ready to flame as soon as a Coal or a small Brand shall roul [roll] against them.

Once more; if Chimneys were more frequently and more carefully clean'd, some Fires might thereby be prevented. I have known foul Chimneys burn most furiously a few Days after they were swept: People in Confidence that they are clean, making large Fires. Every Body among us is allow'd to sweep Chimneys, that please to undertake that Business; and if a Chimney fires thro' fault of the Sweeper, the Owner pays the Fine, and the Sweeper goes free. This Thing is not right. Those who undertake Sweeping of Chimneys, and employ Servants for that Purpose, ought to be licensed by the Mayor; and if any Chimney fires and flames out 15 Days after Sweeping, the Fine should be paid by the Sweeper; for it is his Fault.

We have at present got Engines enough in the Town, but I question, whether in many Parts of the Town, Water enough can be had to keep them going for half an Hour together. It seems to me some Publick Pumps are wanting; but that I submit to better Judgments.

As to our Conduct in the Affair of Extinguishing Fires, tho' we do not want Hands or Good-will, yet we seem to want Order and Method, and therefore I believe I cannot do better than to offer for our Imitation, the Example of a City in a Neighbouring Province. There is, as I am well inform'd, a Club or Society of active Men belonging to each Fire Engine; whose Business is to attend all Fires with it whenever they happen; and to work it once a Quarter, and see it kept in order: Some of these are to handle the Firehooks, and others the Axes, which are always kept with the Engine; and for this Service they are consider'd in an Abatement or Exemption in the Taxes. In Time of Fire, they are commanded by Officers appointed by Law, called *Firewards*, who are distinguish'd by a Red Staff of five Feet long, headed with a Brass Flame of 6 Inches; And being Men of Prudence and Authority, they direct the opening and stripping of Roofs by the Ax-Men, the pulling down burning Timbers by the Hookmen, and the playing of the Engines, and command the making of Lanes, &c. and they are impowered to require Assistance for the Removing of Goods out of Houses on fire or in Danger of Fire, and to appoint Guards for securing such Goods; and Disobedience, to these Officers in any, at such Times, is punished by a Fine of 40*s.* or Ten Days Imprisonment. These Officers, with the Men belonging to the Engine, at their Quarterly Meetings, discourse of Fires, of the Faults committed at some, the good Management in some Cases at others, and thus communicating their Thoughts and Experience they grow wise in the Thing, and know how to command and to execute in the best manner upon every Emergency. Since the Establishment of this Regulation, it seems there has been no extraordinary Fire in that Place; and I wish there never may be any here. But they suffer'd before they made such a Regulation, and so must we; for Englishmen feel but cannot see; as the Italian says of us. And it has pleased God, that in the Fires we have hitherto had, all the bad Circumstances have never happened together, such as dry Season, high Wind, narrow Street, and little or low Water: which perhaps tends to makes us secure in our own Minds; but if a Fire with those Circumstances, which God forbid, should happen, we should afterwards be careful enough.

Let me say one thing more, and I will be silent. I could wish, that either Tiles would come in use for a Covering to Buildings; or else that those who build, would make their Roofs more safe to walk upon, by carrying the Wall above the Eves, in the Manner of the new Buildings in London, and as Mr. Turner's[1] House in Front-Street, or Mr. Nichols's[2] in Chesnut-Street, are built; which I conceive would tend considerably to their Preservation.

Let others communicate their Thoughts as freely as I have done mine, and perhaps something useful may be drawn from the Whole. I am yours, &c.

A. A.[3]

---

1. Joseph Turner. Later member of the Union Fire Company.

2. The same Mr. Nichols referenced in *Proposals and Queries to be Asked the Junto.*

3. Franklin was instrumental in forming Philadelphia's first fire company the following year, the Union Fire Company, modelled largely on the Boston Fire Society.

A Man of Sense

11 February, 1735

Mr. Franklin,

Being the other Day near the Meeting-House Corner with some Gentlemen, in the open Street, I heard the following Piece of Conversation; and penn'd it down as soon as I came home. I am confident it varies scarce any thing from what really passed; and as it pleased the By-standers, it may possibly please the Publick, if you give it a Place in your Paper.

It not being proper to name the Persons discoursing, I shall call one of them Socrates, his manner of Arguing being in my Opinion, somewhat like that of Socrates: And, if you please, the other may be Crito. I am Yours, &c.

A. A.

Socrates. Who is that well-dress'd Man that passed by just now?

Crito. He is a Gentleman of this City, esteem'd a *Man of Sense*, but not very honest.

S. The Appellation of *a Man of Sense* is of late frequently given, and seems to come naturally into the Character of every Man we are about to praise: But I am at some Loss to know whether a Man who *is not honest* can deserve it.

C. Yes, doubtless; There are many vicious Men who are nevertheless Men of very good Sense.

S. You are of Opinion, perhaps, that a Man of Knowledge is *a Man of Sense*.

C. I am really of that Opinion.

S. Is the Knowledge of Push-pin, or of the Game at Ninepins, or of Cards and Dice, or even of Musick and Dancing, sufficient to constitute the Character of a Man of Sense?

C. No certainly; there are many silly People that understand these Things tolerably well.

S. Will the Knowledge of Languages, or of Logic and Rhetoric serve to make a Man of Sense?

C. I think not; for I have known very senseless Fellows to be Masters of two or three Languages; and mighty full of their Logic, or their Rhetoric.

S. Perhaps some Men may understand all the Forms and Terms of Logic, or all the Figures of Rhetoric, and yet be no more able to convince or to perswade, than others who have not learnt those Things?

C. Indeed I believe they may.

S. Will not the Knowledge of the Mathematicks, Astronomy, and Natural Philosophy, those sublime Sciences, give a Right to the Character of *a Man of Sense?*

C. At first Sight I should have thought they might: But upon Recollection I must own I have known some Men, Masters of those Sciences, who, in the Management of their Affairs, and *Conduct of their Lives*, have acted very weakly, I do not mean viciously but foolishly; and therefore I cannot find in my Heart to allow 'em the Character of *Men of Sense.*

S. It seems then, that no Knowledge will serve to give this Character, but the Knowledge of our *true Interest;* that is, of what is best to be done in all the Circumstances of Humane Life, in order to arrive at our main End in View, HAPPINESS.

C. I am of the same Opinion. And now, as to the Point in Hand, I suppose you will no longer doubt whether a vicious Man may deserve the Character of a Man of Sense, since 'tis certain that there are many Men who *know* their true Interest, &c. and are therefore *Men of Sense*, but are nevertheless vicious and dishonest Men, as appears from the whole Tenour of their Conduct in Life.

S. Can Vice consist with any Man's true Interest, or contribute to his Happiness?

C. No certainly; for in Proportion as a Man is vicious he loses the Favour of God and Man, and brings upon himself many Inconveniences, the least of which is capable of marring and demolishing his Happiness.

S. How then does it appear that those vicious Men have the Knowledge we have been speaking of, which constitutes *a Man of Sense*, since they act directly contrary?

C. It appears by their Discoursing perfectly well upon the Subjects of Vice and Virtue, when they occur in Conversation, and by the just Manner in which they express their Thoughts of the pernicious Consequences of the one, and the happy Effects of the other.

S. Is it the Knowledge of all the Terms and Expressions proper to be used in Discoursing well upon the Subject of making a good Shoe, that constitutes a Shoemaker; or is it the Knowing how to go about it and do it?

C. I own it is the latter, and not the former.

S. And if one who could only *talk finely* about Shoemaking, were to be set to work, would he not presently discover his Ignorance in that Art?

C. He would, I confess.

S. Can the Man who is only able to talk justly of Virtue and Vice, and to say that "Drunkenness, Gluttony and Lewdness destroy a Man's Constitution; waste his Time and Substance, and bring him under many Misfortunes, (to the Destruction of his Happiness) which the contrary Virtues would enable him to avoid;" but notwithstanding his talking thus, continues in those Vices; can such a Man deserve the Character of a Temperate and Chaste Man? Or does not that Man rather deserve it, who having *a thorough Sense* that what the other has said is true, *knows* also *how* to resist the Temptation to those Vices, and embrace Virtue with a hearty and steady Affection?

C. The latter, I acknowledge. And since Virtue is really the true Interest of all Men; and some of those who talk well of it, do not put it in Practice, I am now inclined to believe they speak only by rote, retailing to us what they have pick'd out of the Books or Conversation of wise and virtuous Men; but what having never enter'd or made any Impression on their Hearts, has therefore no Influence on the Conduct of their Lives.

S. Vicious Men, then, do not appear to have that Knowledge which constitutes *the Man of Sense*.

C. No, I am convinced they do not deserve the Name. However, I am afraid, that instead of *defining* a Man of Sense we have now entirely *annihilated* him: For if the Knowledge of his true Interest in all Parts of the Conduct of Life, and a constant Course of Practice agreeable to it, are essential to his Character, I do not know where we shall find him.

S. There seems no necessity that to be a Man of Sense, he should never make a Slip in the Path of Virtue, or in Point of Morality; provided he is sensible of his Failing and diligently applys himself to rectify what is done amiss, and to prevent the like for the future. The best Arithmetician may err in casting up a long Account; but having found that Error, he *knows how* to mend it, and immediately does so; and is notwithstanding that Error, an Arithmetician; But he who *always* blunders, and cannot correct his Faults in Accounting, is no Arithmetician; nor is the habitually-vicious Man *a Man of Sense*.

C. But methinks 'twill look hard, that all other Arts and Sciences put together, and possess'd by one Man in the greatest Perfection, are not able to dignify him with the Title of *a Man of Sense*, unless he be also a Man of Virtue.

S. We shall agree, perhaps, that one who is *a Man of Sense*, will not spend his Time in learning such Sciences as, if not useless in themselves, will probably be useless to him?

C. I grant it.

S. And of those which may be useful to him, that is, may contribute to his Happiness, he ought, if he is a Man of Sense to know how to make them so.

C. To be sure.

S. And of those which may be useful, he will not (if he is a Man of Sense) acquire all, except that One only which is the most useful of all, to wit, the Science of Virtue.

C. It would, I own, be inconsistent with his Character to do so.

S. It seems to follow then, that the vicious Man, tho' Master of many Sciences, must needs be an ignorant and foolish Man; for being, as he is vicious, of consequence unhappy, either he has acquired only the useless Sciences, or having acquired such as might be useful, he knows not how to make them contribute to his Happiness; and tho' he may have every other Science, he is ignorant that the SCIENCE OF VIRTUE is of more worth, and of more consequence to his Happiness than all the rest put together. And since he is ignorant of what *principally* concerns him, tho' it has been told him a thousand Times from Parents, Press, and Pulpit, the Vicious Man however learned, cannot be *a Man of Sense*, but is a Fool, a Dunce, and a Blockhead.

Self-Denial Not the Essence of Virtue

18 February, 1735

To the Printer of the *Gazette*.

That Self-Denial *is not the* Essence of Virtue.

It is commonly asserted, that without *Self-Denial* there is no Virtue, and that the greater the *Self-Denial* the greater the Virtue.

If it were said, that he who cannot deny himself in any Thing he inclines to, tho' he knows it will be to his Hurt, has not the Virtue of *Resolution* or *Fortitude*, it would be intelligible enough; but as it stands it seems obscure or erroneous.

Let us consider some of the Virtues singly.

If a Man has no inclination to *wrong* People in his Dealings, if he feels no Temptation to it, and therefore never does it; can it be said that he is not a just Man? If he is a just Man, has he not the Virtue of Justice?

If to a certain Man, idle Diversions have nothing in them that is tempting, and therefore he never relaxes his Application to Business for their Sake; is he not an Industrious Man? Or has he not the Virtue of Industry?

I might in like manner instance in all the rest of the Virtues: But to make the Thing short, As it is certain, that the more we strive against the Temptation to any Vice, and practise the contrary Virtue, the weaker will that Temptation be, and the stronger will be that Habit; 'till at length the Temptation has no Force, or entirely vanishes: Does it follow from thence, that in our Endeavours to overcome Vice, we grow continually less and less Virtuous; till at length we have no Virtue at all?

If Self-Denial be the Essence of Virtue, then it follows, that the Man who is naturally temperate, just, &c. is not virtuous; but that in order to be virtuous, he must, in spight of his natural Inclinations, wrong his Neighbours, and eat and drink, &c. to excess.

But perhaps it may be said, that by the Word *Virtue* in the above Assertion, is meant, *Merit;* and so it should stand thus; Without Self-Denial there is no Merit; and the greater the Self-Denial the greater the Merit.

The Self-denial here meant, must be when our Inclinations are towards Vice, or else it would still be Nonsense.

By Merit is understood, Desert; and when we say a Man merits, we mean that he deserves Praise or Reward.

We do not pretend to merit any thing of God, for he is above our Services; and the Benefits he confers on us, are the Effects of his Goodness and Bounty.

All our Merit then is with regard to one another, and from one to another.

Taking then the Assertion as it last stands,

If a Man does me a Service from a natural benevolent Inclination, does he deserve less of me than another who does me the like Kindness against his Inclination?

If I have two Journeymen, one naturally industrious, the other idle, but both perform a Days Work equally good, ought I to give the latter the most Wages?

Indeed, lazy Workmen are commonly observ'd to be more extravagant in their Demands than the Industrious; for if they have not more for their Work, they cannot live so well: But tho' it be true to a Proverb, *That Lazy Folks take the most Pains*, does it follow that they deserve the most Money?

If you were to employ Servants in Affairs of Trust, would you not bid more for one you knew was naturally honest, than for one naturally roguish, but who had lately acted honestly? For Currents whose natural Channel is damm'd up, (till the new Course is by Time worn sufficiently deep and become natural,) are apt to break their Banks. If one Servant is more valuable than another, has he not more Merit than the other? And yet this is not on Account of Superior Self-denial.

Is a Patriot not praise-worthy, if Publick Spirit is natural to him?

Is a Pacing-Horse less valuable for being a natural Pacer?

Nor in my Opinion has any Man less Merit for having in general natural virtuous Inclinations.

The Truth is, that Temperance, Justice, Charity, &c. are Virtues, whether practis'd with or against our Inclinations; and the Man who practises them, merits our Love and Esteem: And Self-denial is neither good nor bad, but as 'tis apply'd: He that denies a Vicious Inclination is Virtuous in proportion to his Resolution, but the most perfect Virtue is above all Temptation, such as the Virtue of the Saints in Heaven: And he who does a foolish, indecent or wicked Thing, meerly because 'tis contrary to his Inclination, (like some mad Enthusiasts I have read of, who ran about naked, under the Notion of taking up the Cross) is not practising the reasonable Science of Virtue, but is lunatick.

The Drinker's Dictionary

13 January, 1737

Nothing more like a Fool than a drunken Man. Poor Richard.

Tis an old Remark, that Vice always endeavours to assume the Appearance of Virtue: Thus Covetousness calls itself *Prudence; Prodigality* would be thought *Generosity;* and so of others. This perhaps arises hence, that, Mankind naturally and universally approve Virtue in their Hearts, and detest Vice; and therefore, whenever thro' Temptation they fall into a Practice of the latter, they would if possible conceal it from themselves as well as others, under some other Name than that which properly belongs to it.

But Drunkenness is a very unfortunate Vice in this respect. It bears no kind of Similitude with any sort of Virtue, from which it might possibly borrow a Name; and is therefore reduc'd to the wretched Necessity of being express'd by distant round-about Phrases, and of perpetually varying those Phrases, as often as they come to be well understood to signify plainly that A Man is drunk.

Tho' every one may possibly recollect a Dozen at least of the Expressions us'd on this Occasion, yet I think no one who has not much frequented Taverns would imagine the number of them so great as it really is. It may therefore surprize as well as divert the sober Reader, to have the Sight of a new Piece, lately communicated to me, entitled

The Drinkers Dictionary.

A

He is Addled, He's casting up his Accounts, He's Afflicted, He's in his Airs.

B

He's Biggy, Bewitch'd, Block and Block, Boozy, Bowz'd, Been at Barbadoes, Piss'd in the Brook, Drunk as a Wheel-Barrow, Burdock'd, Buskey, Buzzey, Has Stole a Manchet out of the Brewer's Basket, His Head is full of Bees, Has been in the Bibbing Plot, Has drank more than he has bled, He's Bungey, As Drunk as a Beggar, He sees the Bears, He's kiss'd black Betty, He's had a Thump over the Head with Sampson's Jawbone, He's Bridgey.

C

He's Cat, Cagrin'd, Capable, Cramp'd, Cherubimical, Cherry Merry, Wamble Crop'd, Crack'd, Concern'd, Half Way to Concord, Has taken a Chirriping-Glass, Got Corns in his Head, A Cup too much, Coguy, Copey, He's heat his Copper, He's Crocus, Catch'd, He cuts his Capers, He's been in the Cellar, He's in his Cups, Non Compos, Cock'd, Curv'd, Cut, Chipper, Chickery, Loaded his Cart, He's been too free with the Creature, Sir Richard has taken off his Considering Cap, He's Chap-fallen.

D

He's Disguiz'd, He's got a Dish, Kill'd his Dog, Took his Drops, It is a Dark Day with him, He's a Dead Man, Has Dipp'd his Bill, He's Dagg'd, He's seen the Devil.

E

He's Prince Eugene, Enter'd, Wet both Eyes, Cock Ey'd, Got the Pole Evil, Got a brass Eye, Made an Example, He's Eat a Toad and half for Breakfast, In his Element.

F

He's Fishey, Fox'd, Fuddled, Sore Footed, Frozen, Well in for 't, Owes no Man a Farthing, Fears no Man, Crump Footed, Been to France, Flush'd, Froze his Mouth, Fetter'd, Been to a Funeral, His Flag is out, Fuzl'd, Spoke with his Friend, Been at an Indian Feast.

G

He's Glad, Groatable, Gold-headed, Glaiz'd, Generous, Booz'd the Gage, As Dizzy as a Goose, Been before George, Got the Gout, Had a Kick in the Guts, Been with Sir John Goa, Been at Geneva, Globular, Got the Glanders.

H

Half and Half, Hardy, Top Heavy, Got by the Head, Hiddey, Got on his little Hat, Hammerish, Loose in the Hilts, Knows not the way Home, Got the Hornson, Haunted with Evil Spirits, Has Taken Hippocrates grand Elixir.

I

He's Intoxicated, Jolly, Jagg'd, Jambled, Going to Jerusalem, Jocular, Been to Jerico, Juicy.

K

He's a King, Clips the King's English, Seen the French King, The King is his Cousin, Got Kib'd Heels, Knapt, Het his Kettle.

L

He's in Liquor, Lordly, He makes Indentures with his Leggs, Well to Live, Light, Lappy, Limber.

M

He sees two Moons, Merry, Middling, Moon-Ey'd, Muddled, Seen a Flock of Moons, Maudlin, Mountous, Muddy, Rais'd his Monuments, Mellow.

N

He's eat the Cocoa Nut, Nimptopsical, Got the Night Mare.

O

He's Oil'd, Eat Opium, Smelt of an Onion, Oxycrocium, Overset.

P

He drank till he gave up his Half-Penny, Pidgeon Ey'd, Pungey, Priddy, As good conditioned as a Puppy, Has Scalt his Head Pan, Been among the Philistines, In his Prosperity, He's been among the Philippians, He's contending with Pharaoh, Wasted his Paunch, He's Polite, Eat a Pudding Bagg.

Q

He's Quarrelsome.

R

He's Rocky, Raddled, Rich, Religious, Lost his Rudder, Ragged, Rais'd, Been too free with Sir Richard, Like a Rat in Trouble.

S

He's Stitch'd, Seafaring, In the Sudds, Strong, Been in the Sun, As Drunk as David's Sow Swampt, His Skin is full, He's Steady, He's Stiff, He's burnt his Shoulder, He's got his Top Gallant Sails out, Seen the yellow Star, As Stiff as a Ring-bolt, Half Seas over, His Shoe pinches him, Staggerish, It is Star-light with him, He carries too much Sail, Stew'd, Stubb'd, Soak'd, Soft, Been too free with Sir John Strawberry, He's right before the Wind with all his Studding Sails out, Has Sold his Senses.

T

He's Top'd, Tongue-ty'd, Tann'd, Tipium Grove, Double Tongu'd, Topsy Turvey, Tipsey, Has Swallow'd a Tavern Token, He's Thaw'd, He's in a Trance, He's Trammel'd.

V

He makes Virginia Fence, Valiant, Got the Indian Vapours.

W

The Malt is above the Water, He's Wise, He's Wet, He's been to the Salt Water, He's Water-soaken, He's very Weary, Out of the Way.

The Phrases in this Dictionary are not (like most of our Terms of Art) borrow'd from Foreign Languages, neither are they collected from the Writings of the Learned in our own, but gather'd wholly from the modern Tavern-Conversation of Tiplers. I do not doubt but that there are many more in use; and I was even tempted to add a new one my self under the Letter B, to wit, *Brutify'd:* But upon Consideration, I fear'd being guilty of Injustice to the Brute Creation, if I represented Drunkenness as a beastly Vice, since, 'tis well-known, that the Brutes are in general a very sober sort of People.

Part IV

14 MAY, 1743 – 9 MAY, 1751

A Proposal for Promoting Useful Knowledge

An Account on the New Invented Pennsylvania Fireplaces

Plain Truth

Rules for Making Oneself a Disagreeable Companion

Observations Concerning the Increase of Mankind, Peopling of Countries, &c.

Felons and Rattlesnakes

A Proposal for Promoting Useful Knowledge

14 May, 1743

A PROPOSAL for Promoting Useful Knowledge among the British Plantations in America.

The English are possess'd of a long Tract of Continent, from Nova Scotia to Georgia, extending North and South thro' different Climates, having different Soils, producing different Plants, Mines and Minerals, and capable of different Improvements, Manufactures, &c.

The first Drudgery of Settling new Colonies, which confines the Attention of People to mere Necessaries, is now pretty well over; and there are many in every Province in Circumstances that set them at Ease, and afford Leisure to cultivate the finer Arts, and improve the common Stock of Knowledge. To such of these who are Men of Speculation, many Hints must from time to time arise, many Observations occur, which if well-examined, pursued and improved, might produce Discoveries to the Advantage of some or all of the British Plantations, or to the Benefit of Mankind in general.

But as from the Extent of the Country such Persons are widely separated, and seldom can see and converse or be acquainted with each other, so that many useful Particulars remain uncommunicated, die with the Discoverers, and are lost to Mankind; it is, to remedy this Inconvenience for the future, proposed,

That One Society be formed of Virtuosi or ingenious Men residing in the several Colonies, to be called *The American Philosophical Society;* who are to maintain a constant Correspondence.

That Philadelphia being the City nearest the Centre of the Continent-Colonies, communicating with all of them northward and southward by Post, and with all the Islands by Sea, and having the Advantage of a good growing Library, be the Centre of the Society.

That at Philadelphia there be always at least seven Members, viz. a Physician, a Botanist, a Mathematician, a Chemist, a Mechanician, a Geographer, and a general Natural Philosopher, besides a President, Treasurer and Secretary.

That these Members meet once a Month, or oftner, at their own Expence, to communicate to each other their Observations, Experiments, &c. to receive, read and consider such Letters, Communications, or Queries as shall be sent from distant Members; to direct the Dispersing of Copies of such Communications as are valuable, to other distant Members, in order to procure their Sentiments thereupon, &c.

That the Subjects of the Correspondence be, All new-discovered Plants, Herbs, Trees, Roots, &c. their Virtues, Uses, &c. Methods of Propagating them, and making such as are useful, but particular to some Plantations, more general. Improvements of vegetable Juices, as Cyders, Wines, &c. New Methods of Curing or Preventing Diseases. All new-discovered Fossils in different Countries, as Mines, Minerals, Quarries, &c. New and useful Improvements in any Branch of Mathematicks. New Discoveries in Chemistry, such as Improvements in Distillation, Brewing, Assaying of Ores, &c. New Mechanical Inventions for saving Labour; as Mills, Carriages, &c. and for Raising and Conveying of Water, Draining of Meadows, &c. All new Arts, Trades, Manufactures, &c. that may be proposed or thought of. Surveys, Maps and Charts of particular Parts of the Sea-coasts, or Inland Countries; Course and Junction of Rivers and great Roads, Situation of Lakes and Mountains, Nature of the Soil and Productions, &c. New Methods of Improving the Breed of useful Animals, Introducing other Sorts from foreign Countries. New Improvements in Planting, Gardening, Clearing Land, &c. And all philosophical Experiments that let

Light into the Nature of Things, tend to increase the Power of Man over Matter, and multiply the Conveniencies or Pleasures of Life.

That a Correspondence already begun by some intended Members, shall be kept up by this Society with the ROYAL SOCIETY of London, and with the DUBLIN SOCIETY.

That every Member shall have Abstracts sent him Quarterly, of every Thing valuable communicated to the Society's Secretary at Philadelphia; free of all Charge except the Yearly Payment hereafter mentioned.

That by Permission of the Postmaster-General, such Communications pass between the Secretary of the Society and the Members, Postage-free.

That for defraying the Expence of such Experiments as the Society shall judge proper to cause to be made, and other contingent Charges for the common Good, every Member send a Piece of Eight *per Annum* to the Treasurer, at Philadelphia, to form a Common Stock, to be disburs'd by Order of the President with the Consent of the Majority of the Members that can conveniently be consulted thereupon, to such Persons and Places where and by whom the Experiments are to be made, and otherwise as there shall be Occasion; of which Disbursements an exact Account shall be kept, and communicated yearly to every Member.

That at the first Meetings of the Members at Philadelphia, such Rules be formed for Regulating their Meetings and Transactions for the General Benefit, as shall be convenient and necessary; to be afterwards changed and improv'd as there shall be Occasion, wherein due Regard is to be had to the Advice of distant Members.

That at the End of every Year, Collections be made and printed, of such Experiments, Discoveries, Improvements, &c. as may be thought of publick Advantage: And that every Member have a Copy sent him.

That the Business and Duty of the Secretary be, To receive all Letters intended for the Society, and lay them before the President and Members at their Meetings; to abstract, correct and methodize such Papers, &c. as require it, and as he shall be directed to do by the President, after they have been considered, debated and digested in the Society; to enter Copies thereof in the Society's Books, and make out Copies for distant Members; to answer their Letters by Direction of the President, and keep Records of all material Transactions of the Society, &c.

Benjamin Franklin, the Writer of this Proposal, offers himself to serve the Society as their Secretary, 'till they shall be provided with one more capable.

An Account on the New Invented Pennsylvania Fireplaces

15 November, 1744

Advertisement.

These Fire-Places are made in the best Manner, and sold by R. Grace in Philadelphia. They are sold also by J. Parker in New-York, and by J. Franklin in Boston.

The within-describ'd is of the middle and most common Size: There are others to be had both larger and smaller.

An Account Of the New-Invented Fire-Places.

In these Northern Colonies the Inhabitants keep Fires to sit by, generally *Seven Months* in the Year; that is, from the Beginning of October to the End of April; and in some Winters near *Eight Months*, by taking in part of September and May.

Wood, our common Fewel, which within these 100 Years might be had at every Man's Door, must now be fetch'd near 100 Miles to some Towns, and makes a very considerable Article in the Expence of Families.

As therefore so much of the Comfort and Conveniency of our Lives, for so great a Part of the Year, depends on the Article of Fire; since Fuel is become so expensive, and (as the Country is more clear'd and settled) will of course grow scarcer and dearer; any new Proposal for Saving the Wood, and for lessening the Charge and augmenting the Benefit of Fire, by some particular Method of Making and Managing it, may at least be thought worth Consideration.

The New Fire-Places are a late Invention to that purpose (experienced now three Winters by a great Number of Families in Pennsylvania) of which this Paper is intended to give a particular Account.

That the Reader may the better judge whether this Method of Managing Fire has any Advantage over those heretofore in Use, it may be proper to consider both the old and new Methods separately and particularly, and afterwards make the Comparison.

In order to this, 'tis necessary to understand well some few of the Properties of Air and Fire, viz.

1. Air is rarified by *Heat*, and condens'd by *Cold;* i.e. the same Quantity of Air takes up more Space when warm than when cold. This may be shown by several very easy Experiments. Take any clear Glass Bottle (a Florence Flask stript of the Straw is best) place it before the Fire, and as the Air within is warm'd and rarified, part of it will be driven out of the Bottle; turn it up, place its Mouth in a Vessel of Water, and remove it from the Fire; then, as the Air within cools and contracts, you will see the Water rise in the Neck of the Bottle, supplying the Place of just so much Air as was driven out. Hold a large hot Coal near the Side of the Bottle, and as the Air within feels the Heat, it will again distend and force out the Water. Or, Fill a Bladder half-full of Air, tie the Neck tight, and lay it before a Fire as near as may be without scorching the Bladder; as the Air within heats, you will perceive it to swell and fill the Bladder, till it becomes tight as if full-blown: Remove it to a cool Place, and you will see it fall gradually, till it become as lank as at first.

2. Air rarified and distended by Heat, is specifically lighter than it was before, and will rise in other Air of greater Density. As Wood, Oil, or any other Matter specifically lighter than Water, if plac'd at the Bottom of a Vessel of Water, will rise till it comes to the Top; so rarified Air will rise in common Air, till it either comes to Air of equal Weight, or is by Cold reduc'd to its former Density.

A Fire then being made in any Chimney, the Air over the Fire is rarified by the Heat, becomes lighter and therefore immediately rises in the Funnel and goes out; the other Air in the Room (flowing towards the Chimney) supplies its Place, is rarified in its turn, and rises likewise; the Place of the Air thus carried out of the Room is supplied by fresh Air coming in thro' Doors and Windows, or, if they be shut, thro' every Crevice with Violence, as may be seen by holding a Candle to a Keyhole: If the Room be so tight as that all the Crevices together will not supply so much Air as is continually carried off, then in a little time the Current up the Funnel must flag, and the Smoke being no longer driven up must come into the Room.

1. FIRE throws out Light, Heat, and Smoke (or Fume). The two first move in right Lines and with great Swiftness; the latter is but just separated from the Fuel, and then moves only as it is carried by the Stream of rarified Air. And without a continual Accession and Recession of Air to carry off the Smoaky Fumes, they would remain crouded about the Fire, and stifle it.

2. HEAT may be separated from the Smoke as well as from the Light, by means of a Plate of Iron, which will suffer Heat to pass through it without the others.

3. FIRE sends out its Rays of Heat, as well as Rays of Light, equally every way: But the greatest sensible Heat is over the Fire, where there is, besides the Rays of Heat shot upwards, a continual rising Stream of hot Air, heated by the Rays shot round on every Side.

THESE Things being understood, we proceed to consider the Fire-places heretofore in Use, viz.

1. The large open Fire-places used in the Days of our Fathers, and still generally in the Country, and in Kitchens.

2. The newer-fashion'd Fire-places, with low Breasts, and narrow Hearths.

3. Fire-places with hollow Backs, Hearths and Jams of Iron, (described by Mons. Gauger) for warming the Air as it comes into the Room.

4. The Holland Stoves, with Iron Doors opening into the Room.

5. The German Stoves, which have no Opening in the Room where they are us'd, but the Fire is put in from some other Room, or from without.

6. Iron Pots, with open Charcoal Fires, plac'd in the middle of a Room.

1. The first of these Methods has generally the Conveniency of two warm Seats, one in each Corner; but they are sometimes too hot to abide in, and at other times incommoded with the Smoke; there is likewise good Room for the Cook to move, to hang on Pots, &c. Their Inconveniencies are, that they almost always smoke if the Door be not left open; that they require a large Funnel, and a large Funnel carries off a great Quantity of Air, which occasions what is called a strong Draft to the Chimney; without which strong Draft the Smoke would come out of some Part or other of so large an Opening, so that the Door can seldom be shut; and the cold Air so nips the Backs and Heels of those that sit before the Fire, that they have no Comfort, 'till either Screens or Settles are provided (at a considerable Expence) to keep it off, which both cumber the Room and darken the Fireside. A moderate Quantity of Wood on the Fire in so large a Hearth, seems but little; and, in so strong and cold a Draught, warms but little; so that People are continually laying on more. In short, 'tis next to impossible to warm a Room with such a Fire-place: And I suppose our Ancestors never thought of warming Rooms to sit in; all they purpos'd was to have a Place to make a Fire in, by which they might warm themselves when acold.

2. Most of these old-fashion'd Chimneys in Towns and Cities, have been, of late Years, reduc'd to the second Sort mention'd, by building Jambs within them, narrowing the Hearth, and making a low Arch or Breast. 'Tis strange, methinks, that tho' Chimneys have been so long in Use, their Construction should be so little understood till lately, that no Workman pretended to make one which should always carry off all the Smoke, but a Chimney-cloth was look'd upon as essential to a Chimney: This Improvement, however, by small Openings and low Breasts, has been made in our Days; and Success in the first Experiments has brought it into general Use in Cities, so that almost all new Chimneys are now made of that sort, and much fewer Bricks will make a Stack of Chimneys now than formerly. An Improvement so lately made, may give us Room to believe that still farther Improvements may be found, to remedy the Inconveniencies yet

remaining. For these new Chimneys, tho' they keep Rooms generally free from Smoke, and, the Opening being contracted, will allow the Door to be shut, yet the Funnel still requiring a considerable Quantity of Air, it rushes in at every Crevice so strongly, as to make a continual Whistling or Howling; and 'tis very uncomfortable as well as dangerous to sit against any such Crevice. Many Colds are caught from this Cause only; it being safer to sit in the open Street; for then the Pores do all close together, and the Air does not strike so sharply against any particular Part. The Spaniards have a Proverbial Saying, *If the Wind blows on you thro' a Hole, Make your Will, and take Care of your Soul.* Women, particularly, from this Cause, (as they sit much in the House) get Colds in the Head, Rheums and Defluctions, which fall into their Jaws and Gums, and have destroy'd early many a fine Set of Teeth in these Northern Colonies. Great and bright Fires do also very much contribute to damage the Eyes, dry and shrivel the Skin, and bring on early the Appearances of Old-Age. In short, many of the Diseases proceeding from Colds, as Fevers, Pleurisies, &c. fatal to very great Numbers of People, may be ascrib'd to strong-drawing Chimneys, whereby, in severe Weather, a Man is scorch'd before, while he's froze behind. In the mean time very little is done by these Chimneys towards warming the Room; for the Air round the Fire-place which is warm'd by the direct Rays from the Fire, does not continue in the Room, but is continually crouded and gather'd into the Chimney by the Current of cold Air coming behind it, and so is presently carried off.

In both these Sorts of Fire-places, the greatest Part of the Heat from the Fire is lost: For as Fire naturally darts Heat every way, the Back, the two Jambs, and the Hearth, drink up almost all that's given them, very little being reflected from Bodies so dark, porous and unpolish'd; and the upright Heat, which is by far the greatest, flies directly up the Chimney. Thus Five Sixths at least of the Heat (and consequently of the Fewel) is wasted, and contributes nothing towards warming the Room.

3. To remedy this, the Sieur Gauger gives us, in his Book entitled *La Mechanique de Feu*, published 1709, seven different Constructions of the

third Sort of Chimneys mentioned above, in which there are hollow Cavities made by Iron Plates in the Back, Jambs and Hearth, thro' which Plates the Heat passing, warms the Air in those Cavities, which is continually coming into the Room fresh and warm. The Invention was very ingenious, and had many Conveniencies: The Room was warm'd in all Parts, by the Air flowing into it through the heated Cavities: Cold Air was prevented rushing thro' the Crevices, the Funnel being sufficiently supply'd by those Cavities: Much less Fuel would serve, &c. But the first Expence, which was very great; the Intricacy of the Design, and the Difficulty of the Execution, especially in old Chimneys, discouraged the Propagation of the Invention; so that there are (I suppose) very few such Chimneys now in Use. [The upright Heat, too, was almost all lost in these, as in the common Chimneys.]

4. The Holland Iron Stove, which has a Flue proceeding from the Top, and a small Iron Door opening into the Room, comes next to be considered. Its Conveniences are, that it makes a Room all over warm; for the Chimney being wholly closed, except the Flue of the Stove, very little Air is required to supply that, and therefore not much rushes in at Crevices, or at the Door when 'tis opened. Little Fewel serves, the Heat being almost all saved; for it rays out almost equally from the four Sides, the Bottom and the Top, into the Room, and presently warms the Air around it, which being rarified rises to the Cieling, and its Place is supplied by the lower Air of the Room, which flows gradually towards the Stove, and is there warm'd and rises in its Turn, so that there is a continual Circulation till all the Air in the Room is warmed. The Air, too, is gradually changed by the Stove-Door's being in the Room, thro' which, part of it is continually passing, and that makes these Stoves wholesomer, or at least pleasanter, than the German Stoves next to be spoke of. But they have these Inconveniences. There is no Sight of the Fire, which is in itself a pleasant Thing. One cannot conveniently make any other Use of the Fire but that of warming the Room. When the Room is warm, People not seeing the Fire are apt to forget supplying it with Fuel 'til 'tis almost out, then, growing cold, a great deal of Wood is put in, which soon makes it too hot. The

Change of Air is not carried on quite quick enough, so that if any Smoke or ill Smell happens in the Room, 'tis a long Time before 'tis discharg'd. For these Reasons the Holland Stove has not obtain'd much among the English (who love the Sight of the Fire) unless in some Workshops, where People are oblig'd to sit near Windows for the Light, and in such Places they have been found of good Use.

5. The German Stove is like a Box, one Side wanting. 'Tis compos'd of Five Iron Plates scru'd together; and fix'd so as that you may put the Fuel into it from another Room, or from the Outside of the House. 'Tis a kind of Oven revers'd, its Mouth being without, and Body within the Room that is to be warm'd by it. This Invention certainly warms a Room very speedily and thoroughly with little Fuel: No Quantity of cold Air comes in at any Crevice, because there is no Discharge of Air which it might Supply, there being no Passage into the Stove from the Room. These are its Conveniencies. Its Inconveniences are, That People have not even so much Sight or Use of the Fire as in the Holland Stoves, and are moreover oblig'd to breathe the same unchang'd Air continually, mix'd with the Breath and Perspiration from one anothers Bodies, which is very disagreeable to those who have not been accustomed to it.

6. Charcoal Fires, in Pots, are us'd chiefly in the Shops of Handicraftsmen. They warm a Room (that is kept close and has no Chimney to carry off the warm'd Air) very speedily and uniformly: But there being no Draught to change the Air, the sulphurous Fumes from the Coals [be they ever so well kindled before they are brought in, there will be some] mix with it, render it disagreeable, hurtful to some Constitutions, and sometimes, when the Door is long kept shut, produce fatal Consequences.

To avoid the several Inconveniences, and at the same time retain all the Advantages of other Fire-places, was contrived the PENNSYLVANIA FIRE-PLACE now to be described.

This Machine consists of

- A Bottom Plate, (i) [*See the Cut.*] [below]

- A Back Plate, (ii)
- Two Side Plates, (iii iii)
- Two Middle Plates, (iv iv) which join'd together form a tight Box with winding Passages in it for warming the Air.
- A Front Plate, (v)
- A Top Plate, (vi)

These are all of cast Iron, with Mouldings or Ledges where the Plates come together, to hold them fast, and retain the Mortar us'd for Pointing to make tight Joints. When the Plates are all in their Places, a Pair of slender Rods with Screws, are sufficient to bind the Whole very firmly together, as it appears in *Fig.* 2.

There are, moreover, two thin Plates of wrought Iron, viz. The Shutter, (vii) and the Register, (viii); besides the Screw-Rods *O P*, all which we shall explain in their Order.

(i) The Bottom Plate, or Hearth-Piece, is round before, with a rising Moulding that serves as a Fender to keep Coals and Ashes from coming to the Floor, &c. It has two Ears, *F G*, perforated to receive the Screw-Rods *O P*; a long Air-hole, *a a*, thro' which the fresh outward Air passes up into the Air-Box; and three Smoke-Holes *B C* thro' which the Smoke descends and passes away; also a square Hole *b* for the Bellows; all represented by dark Squares. It has also double Ledges to receive between them the Bottom Edges of the Back-Plate, the two Side Plates, and the two middle Plates. These Ledges are about an Inch asunder, and half an Inch high; a Profile of two of them join'd to a Fragment of Plate appears in *Fig.* 3.

(ii) The Back Plate is without Holes, having only a Pair of Ledges on each Side, to receive the Back Edges of the two

(iii iii) Side Plates: These have each a Pair of Ledges to receive the Side-Edges of the Front Plate, and a little Shoulder for it to rest on; also two Pair of Ledges to receive the Side-Edges of the two Middle Plates which form the Air-Box; and an oblong Airhole near the Top, thro' which is discharg'd into the Room the Air warm'd in the Air-Box. Each has also a Wing or Bracket, *H* and *I*, to keep in falling Brands, Coals, &c. and a small Hole *Q* and *R*, for the Axis of the Register to turn in.

(iv iv) The Air-Box is compos'd of the two Middle Plates *D E* and *F G*. The first has five thin Ledges or Partitions, cast on it, two Inches deep, the Edges of which are receiv'd in so many Pair of Ledges cast in the other. The Tops of all the Cavities form'd by these thin deep Ledges are also covered by a Ledge of the same Form and Depth, cast with them; so that when the Plates are put together, and the Joints luted, there is no Communication between the Air-Box and the Smoke. In the winding Passages of this Box, fresh Air is warm'd as it passes into the Room.

(v) The Front Plate is arch'd on the under Side, and ornamented with Foliages, &c. It has no Ledges.

(vi) The Top Plate has a Pair of Ears *M N*, answerable to those in the Bottom Plate, and perforated for the same Purpose: It has also a Pair of Ledges running round the under Side, to receive the Top-Edges of the Front, Back and Side Plates. The Air-Box does not reach up to the Top Plate by two Inches and half.

(vii) The Shutter is of thin wrought Iron and light, of such a Length and Breadth as to close well the Opening of the Fire-Place. It is us'd to blow up the Fire, and to shut up and secure it a Nights. It has two brass Knobs for Handles *d d*, and commonly slides up and down in a Groove, left, in putting up the Fire-place, between the foremost Ledge of the Side Plates, and the Face of the Front Plate; but some choose to set it aside when it is not in Use, and apply it on Occasion.

(viii) The Register, is also of thin wrought Iron. It is plac'd between the Back Plate and Air-Box, and can, by Means of the Key *S* be turn'd on its Axis so as to lie in any Position between level and upright.

The Screw-Rods *O P* are of wrought Iron, about a third of an Inch thick, with a Button at Bottom, and a Screw and Nut at Top; and may be ornamented with two small Brasses screw'd on above the Nuts.

To put this Machine to work,

1. A false Back of four Inch- (or, in shallow small Chimneys, two Inch-) Brick-work is to be made in the Chimney, four Inches or more from the true Back: From the Top of this false Back, a Closing is to be made over to the Breast of the Chimney, that no Air may pass into the Chimney, but what goes under the false Back, and up behind it.

2. Some Bricks of the Hearth are to be taken up, to form a Hollow under the Bottom Plate; across which Hollow runs a thin tight Partition to keep apart the Air entring the Hollow, and the Smoke; and is therefore plac'd between the Air-hole and Smoke-holes.

3. A Passage is made, communicating with the outward Air, to introduce that Air into the forepart of the Hollow under the Bottom Plate, whence it may rise thro' the Air-hole into the Air-box.

4. A Passage is made from the back Part of the Hollow, communicating with the Flue behind the false Back: Through this Passage the Smoke is to pass.

The Fire-place is to be erected upon these Hollows, by putting all the Plates in their Places, and screwing them together.

Its Operation may be conceiv'd by observing the following

PROFILE of the Chimney and FIRE-PLACE

The Fire being made at *A*, the Flame and Smoke will ascend and strike the Top *T*, which will thereby receive a considerable Heat. The Smoke finding no Passage upwards, turns over the Top of the Air-box, and descends between it and the Back Plate to the Holes at *B* in the Bottom Plate, heating, as it passes, both Plates of the Air-box and the said Back Plate; the Front Plate, Bottom and Side Plates are also all heated at the same Time. The Smoke proceeds in the Passage that leads it under and behind the false Back, and so rises into the Chimney. The Air justof the Room, warm'd behind the Back Plate, and by the Sides, Front and Top Plates, becoming specifically lighter than the other Air in the Room, is oblig'd to rise; but the Closure over the Fire-place hindring it from going up the Chimney, it is forc'd out into the Room, rises by the Mantle-piece to the Cieling and spreads all over the Top of the Room, whence being crouded down gradually by the Stream of newly warm'd Air that follows and rises above it, the whole Room becomes in a short time equally warmed.

At the same Time the Air, warmed under the Bottom Plate and in the Air-Box, rises, and comes out of the Holes in the Side-Plates, very swiftly if the Door of the Room be shut, and joins its Current with the Stream before mentioned rising from the Side, Back and Top Plates.

The Air that enters the Room thro' the Air-box is fresh, tho' warm; and computing the Swiftness of its Motion with the Areas of the Holes, 'tis found that near 10 Barrels of fresh Air are hourly introduc'd by the Air-Box; and by this Means the Air in the Room is continually changed, and kept at the same Time sweet and warm.

'Tis to be observed that the entring Air will not be warm at first Lighting the Fire, but heats gradually as the Fire encreases.

A square Opening for a Trap-Door should be left in the Closing of the Chimney, for the Sweeper to go up: The Door may be made of Slate or Tin, and commonly kept close shut, but so plac'd as that turning up against the Back of the Chimney when open, it closes the Vacancy behind the false Back, and shoots the Soot that falls in Sweeping, out upon the Hearth. This Trap-Door is a very convenient Thing.

In Rooms where much Smoking of Tobacco is used, 'tis also convenient to have a small Hole about five or six Inches square, cut near the Cieling through into the Funnel: This Hole must have a Shutter, by which it may be clos'd or open'd at Pleasure. When open, there will be a strong Draught of Air through it into the Chimney, which will presently carry off a Cloud of Smoke, and keep the Room clear: If the Room be too hot likewise, it will carry off as much of the warm Air as you please, and then you may stop it intirely, or in part, as you think fit. By this Means it is that the Tobacco-Smoke does not descend among the Heads of the Company near the Fire, as it must do before it can get into common Chimneys.

The Manner of Using this FIREPLACE.

YOUR Cord-wood must be cut into three Lengths; or else a short Piece, fit for the Fire-place, cut off, and the longer left for the Kitchin or other Fires. Dry Hickery, or Ash, or any Woods that burn with a clear Flame, are rather to be chosen; because such are less apt to foul the Smoke-Passages with Soot; and Flame communicates, with its Light, as well as by Contact, greater Heat to the Plates and Room. But where more ordinary Wood is used, half a dry Faggot of Brush-wood burnt at the first making of Fire in the Morning, is very advantageous; as it immediately by its sudden Blaze heats the Plates and warms the Room (which with bad Wood slowly kindling would not be done so soon) and at the same time, by the Length of its Flame turning in the Passages, consumes and cleanses away the Soot that such bad smoaky Wood had produc'd therein the preceding Day, and so keeps them always free and clean. When you have laid a little Back-log, and plac'd your Billets on small Dogs, as in common Chimneys, and put some Fire to them; then slide down your Shutter as low as the Dogs, and the Opening being by that Means contracted, the Air rushes in briskly and presently blows up the Flames. When the Fire is sufficiently kindled, slide it up again. In some of these Fire-places there is a little six-inch square Trap-door of thin wrought Iron or Brass, covering a Hole of like Dimensions near the Fore-part of the Bottom-Plate, which being by a Ring lifted up towards the Fire, about an Inch, where it will be retain'd by two springing Sides fix'd to it perpendicularly, [*See the Plate, Fig.* 4] the Air rushes in from the Hollow under the Bottom Plate, and blows the Fire. Where this is us'd, the Shutter serves only to close the Fire a Nights. The more forward you can make your Fire on the Hearth-Plate, not to be incommoded by the Smoke, the sooner and more will the Room be warmed. At Night when you go to Bed, cover the Coals or Brands with Ashes as usual; then take away the Dogs and slide down the Shutter close to the Bottom-Plate, sweeping a little Ashes against it that no Air may pass under it; then turn the Register, so as very near to stop the Flue behind. If no Smoke then comes out at Crevices into the Room, 'tis right: If any Smoke is perceiv'd to come out, move the Register so as to give a little

Draught, and 'twill go the right way. Thus the Room will be kept warm all Night; for the Chimney being almost entirely stopt, very little, if any, cold Air will enter the Room at any Crevice. When you come to rekindle the Fire in the Morning, turn open the Register before you lift up the Slider, otherwise if there be any Smoke in the Fire-Place, it will come out into the Room. By the same Use of the Shutter and Register, a blazing Fire may be presently stifled, as well as secured, when you have Occasion to leave it for any Time; and at your Return, you will find the Brands warm and ready for a speedy Re-kindling. The Shutter alone will not stifle a Fire; for it cannot well be made to fit so exactly, but that Air will enter, and that in a violent Stream, so as to blow up and keep alive the Flames, and consume the Wood, if the Draught be not check'd by turning the Register to shut the Flue behind. The Register has also two other Uses. If you observe the Draught of Air into your Fire-place, to be stronger than is necessary, (as in extream cold Weather it often is) so that the Wood is consum'd faster than usual; in that Case, a quarter, half, or two thirds Turn of the Register, will check the Violence of the Draught, and let your Fire burn with the Moderation you desire: And at the same Time both the Fire-Place and the Room will be the warmer, because less cold Air will enter and pass through them. And if the Chimney should happen to take Fire (which indeed there is very little Danger of, if the preceding Direction be observ'd in making Fires, and it be well swept once a Year; for, much less Wood being burnt, less Soot is proportionably made; and the Fuel being soon blown into Flame by the Shutter (or the Trap-door Bellows) there is consequently less Smoke from the Fuel to make Soot; then, tho' the Funnel should be foul, yet the Sparks have such a crooked up and down round-about Way to go, that they are out before they get at it) I say, if it should ever be on fire, a Turn of the Register shuts all close, and prevents any Air going into the Chimney, and so the Fire may be easily stifled and mastered.

The Advantages of this FIRE-PLACE.

ITS Advantages above the common Fire-Places are,

1. That your whole Room is equally warmed; so that People need not croud so close round the Fire, but may sit near the Window and have the Benefit of the Light for Reading, Writing, Needle-work, &c. They may sit with Comfort in any Part of the Room; which is a very considerable Advantage in a large Family, where there must often be two Fires kept, because all cannot conveniently come at One.

2. If you sit near the Fire, you have not that cold Draught of uncomfortable Air nipping your Back and Heels, as when before common Fires, by which many catch Cold, being scorcht before and as it were froze behind.

3. If you sit against a Crevice, there is not that sharp Draught of cold Air playing on you, as in Rooms where there are Fires in the common way; by which many catch Cold, whence proceed Coughs, Catarrhs, Tooth-Achs, Fevers, Pleurisies and many other Diseases.

4. In Case of Sickness, they make most excellent Nursing-Rooms; as they constantly supply a Sufficiency of fresh Air, so warmed at the same time as to be no way inconvenient or dangerous. A small One does well in a Chamber; and, the Chimneys being fitted for it, it may be remov'd from one Room to another as Occasion requires, and fix'd in half an Hour. The equal Temper, too, and Warmth, of the Air of the Room, is thought to be particularly advantageous in some Distempers: For 'twas observ'd in the Winters of 1730 and 1736, when the Small Pox spread in Pennsylvania, that very few of the Children of the Germans died of that Distemper, in Proportion to those of the English; which was ascrib'd by some to the Warmth and equal Temper of Air in their Stove-Rooms; which made the Disease as favourable as it commonly is in the West-Indies. But this Conjecture we submit to the Judgment of Physicians.

5. In common Chimneys the strongest Heat from the Fire, which is upwards, goes directly up the Chimney, and is lost; and there is such a strong Draught into the Chimney, that not only the upright Heat, but also the back, sides and downward Heats, are carried up the Chimney by that Draught of Air; and the Warmth given before the Fire by the Rays that strike out towards the Room, is continually driven back, crouded

into the Chimney, and carried up, by the same Draught of Air. But here the upright Heat, strikes and heats the Top Plate, which warms the Air above it, and that comes into the Room. The Heat likewise which the Fire communicates to the Sides, Back, Bottom and Air-Box, is all brought into the Room; for you will find a constant Current of warm Air coming out of the Chimney-Corner into the Room. Hold a Candle just under the Mantle-Piece or Breast of your Chimney, and you will see the Flame bent outwards: By laying a Piece of smoaking Paper on the Hearth, on either Side, you may see how the Current of Air moves, and where it tends, for it will turn and carry the Smoke with it.

6. Thus as very little of the Heat is lost, when this Fire-Place is us'd, *much less Wood* will serve you, which is a considerable Advantage where Wood is dear.

7. When you burn Candles near this Fire-Place, you will find that the Flame burns quite upright, and does not blare and run the Tallow down, by drawing towards the Chimney, as against common Fires.

8. This Fire-place cures most smoaky Chimneys, and thereby preserves both the Eyes and Furniture.

9. It prevents the Fouling of Chimneys; much of the Lint and Dust that contributes to foul a Chimney, being by the low Arch oblig'd to pass thro' the Flame, where 'tis consum'd. Then, less Wood being burnt, there is less Smoke made. Again, the Shutter, or Trap-Bellows, soon blowing the Wood into a Flame, the same Wood does not yield so much Smoke as if burnt in a common Chimney: For as soon as Flame begins, Smoke, in proportion, ceases.

10. And if a Chimney should be foul, 'tis much less likely to take Fire. If it should take Fire, 'tis easily stifled and extinguished.

11. A Fire may be very speedily made in this Fire-Place, by the Help of the Shutter, or Trap-Bellows, as aforesaid.

12. A Fire may be soon extinguished, by closing it with the Shutter before, and turning the Register behind, which will stifle it, and the Brands will remain ready to rekindle.

13. The Room being once warm, the Warmth may be retain'd in it all Night.

14. And lastly, the Fire is so secur'd at Night, that not one Spark can fly out into the Room to do Damage.

With all these Conveniencies, you do not lose the pleasant Sight nor Use of the Fire, as in the Dutch Stoves, but may boil the Tea-Kettle, warm the Flat-Irons, heat Heaters, keep warm a Dish of Victuals by setting it on the Top, &c. &c. &c.

Objections answered.

THERE are some Objections commonly made by People that are unacquainted with these Fire-Places, which it may not be amiss to endeavour to remove, as they arise from Prejudices which might otherwise obstruct in some Degree the general Use of this beneficial Machine. We frequently hear it said, *They are of the Nature of the Dutch Stoves; Stoves have an unpleasant Smell; Stoves are unwholesome;* and, *Warm Rooms make People tender ana apt to catch Cold*. As to the first, that they are of the Nature of Dutch Stoves, the Description of those Stoves in the Beginning of this Paper, compar'd with that of these Machines, shows that there is a most material Difference, and that these have vastly the Advantage, if it were only in the single Article of the Admission and Circulation of fresh Air. But it must be allowed there has been some Cause to complain of the offensive Smell of Iron Stoves. This Smell, however, never proceeded from the Iron itself, which in its Nature, whether hot or cold, is one of the sweetest of Metals, but from the general uncleanly Manner of using those Stoves. If they are kept clean, they are as sweet as an Ironing-Box, which, tho' ever so hot, never offends the Smell of the nicest Lady: But it is common, to let them be greased by setting Candlesticks on them, or otherwise; to rub greasy Hands on them, and, above all, to spit upon them to try how hot they are, which is an inconsiderate, filthy unmannerly Custom; for the slimy Matter of Spittle drying on, burns and fumes when the Stove is hot, as well as the Grease, and smells most nauseously; which makes such close Stove-Rooms, where there is no Draught to carry off those filthy Vapours, almost intolerable to those that are not from their Infancy accustomed to them. At the same time, nothing is more easy than to keep them clean; for when by any Accident they happen to be fouled, a Lee made of Ashes and Water, with a Brush, will scour them perfectly; as will also a little strong Soft-Soap and Water.

That hot Iron of itself gives no offensive Smell, those know very well, who have (as the Writer of this has) been present at a Furnace, when the Workmen were pouring out the flowing Metal to cast large Plates, and not the least Smell of it to be perceived. That hot Iron does not, like Lead, Brass, and some other Metals, give out unwholesome Vapours, is plain from the general Health and Strength of those who constantly work in Iron, as Furnace-men, Forge-Men, and Smiths; That it is in its Nature a Metal perfectly wholesome to the Body of Man, is known from the beneficial Use of Chalybeat or Iron-Mine Waters; from the Good done by taking Steel Filings in several Disorders; and that even the Smithy Water in which hot Irons are quench'd, is found advantageous to the human Constitution. The ingenious and learned Dr. Desaguliers, to whose instructive Writings the Contriver of this Machine acknowledges himself much indebted, relates an Experiment he made, to try whether heated Iron would yield unwholesome Vapours; He took a Cube of Iron, and having given it a very great Heat, he fix'd it so to a Receiver, exhausted by the Air Pump, that all the Air rushing in to fill the Receiver, should first pass thro' a Hole in the hot Iron. He then put a small Bird into the Receiver, who breath'd that Air without any Inconvenience or suffering the least Disorder. But the same Experiment being made with a Cube of hot Brass, a Bird put into that Air dy'd in a few Minutes. Brass indeed stinks even when cold, and much more when hot; Lead too, when hot, yields a very unwholesome Steam; but IRON is always sweet, and every way taken is wholesome and friendly to the human Body——except in Weapons.

That warm Rooms make People tender and apt to catch Cold, is a Mistake as great as it is (among the English) general. We have seen in the preceding Pages how the common Rooms are apt to give Colds; but the Writer of this Paper may affirm, from his own Experience, and that of his Family and Friends who have used warm Rooms for these four Winters past, that by the Use of such Rooms, People are rendered *less liable* to take Cold, and indeed *actually hardened*. If sitting warm in a Room made One subject to take Cold on going out, lying warm in Bed should, by a Parity of Reason, produce the same Effect when we rise; Yet we find we can leap out of the warmest Bed naked in the coldest Morning, without any such Danger; and in the same Manner out of warm Clothes into a cold Bed. The Reason is, that in these Cases the Pores all close at once, the Cold is shut out, and the Heat within augmented, as we soon after feel by the glowing of the Flesh and Skin. Thus no one was ever known to catch Cold by the Use of the Cold Bath: And are not cold Baths allowed to harden the Bodies of those that use them? Are they not therefore frequently prescrib'd to the tenderest Constitutions? Now every Time you go out of a warm Room into the cold freezing Air, you do as it were plunge into a Cold Bath, and the Effect is in proportion the same; for (tho' perhaps you may feel somewhat chilly at first) you find in a little Time your Bodies hardened and strengthened, your Blood is driven round with a brisker Circulation, and a comfortable steady uniform inward Warmth succeeds that equal outward Warmth you first received in the Room. Farther to confirm this Assertion, we instance the Swedes, the Danes, the Russians: These Nations are said to live in Rooms, compar'd to ours, as hot as Ovens; yet where are the hardy Soldiers, tho' bred in their boasted cool Houses, that can, like these People, bear the Fatigues of a Winter Campaign in so severe a Climate, march whole Days to the Neck in Snow, and at Night entrench in Ice, as they do?

The Mentioning of those Northern Nations puts me in Mind of a considerable *Publick Advantage* that may arise from the general Use of these Fire-places. It is observable, that tho' those Countries have been well inhabited for many Ages, Wood is still their Fuel, and yet at no very great Price; which could not have been if they had not universally used Stoves, but consum'd it as we do, in great Quantities by open Fires. By the Help of this saving Invention, our Wood may grow as fast as we consume it, and our

Posterity may warm themselves at a moderate Rate, without being oblig'd to fetch their Fuel over the Atlantick; as, if Pit-Coal should not be here discovered (which is an Uncertainty) they must necessarily do.

We leave it to the *Political Arithmetician* to compute, how much Money will be sav'd to a Country, by its spending two thirds less of Fuel; how much Labour sav'd in Cutting and Carriage of it; how much more Land may be clear'd for Cultivation; how great the Profit by the additional Quantity of Work done, in those Trades particularly that do not exercise the Body so much, but that the Workfolks are oblig'd to run frequently to the Fire to warm themselves: And to Physicians to say, how much healthier thick-built Towns and Cities will be, now half suffocated with sulphury Smoke, when so much less of that Smoke shall be made, and the Air breath'd by the Inhabitants be consequently so much purer. These Things it will suffice just to have mentioned; let us proceed to give some necessary Directions to the Workman who is to fix or set up these Fire-Places.

Directions to the Bricklayer.

The Chimney being first well swept and cleans'd from Soot, &c. lay the Bottom Plate down on the Hearth in the Place where the Fire-Place is to stand, which may be as forward as the Hearth will allow. Chalk a Line from one of its back Corners round the Plate to the other Corner, that you may afterwards know its Place when you come to fix it; and from those Corners two parallel Lines to the Back of the Chimney: Make Marks also on each Side, that you may know where the Partition is to stand, which is to prevent any Communication between the Air and Smoke. Then removing the Plate, make a Hollow under it and beyond it, by taking up as many of the Bricks or Tiles as you can within your chalk'd Lines, quite to the Chimney-Back. Dig out six or eight Inches deep of the Earth or Rubbish all the Breadth and Length of your Hollow; then make a Passage of four Inches square, (if the Place will allow so much) leading from the Hollow to some Place communicating with the outer Air; by *outer Air* we mean Air without the Room you intend to warm. This Passage may be made to enter your Hollow on either Side, or in the Fore-part, just as you find most convenient, the Circumstances of your Chimney considered. If the Fire-Place is to be put up in a Chamber, you may have this Communication of outer Air from the Staircase; or sometimes more easily from between the Chamber Floor and the Cieling of the lower Room, making only a small Hole in the Wall of the House entring the Space betwixt those two Joists with which your Air-Passage in the Hearth communicates. If this Air-Passage be so situated, as that Mice may enter it and nestle in the Hollow, a little Grate of Wire will keep them out. This Passage being made, and, if it runs under any Part of the Hearth, til'd over securely; you may proceed to raise your false Back. This may be of four Inches or two Inches Thickness, as you have Room, but let it stand at least four Inches from the true Chimney-Back. In narrow Chimnies this false Back runs from Jamb to Jamb, but in large old-fashion'd Chimnies you need not make it wider than the Back of the Fire-place. To begin it, you may form an Arch nearly flat of three Bricks End to End, over the Hollow, to leave a Passage the Breadth of the Iron Fire-Place, and five or six Inches deep, rounding at Bottom, for the Smoke to turn and pass under the false Back, and so behind it up the Chimney. The false Back is to rise till it is as high as the Breast of the Chimney, and then to close over to the Breast; always observing, if there is a wooden Mantle-Tree, to close above it. If there is no Wood in the Breast, you may arch over and close even with the lower Part of the Breast. By this Closing the Chimney is made tight, that no Air or Smoke can pass up it, without going under the false Back. Then from Side to Side of your Hollow, against the Marks you made with Chalk, raise a tight Partition, Brick-on-Edge, to separate the Air from the Smoke, bevelling away to half an Inch the Brick that comes just under the Air-Hole, that the Air may have a free Passage up into the Air-Box: Lastly, close the Hearth over that Part of the Hollow that is between the false Back and the Place of the Bottom Plate, coming about half an Inch under the Plate, which Piece of hollow Hearth may be supported by a Bit or two of old Iron Hoop; then is your Chimney fitted to receive the Fire-Place.

To set it, Lay first a little Bed of Mortar all round the Edges of the Hollow and over the Top of the Partition: Then lay down your Bottom Plate in its Place (with the Rods in it) and tread it till it lies firm. Then put a little fine Mortar (made of Loam and Lime with a little Hair) into its Joints, and set in your back Plate, leaning it for the present against the false Back; Then set in your Air-Box, with a little Mortar in its Joints; Then put in the two Sides, closing them up against the Air-Box with Mortar in their Grooves, and fixing at the same time your Register; Then bring up your Back to its Place, with Mortar in its Grooves, and that will bind the Sides together. Then put in your Front-Plate, placing it as far back in the Groove as you can, to leave Room for the sliding Plate; Then lay on your Top-Plate, with Mortar in its Grooves also, screwing the whole firmly together by means of the Rods. The Capital Letters *A B D E*, &c. in the annex'd Cut, show the corresponding Parts of the several Plates. Lastly the Joints being pointed all round on the Out-side, the Fire-Place is fit for Use.

When you make your first Fire in it, perhaps, if the Chimney be thoroughly cold, it may not draw, the Work too being all cold and damp. In such Case put first a few Shovels of hot Coals in the Fire-Place, then lift up the Chimney-sweeper's Trap-Door, and putting in a Sheet or two of flaming Paper, shut it again, which will set the Chimney a Drawing immediately, and when once 'tis fill'd with a Column of warm Air, it will draw strongly and continually.

The Drying of the Mortar and Work by the first Fire, may smell unpleasantly; but that will soon be over.

In some shallow Chimneys, to make more Room for the false Back and its Flue, four Inches or more of the Chimney-Back may be pick'd away.

Let the Room be made as tight as conveniently it may be, so will the outer Air that must come in to supply the Room and Draught of the Fire, be all obliged to enter thro' the Passage under the Bottom-Plate, and up thro' the Air-Box; by which Means it will not come cold to your Backs, but be warmed as it comes in, and mixed with the warm Air round the Fire-Place before it spreads in the Room.

But as a great Quantity of cold Air, in extream cold Weather especially, will presently enter a Room if the Door be carelessly left open, 'tis good to have some Contrivance to shut it, either by Means of Screw Hinges, a Spring, or a Pulley.

When the Pointing in the Joints is all dry and hard, get some Powder of Black-Lead, (broken Bits of Black-Lead Crucibles from the Silver-smith's, pounded fine, will do) and mixing it with a little Rum and Water, lay it on, when the Plates are warm, with a hard Brush, over the Top and Front-Plates, part of the Side and Bottom Plates, and over all the Pointing; and as it dries rub it to a Gloss with the same Brush, so the Joints will not be discern'd, but it will look all of a Piece, and shine like new Iron. And the false Back being plaister'd and whitewash'd, and the Hearth redden'd, the whole will make a pretty Appearance. Before the Black Lead is laid on, it would not be amiss to wash the Plates with strong Lee and a Brush, or Soap and Water, to cleanse them from any Spots of Grease or Filth that may be on them. If any Grease should afterwards come on them, a little wet Ashes will get it out.

If it be well set up, and in a tolerable good Chimney, Smoke will draw in from as far as the Fore-Part of the Bottom Plate, as you may try by a Bit of burning Paper.

People are at first apt to make their Rooms too warm, not imagining how little a Fire will be sufficient. When the Plates are no hotter than that one may just bear the Hand on them, the Room will generally be as warm as you desire it.

THE END

EXPLANATION of the Plate,

Referring to the Pages where the several Parts are describ'd, or their Uses shewn.

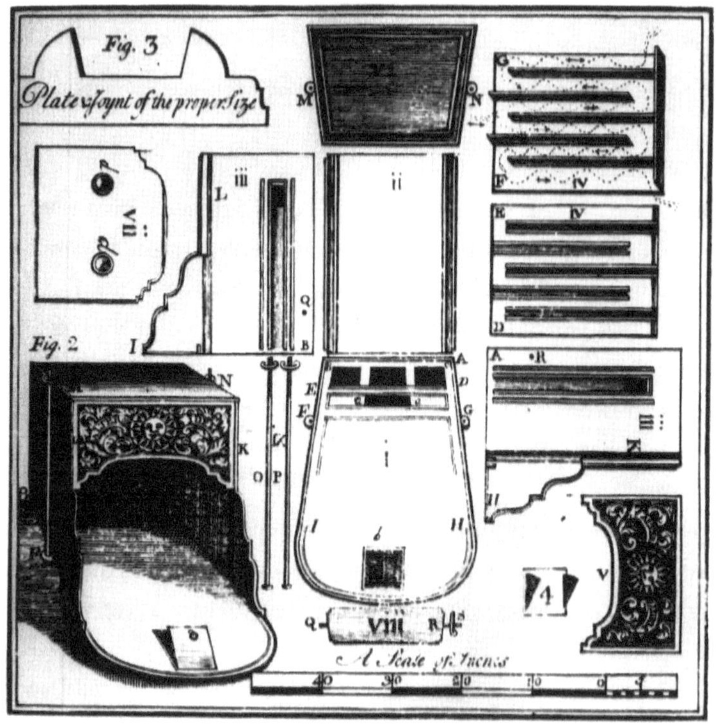

Plate of the Pennsylvania Fireplace

i The Bottom Plate

ii The Back Plate

iii iii The two Side Plates

iv iv The two Plates that make up the Air-box

v The Front Plate

vi The Top Plate

vii The Shutter or Slider

viii The Register

Fig. 2. The Fire-Place put together

3. The Section of a Fragment of a Plate, shewing the quarter-round Regulets that make the Joints

4. The Blower, (Bottom upwards)

OP The two Screw Rods

↥↥ With the prick'd Lines, shew the Course of the Air thro' the Windings of the Air-Box.

The Capital Letters show the corresponding Parts of the several Plates.

On the DEVICE of the NEW FIRE-PLACE,
A SUN; *with this Motto*, ALTER IDEM.
i.e. *A second Self;* or, *Another, the same.*
By a Friend.

ANOTHER Sun!—'tis true;—but not THE SAME.
Alike, I own, in Warmth and genial Flame:
But, more obliging than his elder Brother,
This will not scorch in Summer, like *the other;*
Nor, when sharp Boreas chills our shiv'ring Limbs,
Will *this Sun* leave us for more Southern Climes;
Or, in long Winter Nights, forsake us here,
To chear new Friends in t'other Hemisphere:
But, faithful still to us, this *new Sun*'s Fire,
Warms when we please, and just as we desire.

Plain Truth

17 November, 1747

It is said the wise Italians make this proverbial Remark on our Nation, viz. *The English* FEEL, *but they do not* SEE. That is, they are sensible of Inconveniencies when they are present, but do not take sufficient Care to prevent them: Their natural Courage makes them too little apprehensive of Danger, so that they are often surpriz'd by it, unprovided of the proper Means of Security. When 'tis too late they are sensible of their Imprudence: After great Fires, they provide Buckets and Engines: After a Pestilence they think of keeping clean their Streets and common Shores: and when a Town has been sack'd by their Enemies, they provide for its Defence, &c. This Kind of AFTER- WISDOM is indeed so common with us, as to occasion the vulgar, tho' very significant Saying, *When the Steed is stolen, you shut the Stable Door.*

But the more insensible we generally are of publick Danger, and indifferent when warn'd of it, so much the more freely, openly, and earnestly, ought such as apprehend it, to speak their Sentiments; that if possible, those who seem to sleep, may be awaken'd, to think of some Means of Avoiding or Preventing the Mischief before it be too late.

Believing therefore that 'tis my DUTY, I shall honestly speak my Mind in the following Paper.

War, at this Time, rages over a great Part of the known World; our News-Papers are Weekly filled with fresh Accounts of the Destruction it every where occasions. Pennsylvania, indeed, situate in the Center of the Colonies, has hitherto enjoy'd profound Repose; and tho' our Nation is engag'd in a bloody War, with two great and powerful Kingdoms, yet, defended, in a great Degree, from the French on the one Hand by the Northern Provinces, and from the Spaniards on the other by the Southern, at no small Expence to each, our People have, till lately, slept securely in their Habitations.

There is no British Colony excepting this, but has made some Kind of Provision for its Defence; many of them have therefore never been attempted by an Enemy; and others that were attack'd, have generally defended themselves with Success. The Length and Difficulty of our Bay and River has been thought so effectual a Security to us, that hitherto no Means have been entered into that might discourage an Attempt upon us, or prevent its succeeding.

But whatever Security this might have been while both Country and City were poor, and the Advantage to be expected scarce worth the Hazard of an Attempt, it is now doubted whether we can any longer safely depend upon it. Our Wealth, of late Years much encreas'd, is one strong Temptation, our defenceless State another, to induce an Enemy to attack us; while the Acquaintance they have lately gained with our Bay and River, by Means of the Prisoners and Flags of Truce they have had among us; by Spies which they almost every where maintain, and perhaps from Traitors among ourselves; with the Facility of getting Pilots to conduct them; and the known Absence of Ships of War, during the greatest Part of the Year, from both Virginia and New-York, ever since the War began, render the Appearance of Success to the Enemy far more promising, and therefore highly encrease our DANGER.

That our Enemies may have Spies abroad, and some even in these Colonies, will not be made much doubt of, when 'tis considered, that such has been the Practice of all Nations in all Ages, whenever they were engaged, or intended to engage in War. Of this we have an early Example in the Book of Judges (too too [*sic*] pertinent to our Case, and therefore I must beg leave a little to enlarge upon it) where we are told, Chap. xviii, v. 2, That *the Children of Dan sent of their Family five Men from their*

Coasts to spie out the Land, and search it, saying, Go, search the LAND. These Danites it seems were at this Time not very orthodox in their Religion, and their Spies met with a certain idolatrous Priest of their own Persuasion, v. 3, and they said to him, *Who brought thee hither! what makest thou in this Place? and what hast thou here?* [would to God no such Priests were to be found among us.] And they said unto him, verse 5, *Ask Counsel of God, that we may know whether our Way which we go shall be prosperous? And the Priest said unto them, Go in Peace; before the Lord is your Way wherein you go*. [Are there no Priests among us, think you, that might, in the like Case, give an Enemy as good Encouragement? 'Tis well known, that we have Numbers of the same Religion with those who of late encouraged the French to invade our Mother-Country.] *And they came*, Verse 7, *to Laish, and saw the People that were therein, how they dwelt* CARELESS, *after the Manner of the Zidonians*, QUIET *and* SECURE. They *thought* themselves secure, no doubt; and as they *never had been* disturbed, vainly imagined they *never should*. 'Tis not unlikely that some might see the Danger they were exposed to by living in that *careless* Manner; but that if these publickly expressed their Apprehensions, the rest reproached them as timorous Persons, wanting Courage or Confidence in their Gods, who (they might say) had hitherto protected them. But the Spies, Verse 8, returned, and said to their Countrymen, Verse 9, *Arise that we may go up against them; for we have seen the Land, and behold it is very good! And are ye still? Be not slothful to go*. Verse 10, *When ye go, ye shall come unto a People* SECURE; [that is, a People that apprehend no Danger, and therefore have made no Provision against it; great Encouragement this!] *and to a large Land, and a Place where there is no Want of any Thing*. What could they desire more? Accordingly we find, in the following Verses, that *Six hundred Men* only, *appointed with Weapons of War*, undertook the Conquest of this *large Land;* knowing that 600 Men, armed and disciplined, would be an Over-match perhaps for 60,000, unarmed, undisciplined, and off their Guard. And when they went against it, the idolatrous Priest, Verse 17, *with his graven Image, and his Ephod, and his Teraphim, and his molten*

Image, [Plenty of superstitious Trinkets] joined with them, and, no doubt, gave them all the Intelligence and Assistance in his Power; his Heart, as the Text assures us, *being glad*, perhaps for Reasons more than one. And now, what was the Fate of poor Laish! The 600 Men being arrived, found, as the Spies had reported, a People QUIET and SECURE, Verse 20, 21. *And they smote them with the Edge of the Sword, and burnt the City with* Fire; *and there was no* DELIVERER, *because it was far from Zidon*. Not so far from Zidon, however, as Pennsylvania is from Britain; and yet we are, if possible, more *careless* than the People of Laish! As the Scriptures are given for our Reproof, Instruction and Warning, may we make a due Use of this Example, before it be too late!

And is our *Country*, any more than our City, altogether free from Danger? Perhaps not. We have, 'tis true, had a long Peace with the Indians: But it is a long Peace indeed, as well as a long Lane, that has no Ending. The French know the Power and Importance of the Six Nations, and spare no Artifice, Pains or Expence, to gain them to their Interest. By their Priests they have converted many to their Religion, and these‡ have openly espoused their Cause. The rest appear irresolute which Part to take; no Persuasions, tho' enforced with costly Presents, having yet been able to engage them generally on our Side, tho' we had numerous Forces on their Borders, ready to second and support them. What then may be expected, now those Forces are, by Orders from the Crown, to be disbanded; when our boasted Expedition is laid aside, thro' want (as it may appear to them) either of Strength or Courage; when they see that the French, and their Indians, boldly, and with Impunity, ravage the Frontiers of New-York, and scalp the Inhabitants; when those few Indians that engaged with us against the French, are left exposed to their Resentment: When they consider these Things, is there no Danger that, thro' Disgust at our Usage, joined with Fear of the French Power, and greater Confidence in their Promises and Protection than in ours, they may be wholly gained over by our Enemies, and join in the War against us? If such should be the Case, which God forbid, how soon may the Mischief spread to our Frontier Counties? And what may we expect to be the Consequence, but deserting of Plantations, Ruin, Bloodshed and Confusion!

Perhaps some in the City, Towns and Plantations near the River, may say to themselves, *An Indian War on the Frontiers will not affect us; the Enemy will never come near our Habitations; let those concern'd take Care of themselves.* And others who live in the Country, when they are told of the Danger the City is in from Attempts by Sea, may say, *What is that to us? The Enemy will be satisfied with the Plunder of the Town, and never think it worth his while to visit our Plantations: Let the Town take care of itself.* These are not mere Suppositions, for I have heard some talk in this strange Manner. But are these the Sentiments of true Pennsylvanians, of Fellow-Countrymen, or even of Men that have common Sense or Goodness? Is not the whole Province one Body, united by living under the same Laws, and enjoying the same Priviledges? Are not the People of City and Country connected as Relations both by Blood and Marriage, and in Friendships equally dear? Are they not likewise united in Interest, and mutually useful and necessary to each other? When the Feet are wounded, shall the Head say, *It is not me; I will not trouble myself to contrive Relief!* Or if the Head is in Danger, shall the Hands say, *We are not affected, and therefore will lend no Assistance!* No. For so would the Body be easily destroyed: But when all Parts join their Endeavours for its Security, it is often preserved. And such should be the Union between the Country and the Town; and such their mutual Endeavours for the Safety of the Whole. When New-England, a distant Colony, involv'd itself in a grievous Debt to reduce Cape-Breton, we freely gave *Four Thousand Pounds* for *their* Relief. And at another Time, remembring that Great Britain, still more distant, groan'd under heavy Taxes in Supporting the War, we threw in our Mite to their Assistance, by a free Gift of *Three Thousand Pounds:* And shall Country and Town join in helping Strangers (as those comparatively are) and yet refuse to assist each other?

But whatever different Opinions we have of our Security in other Respects, our TRADE, all seem to agree, is in Danger of being ruin'd in another

Year. The great Success of our Enemies, in two different Cruizes this last Summer in our Bay, must give them the greatest Encouragement to repeat more frequently their Visits, the Profit being almost certain, and the Risque next to nothing. Will not the first Effect of this be, an Enhauncing of the Price of all foreign Goods to the Tradesman and Farmer, who use or consume them? For the Rate of Insurance will increase in Proportion to the Hazard of Importing them; and in the same Proportion will the Price of those Goods increase. If the Price of the Tradesman's Work and the Farmer's Produce would encrease equally with the Price of foreign Commodities, the Damage would not be so great: But the direct contrary must happen. For the same Hazard, or Rate of Insurance, that raises the Price of what is imported, must be deducted out of, and lower the Price of what is exported. Without this Addition and Deduction, as long as the Enemy cruize at our Capes, and take those Vessels that attempt to *go out*, as well as those that endeavour to *come in*, none can afford to trade, and Business must be soon at a Stand. And will not the Consequences be, A discouraging of many of the Vessels that us'd to come from other Places to purchase our Produce, and thereby a Turning of the Trade to Ports that can be entered with less Danger, and capable of furnishing them with the same Commodities, as New-York, &c? A Lessening of Business to every Shopkeeper, together with Multitudes of bad Debts; the high Rate of Goods discouraging the Buyers, and the low Rates of their Labour and Produce rendering them unable to pay for what they had bought: Loss of Employment to the Tradesman, and bad Pay for what little he does: And lastly, Loss of many Inhabitants, who will retire to other Provinces not subject to the like Inconveniencies; whence a Lowering of the Value of Lands, Lots, and Houses.

The Enemy, no doubt, have been told, That the People of Pennsylvania are Quakers, and against all Defence, from a Principle of Conscience; this, tho' true of a Part, and that a small Part only of the Inhabitants, is commonly said of the Whole; and what may make it look probable to Strangers, is, that in Fact, nothing is done by any Part of the People towards their Defence. But to refuse Defending one's self or one's Country, is so unusual a Thing among Mankind, that possibly they may not believe it, till by Experience they find, they can come higher and higher up our River, seize our Vessels, land and plunder our Plantations and Villages, and retire with their Booty unmolested. Will not this confirm the Report, and give them the greatest Encouragement to strike one bold Stroke for the City, and for the whole Plunder of the River?

It is said by some, that the Expence of a Vessel to guard our Trade, would be very heavy, greater than perhaps all the Enemy can be supposed to take from us at Sea would amount to; and that it would be cheaper for the Government to open an Insurance-Office, and pay all Losses. But is this right Reasoning? I think not: For what the Enemy takes is clear Loss to us, and Gain to him; encreasing his Riches and Strength as much as it diminishes ours, so making the Difference double; whereas the Money paid our own Tradesmen for Building and Fitting out a Vessel of Defence, remains in the Country, and circulates among us; what is paid to the Officers and Seamen that navigate her, is also spent ashore, and soon gets into other Hands; the Farmer receives the Money for her Provisions; and on the whole, nothing is clearly lost to the Country but her Wear and Tear, or so much as she sells for at the End of the War less than her first Cost. This Loss, and a trifling one it is, is all the Inconvenience; But how many and how great are the Conveniencies and Advantages! And should the Enemy, thro' our Supineness and Neglect to provide for the Defence both of our Trade and Country, be encouraged to attempt this City, and after plundering us of our Goods, either *burn it*, or put it to Ransom; how great would that Loss be! Besides the Confusion, Terror, and Distress, so many Hundreds of Families would be involv'd in!

The Thought of this latter Circumstance so much affects me, that I cannot forbear expatiating somewhat more upon it. You have, my dear Countrymen, and Fellow Citizens, Riches to tempt a considerable Force to unite and attack you, but are under no Ties or Engagements to unite for your Defence. Hence, on the first Alarm, *Terror* will spread over All;

and as no Man can with Certainty depend that another will stand by him, beyond Doubt very many will seek Safety by a speedy Flight. Those that are reputed rich, will flee, thro' Fear of Torture, to make them produce more than they are able. The Man that has a Wife and Children, will find them hanging on his Neck, beseeching him with Tears to quit the City, and save his Life, to guide and protect them in that Time of general Desolation and Ruin. All will run into Confusion, amidst Cries and Lamentations, and the Hurry and Disorder of Departers, carrying away their Effects. The Few that remain will be unable to resist. *Sacking* the City will be the first, and *Burning* it, in all Probability, the last Act of the Enemy. This, I believe, will be the Case, if you have timely Notice. But what must be your Condition, if suddenly surprized, without previous Alarm, perhaps in the Night! Confined to your Houses, you will have nothing to trust to but the Enemy's Mercy. Your best Fortune will be, to fall under the Power of Commanders of King's Ships, able to controul the Mariners; and not into the Hands of *licentious Privateers*. Who can, without the utmost Horror, conceive the Miseries of the Latter! when your Persons, Fortunes, Wives and Daughters, shall be subject to the wanton and unbridled Rage, Rapine and Lust, of *Negroes, Molattoes*, and others, the vilest and most abandoned of Mankind. A dreadful Scene! which some may represent as exaggerated. I think it my Duty to warn you: Judge for yourselves.

'Tis true, with very little Notice, the Rich may shift for themselves. The Means of speedy Flight are ready in their Hands; and with some previous Care to lodge Money and Effects in distant and secure Places, tho' they should lose much, yet enough may be left them, and to spare. But most unhappily circumstanced indeed are we, the middling People, the Tradesmen, Shopkeepers, and Farmers of this Province and City! We cannot all fly with our Families; and if we could, how shall we subsist? No; we and they, and what little we have gained by hard Labour and Industry, must bear the Brunt: The Weight of Contributions, extorted by the Enemy (as it is of Taxes among ourselves) must be surely borne by us. Nor can it be avoided as we stand at present; for tho' we are numerous, we are quite defenceless, having neither Forts, Arms, Union, nor Discipline. And tho' it were true, that our Trade might be protected at no great Expence, and our Country and our City easily defended, if proper Measures were but taken; yet who shall take these Measures? Who shall pay that Expence? On whom may we fix our Eyes with the least Expectation that they will do any one Thing for our Security? Should we address that wealthy and powerful Body of People, who have ever since the War governed our Elections, and filled almost every Seat in our Assembly; should we intreat them to consider, if not as Friends, at least as Legislators, that *Protection* is as truly due from the Government to the People, as *Obedience* from the People to the Government; and that if on account of their religious Scruples, they themselves could do no Act for our Defence, yet they might retire, relinquish their Power for a Season, quit the Helm to freer Hands during the present Tempest, to Hands chosen by their own Interest too, whose Prudence and Moderation, with regard to them, they might safely confide in; secure, from their own native Strength, of resuming again their present Stations, whenever it shall please them: Should we remind them, that the Publick Money, raised *from All*, belongs *to All;* that since they have, for their own Ease, and to secure themselves in the quiet Enjoyment of their Religious Principles (and may they long enjoy them) expended such large Sums to oppose Petitions, and engage favourable Representations of their Conduct, if they themselves could by no Means be free to appropriate any Part of the Publick Money for our Defence; yet it would be no more than Justice to spare us a reasonable Sum for that Purpose, which they might easily give to the King's Use as heretofore, leaving all the Appropriation to others, who would faithfully apply it as we desired: Should we tell them, that tho' the Treasury be at present empty, it may soon be filled by the outstanding Publick Debts collected; or at least Credit might be had for such a Sum, on a single Vote of the Assembly: That tho' *they* themselves may be resigned and easy under this naked, defenceless State of the Country, it is far otherwise with a very great Part of the People; with *us*, who can have no Confidence that God will protect those that neglect the Use of rational Means for their Security; nor have any Reason to hope, that our Losses, if we should suffer any, may be made up by Collections in our Favour at Home? Should we conjure them by all the Ties of Neighbourhood, Friendship, Justice and Humanity, to consider these Things; and what Distraction, Misery and Confusion, what Desolation and Distress, may possibly be the Effect of their *unseasonable* Predominancy and Perseverance; yet all would be in vain: For they have already been by great Numbers of the People petitioned in vain. Our late Governor did for Years sollicit, request, and even threaten them in vain. The Council have since twice remonstrated to them in vain. Their religious Prepossessions are unchangeable, their Obstinacy invincible. Is there then the least Hope remaining, that from that Quarter any Thing should arise for our Security?

And is our Prospect better, if we turn our Eyes to the Strength of the *opposite Party*, those Great and rich Men, Merchants and others, who are ever railing at Quakers for doing what their Principles seem to require, and what in Charity we ought to believe they think their Duty, but take no one Step themselves for the Publick Safety? They have so much Wealth and Influence, if they would use it, that they might easily, by their Endeavours and Example, raise a military Spirit among us, make us fond, studious of, and expert in Martial Discipline, and effect every Thing that is necessary, under God, for our Protection. But Envy seems to have taken Possession of their Hearts, and to have eaten out and destroyed every generous, noble, Publick-spirited Sentiment. *Rage* at the Disappointment of their little Schemes for Power, gnaws their Souls, and fills them with such cordial Hatred to their Opponents, that every Proposal, by the Execution of which *those* may receive Benefit as well as themselves, is rejected with Indignation. *What*, say they, *shall we lay out our Money to protect the Trade of Quakers? Shall we fight to defend Quakers? No; Let the Trade perish, and the City burn; let what will happen, we shall never lift a Finger to prevent it.* Yet the Quakers have *Conscience* to plead for their Resolution not to fight, which these Gentlemen have not: *Conscience* with you, Gentlemen, is on the other Side of the Question: *Conscience* enjoins it as a Duty on you (and indeed

I think it such on every Man) to defend your Country, your Friends, your aged Parents, your Wives, and helpless Children: And yet you resolve not to perform this Duty, but act *contrary* to *your own* Consciences, because the Quakers act *according* to *theirs*. 'Till of late I could scarce believe the Story of him who refused to pump in a sinking Ship, because one on board, whom he hated, would be saved by it as well as himself. But such, it seems, is the Unhappiness of human Nature, that our Passions, when violent, often are too hard for the united Force of *Reason, Duty* and *Religion*.

Thus unfortunately are we circumstanc'd at this Time, my dear Countrymen and Fellow-Citizens; we, I mean, the middling People, the Farmers, Shopkeepers and Tradesmen of this City and Country. Thro' the Dissensions of our Leaders, thro' *mistaken Principles* of *Religion*, join'd with a Love of Worldly Power, on the one Hand; thro' *Pride, Envy* and *implacable Resentment* on the other; our Lives, our Families and little Fortunes, dear to us as any Great Man's can be to him, are to remain continually expos'd to Destruction, from an enterprizing, cruel, now well-inform'd, and by Success encourag'd Enemy. It seems as if Heaven, justly displeas'd at our growing Wickedness, and determin'd to punish* this once favour'd Land, had suffered our Chiefs to engage in these foolish and mischievous Contentions, for *little Posts* and *paltry Distinctions*, that our Hands might be bound up, our Understandings darkned and misled, and every Means of our Security neglected. It seems as if our greatest Men, our *Cives nobilissimi*‡ of both Parties, had *sworn the Ruin of the Country, and invited the French, our most inveterate Enemy, to destroy it*. Where then shall we seek for Succour and Protection? The Government we are immediately under denies it to us; and if the Enemy comes, we are *far from* ZIDON, *and there is no Deliverer near*. Our Case indeed is dangerously bad; but perhaps there is yet a Remedy, if we have but the Prudence and the Spirit to apply it.

If this now flourishing City, and greatly improving Colony, is destroy'd and ruin'd, it will not be for want of Numbers of Inhabitants able to bear Arms in its Defence. 'Tis computed that we have at least (exclusive of the Quakers) 60,000 Fighting Men, acquainted with Fire- Arms, many of them Hunters and Marksmen, hardy and bold. All we want is Order, Discipline, and a few Cannon. At present we are like the separate Filaments of Flax before the Thread is form'd, without Strength because without Connection; but UNION would make us strong and even formidable: Tho' the *Great* should neither help nor join us; tho' they should even oppose our Uniting, from some mean Views of their own, yet, if we resolve upon it, and it please GOD to inspire us with the necessary Prudence and Vigour, it *may* be effected. Great Numbers of our People are of BRITISH RACE, and tho' the fierce fighting Animals of those happy Islands, are said to abate their native Fire and Intrepidity, when removed to a Foreign Clime, yet with the People 'tis not so; Our Neighbours of New-England afford the World a convincing Proof, that BRITONS, tho' a Hundred Years transplanted, and to the remotest Part of the Earth, may yet retain, even to the third and fourth Descent, that *Zeal* for the *Publick Good*, that *military Prowess*, and that *undaunted Spirit*, which has in every Age distinguished their Nation. What Numbers have we likewise of *those brave People*, whose Fathers in the last Age made so glorious a Stand for our Religion and Liberties, when invaded by a powerful French Army, join'd by Irish Catholicks, under a bigotted Popish King! Let the memorable SIEGE OF LONDONDERRY, and the signal Actions of the INISKILLINGERS, by which the Heart of that Prince's Schemes was broken, be perpetual Testimonies of the *Courage* and *Conduct* of those *noble Warriors!* Nor are there wanting amongst us, Thousands of *that Warlike Nation*, whose Sons have ever since the Time of Caesar maintained the Character he gave their Fathers, of joining the most *obstinate Courage* to all the other military Virtues. I mean the *brave* and *steady* GERMANS. Numbers of whom have actually borne Arms in the Service of their respective Princes; and if they fought well for their Tyrants and Oppressors, would they refuse to unite with us in Defence of their *newly acquired* and most precious *Liberty* and *Property?* Were this Union form'd, were we once united, thoroughly arm'd and disciplin'd, was every Thing in our Power done for our Security, as far as human Means and Foresight could provide, we might then, *with more Propriety*, humbly ask the Assistance of Heaven, and a Blessing on our lawful Endeavours. The very Fame of our Strength and Readiness would be a Means of Discouraging our Enemies; for 'tis a wise and true Saying, that *One Sword often keeps another in the Scabbard.* The Way to secure Peace is to be prepared for War. They that are on their Guard, and appear ready to receive their Adversaries, are in much less Danger of being attack'd, than the supine, secure and negligent. We have yet a Winter before us, which may afford a good and almost sufficient Opportunity for this, if we seize and improve it with a becoming Vigour. And if the Hints contained in this Paper are so happy as to meet with a suitable Disposition of Mind in his Countrymen and Fellow Citizens, the Writer of it will, in a few Days, lay before them a Form of an ASSOCIATION for the Purposes herein mentioned, together with a practicable Scheme for raising the Money necessary for the Defence of our Trade, City, and Country, without laying a Burthen on any Man.

May the God *of* WISDOM, STRENGTH *and* POWER, *the Lord of the Armies of Israel, inspire us with Prudence in this Time of* DANGER; *take away from us all the Seeds of Contention and Division, and unite the Hearts and Counsels of all of us, of whatever* SECT *or* NATION, *in one Bond of Peace, Brotherly Love, and generous Publick Spirit; May he give us Strength and Resolution to amend our Lives, and remove from among us every Thing that is displeasing to him; afford us his most gracious Protection, confound the Designs of our Enemies, and give* Peace *in all our Borders, is the sincere Prayer of*

A TRADESMAN of Philadelphia

Rules for Making Oneself a Disagreeable Companion

15 November, 1750

Rules, by the Observation of which, a Man of Wit and Learning may nevertheless make himself a *disagreeable* Companion.

Your Business is to *shine;* therefore you must by all means prevent the shining of others, for their Brightness may make yours the less distinguish'd. To this End,

1. If possible engross the whole Discourse; and when other Matter fails, talk much of your-self, your Education, your Knowledge, your Circumstances, your Successes in Business, your Victories in Disputes, your own wise Sayings and Observations on particular Occasions, &c. &c. &c.

2. If when you are out of Breath, one of the Company should seize the Opportunity of saying something; watch his Words, and, if possible, find somewhat either in his Sentiment or Expression, immediately to contradict and raise a Dispute upon. Rather than fail, criticise even his Grammar.

3. If another should be saying an indisputably good Thing; either give no Attention to it; or interrupt him; or draw away the Attention of others; or, if you can guess what he would be at, be quick and say it before him; or, if he gets it said, and you perceive the Company pleas'd with it, own it to be a good Thing, and withal remark that it had been said by Bacon, Locke, Bayle, or some other eminent Writer: thus you deprive him of the Reputation he might have gain'd by it, and gain some yourself, as you hereby show your great Reading and Memory.

4. When modest Men have been thus treated by you a few times, they will chuse ever after to be silent in your Company; then you may shine on

without Fear of a Rival; rallying them at the same time for their Dullness, which will be to you a new Fund of Wit.

Thus you will be sure to please *yourself*. The polite Man aims at pleasing *others*, but you shall go beyond him even in that. A Man can be present only in one Company, but may at the same time be absent in twenty. He can please only where he *is*, you whereever you are *not*.

Observations Concerning the Increase of Mankind, Peopling of Countries, &c.

1751

1. Tables of the Proportion of Marriages to Births, of Deaths to Births, of Marriages to the Numbers of Inhabitants, &c. form'd on Obser-vaions made upon the Bills of Mortality, Christnings, &c. of populous Cities, will not suit Countries; nor will Tables form'd on Observations made on full settled old Countries, as Europe, suit new Countries, as America.

2. For People increase in Proportion to the Number of Marriages, and that is greater in Proportion to the Ease and Convenience of supporting a Family. When Families can be easily supported, more Persons marry, and earlier in Life.

3. In Cities, where all Trades, Occupations and Offices are full, many delay marrying, till they can see how to bear the Charges of a Family; which Charges are greater in Cities, as Luxury is more common: many live single during Life, and continue Servants to Families, Journeymen to Trades, &c. hence Cities do not by natural Generation supply themselves with Inhabitants; the Deaths are more than the Births.

4. In Countries full settled, the Case must be nearly the same; all Lands being occupied and improved to the Heighth: those who cannot get Land, must Labour for others that have it; when Labourers are plenty, their Wages will be low; by low Wages a Family is supported with Difficulty; this Difficulty deters many from Marriage, who therefore long continue Servants and single. Only as the Cities take Supplies of People from the

Country, and thereby make a little more Room in the Country; Marriage is a little more incourag'd there, and the Births exceed the Deaths.

5. Europe is generally full settled with Husbandmen, Manufacturers, &c. and therefore cannot now much increase in People: America is chiefly occupied by Indians, who subsist mostly by Hunting. But as the Hunter, of all Men, requires the greatest Quantity of Land from whence to draw his Subsistence, (the Husbandman subsisting on much less, the Gardner on still less, and the Manufacturer requiring least of all), The Europeans found America as fully settled as it well could be by Hunters; yet these having large Tracks, were easily prevail'd on to part with Portions of Territory to the new Comers, who did not much interfere with the Natives in Hunting, and furnish'd them with many Things they wanted.

6. Land being thus plenty in America, and so cheap as that a labouring Man, that understands Husbandry, can in a short Time save Money enough to purchase a Piece of new Land sufficient for a Plantation, whereon he may subsist a Family; such are not afraid to marry; for if they even look far enough forward to consider how their Children when grown up are to be provided for, they see that more Land is to be had at Rates equally easy, all Circumstances considered.

7. Hence Marriages in America are more general, and more generally early, than in Europe. And if it is reckoned there, that there is but one Marriage per Annum among 100 Persons, perhaps we may here reckon two; and if in Europe they have but 4 Births to a Marriage (many of their Marriages being late) we may here reckon 8, of which if one half grow up, and our Marriages are made, reckoning one with another at 20 Years of Age, our People must at least be doubled every 20 Years.

8. But notwithstanding this Increase, so vast is the Territory of North-America, that it will require many Ages to settle it fully; and till it is fully settled, Labour will never be cheap here, where no Man continues long a Labourer for others, but gets a Plantation of his own, no Man continues long a Journeyman to a Trade, but goes among those new Settlers, and sets up for himself, &c. Hence Labour is no cheaper now, in

Pennsylvania, than it was 30 Years ago, tho' so many Thousand labouring People have been imported.

9. The Danger therefore of these Colonies interfering with their Mother Country in Trades that depend on Labour, Manufactures, &c. is too remote to require the Attention of Great-Britain.

10. But in Proportion to the Increase of the Colonies, a vast Demand is growing for British Manufactures, a glorious Market wholly in the Power of Britain, in which Foreigners cannot interfere, which will increase in a short Time even beyond her Power of supplying, tho' her whole Trade should be to her Colonies: Therefore Britain should not too much restrain Manufactures in her Colonies. A wise and good Mother will not do it. To distress, is to weaken, and weakening the Children, weakens the whole Family.

11. Besides if the Manufactures of Britain (by Reason of the American Demands) should rise too high in Price, Foreigners who can sell cheaper will drive her Merchants out of Foreign Markets; Foreign Manufactures will thereby be encouraged and increased, and consequently foreign Nations, perhaps her Rivals in Power, grow more populous and more powerful; while her own Colonies, kept too low, are unable to assist her, or add to her Strength.

12. 'Tis an ill-grounded Opinion that by the Labour of Slaves, America may possibly vie in Cheapness of Manufactures with Britain. The Labour of Slaves can never be so cheap here as the Labour of working Men is in Britain. Any one may compute it. Interest of Money is in the Colonies from 6 to 10 per Cent. Slaves one with another cost £30 Sterling per Head. Reckon then the Interest of the first Purchase of a Slave, the Insurance or Risque on his Life, his Cloathing and Diet, Expences in his Sickness and Loss of Time, Loss by his Neglect of Business (Neglect is natural to the Man who is not to be benefited by his own Care or Diligence), Expence of a Driver to keep him at Work, and his Pilfering from Time to Time, almost every Slave being *by Nature* a Thief, and compare the whole Amount with the Wages of a Manufacturer of Iron or Wool in England, you will see that

Labour is much cheaper there than it ever can be by Negroes here. Why then will Americans purchase Slaves? Because Slaves may be kept as long as a Man pleases, or has Occasion for their Labour; while hired Men are continually leaving their Master (often in the midst of his Business,) and setting up for themselves.

13. As the Increase of People depends on the Encouragement of Marriages, the following Things must diminish a Nation, viz.

1. The being conquered; for the Conquerors will engross as many Offices, and exact as much Tribute or Profit on the Labour of the conquered, as will maintain them in their new Establishment, and this diminishing the Subsistence of the Natives discourages their Marriages, and so gradually diminishes them, while the Foreigners increase. 2. Loss of Territory. Thus the Britons being driven into Wales, and crowded together in a barren Country insufficient to support such great Numbers, diminished 'till the People bore a Proportion to the Produce, while the Saxons increas'd on their abandoned Lands; 'till the Island became full of English. And were the English now driven into Wales by some foreign Nation, there would in a few Years be no more Englishmen in Britain, than there are now People in Wales. 3. Loss of Trade. Manufactures exported, draw Subsistence from Foreign Countries for Numbers; who are thereby enabled to marry and raise Families. If the Nation be deprived of any Branch of Trade, and no new Employment is found for the People occupy'd in that Branch, it will also be soon deprived of so many People. 4. Loss of Food. Suppose a Nation has a Fishery, which not only employs great Numbers, but makes the Food and Subsistence of the People cheaper; If another Nation becomes Master of the Seas, and prevents the Fishery, the People will diminish in Proportion as the Loss of Employ, and Dearness of Provision, makes it more difficult to subsist a Family. 5. Bad Government and insecure Property. People not only leave such a Country, and settling Abroad incorporate with other Nations, lose their native Language, and become Foreigners; but the Industry of those that remain being discourag'd, the Quantity of Subsistence in the Country is lessen'd, and the Support of a Family becomes more difficult. So

heavy Taxes tend to diminish a People. 6. The Introduction of Slaves. The Negroes brought into the English Sugar Islands, have greatly diminish'd the Whites there; the Poor are by this Means depriv'd of Employment, while a few Families acquire vast Estates; which they spend on Foreign Luxuries, and educating their Children in the Habit of those Luxuries; the same Income is needed for the Support of one that might have maintain'd 100. The Whites who have Slaves, not labouring, are enfeebled, and therefore not so generally prolific; the Slaves being work'd too hard, and ill fed, their Constitutions are broken, and the Deaths among them are more than the Births; so that a continual Supply is needed from Africa. The Northern Colonies having few Slaves increase in Whites. Slaves also pejorate the Families that use them; the white Children become proud, disgusted with Labour, and being educated in Idleness, are rendered unfit to get a Living by Industry.

14. Hence the Prince that acquires new Territory, if he finds it vacant, or removes the Natives to give his own People Room; the Legislator that makes effectual Laws for promoting of Trade, increasing Employment, improving Land by more or better Tillage; providing more Food by Fisheries; securing Property, &c. and the Man that invents new Trades, Arts or Manufactures, or new Improvements in Husbandry, may be properly called *Fathers* of their Nation, as they are the Cause of the Generation of Multitudes, by the Encouragement they afford to Marriage.

15. As to Privileges granted to the married, (such as the *Jus trium Liberorum* among the Romans), they may hasten the filling of a Country that has been thinned by War or Pestilence, or that has otherwise vacant Territory; but cannot increase a People beyond the Means provided for their Subsistence.

16. Foreign Luxuries and needless Manufactures imported and used in a Nation, do, by the same Reasoning, increase the People of the Nation that furnishes them, and diminish the People of the Nation that uses them. Laws therefore that prevent such Importations, and on the contrary promote the Exportation of Manufactures to be consumed in Foreign Coun-

tries, may be called (with Respect to the People that make them) *generative Laws*, as by increasing Subsistence they encourage Marriage. Such Laws likewise strengthen a Country, doubly, by increasing its own People and diminishing its Neighbours.

17. Some European Nations prudently refuse to consume the Manufactures of East-India. They should likewise forbid them to their Colonies; for the Gain to the Merchant, is not to be compar'd with the Loss by this Means of People to the Nation.

18. Home Luxury in the Great, increases the Nation's Manufacturers employ'd by it, who are many, and only tends to diminish the Families that indulge in it, who are few. The greater the common fashionable Expence of any Rank of People, the more cautious they are of Marriage. Therefore Luxury should never be suffer'd to become common.

19. The great Increase of Offspring in particular Families, is not always owing to greater Fecundity of Nature, but sometimes to Examples of Industry in the Heads, and industrious Education; by which the Children are enabled to provide better for themselves, and their marrying early, is encouraged from the Prospect of good Subsistence.

20. If there be a Sect therefore, in our Nation, that regard Frugality and Industry as religious Duties, and educate their Children therein, more than others commonly do; such Sect must consequently increase more by natural Generation, than any other Sect in Britain.

21. The Importation of Foreigners into a Country that has as many Inhabitants as the present Employments and Provisions for Subsistence will bear; will be in the End no Increase of People; unless the New Comers have more Industry and Frugality than the Natives, and then they will provide more Subsistence, and increase in the Country; but they will gradually eat the Natives out. Nor is it necessary to bring in Foreigners to fill up any occasional Vacancy in a Country; for such Vacancy (if the Laws are good, § 14, 16) will soon be filled by natural Generation. Who can now find the Vacancy made in Sweden, France or other Warlike Nations, by the Plague of Heroism 40 Years ago; in France, by the Expulsion of the Protestants;

in England, by the Settlement of her Colonies; or in Guinea, by 100 Years Exportation of Slaves, that has blacken'd half America? The thinness of Inhabitants in Spain is owing to National Pride and Idleness, and other Causes, rather than to the Expulsion of the Moors, or to the making of new Settlements.

22. There is in short, no Bound to the prolific Nature of Plants or Animals, but what is made by their crowding and interfering with each others Means of Subsistence. Was the Face of the Earth vacant of other Plants, it might be gradually sowed and overspread with one Kind only; as, for Instance, with Fennel; and were it empty of other Inhabitants, it might in a few Ages be replenish'd from one Nation only; as, for Instance, with Englishmen. Thus there are suppos'd to be now upwards of One Million English Souls in North-America, (tho' 'tis thought scarce 80,000 have been brought over Sea) and yet perhaps there is not one the fewer in Britain, but rather many more, on Account of the Employment the Colonies afford to Manufacturers at Home. This Million doubling, suppose but once in 25 Years, will in another Century be more than the People of England, and the greatest Number of Englishmen will be on this Side the Water. What an Accession of Power to the British Empire by Sea as well as Land! What Increase of Trade and Navigation! What Numbers of Ships and Seamen! We have been here but little more than 100 Years, and yet the Force of our Privateers in the late War, united, was greater, both in Men and Guns, than that of the whole British Navy in Queen Elizabeth's Time. How important an Affair then to Britain, is the present Treaty for settling the Bounds between her Colonies and the French, and how careful should she be to secure Room enough, since on the Room depends so much the Increase of her People?

23. In fine, A Nation well regulated is like a Polypus; take away a Limb, its Place is soon supply'd; cut it in two, and each deficient Part shall speedily grow out of the Part remaining. Thus if you have Room and Subsistence enough, as you may by dividing, make ten Polypes out of one, you may of

one make ten Nations, equally populous and powerful; or rather, increase a Nation ten fold in Numbers and Strength.

And since Detachments of English from Britain sent to America, will have their Places at Home so soon supply'd and increase so largely here; why should the Palatine Boors be suffered to swarm into our Settlements, and by herding together establish their Language and Manners to the Exclusion of ours? Why should Pennsylvania, founded by the English, become a Colony of *Aliens*, who will shortly be so numerous as to Germanize us instead of our Anglifying them, and will never adopt our Language or Customs, any more than they can acquire our Complexion.

24. Which leads me to add one Remark: That the Number of purely white People in the World is proportionably very small. All Africa is black or tawny. Asia chiefly tawny. America (exclusive of the new Comers) wholly so. And in Europe, the Spaniards, Italians, French, Russians and Swedes, are generally of what we call a swarthy Complexion; as are the Germans also, the Saxons only excepted, who with the English, make the principal Body of White People on the Face of the Earth. I could wish their Numbers were increased. And while we are, as I may call it, *Scouring* our Planet, by clearing America of Woods, and so making this Side of our Globe reflect a brighter Light to the Eyes of Inhabitants in Mars or Venus, why should we in the Sight of Superior Beings, darken its People? why increase the Sons of Africa, by Planting them in America, where we have so fair an Opportunity, by excluding all Blacks and Tawneys, of increasing the lovely White and Red? But perhaps I am partial to the Complexion of my Country, for such Kind of Partiality is natural to Mankind.[1]

---

1. Franklin composed this essay largely in response to the Iron Act of 1750. This Act intended to suppress the development of colonial manufacturing in competition with home industry by restricting the growth of the American iron industry to the supply of raw metals. (23 Geo. ii. C. 29)

Felons and Rattlesnakes

9 May, 1751

To the Printers of the Gazette.

By a Passage in one of your late Papers, I understand that the Government at home will not suffer our mistaken Assemblies to make any Law for preventing or discouraging the Importation of Convicts from Great Britain, for this kind Reason, "*That such Laws are against the Publick Utility, as they tend to prevent the* IMPROVEMENT *and* WELL PEOPLING of the Colonies."

Such a tender *parental* Concern in our *Mother Country* for the *Welfare* of her Children, calls aloud for the highest *Returns* of Gratitude and Duty. This every one must be sensible of: But 'tis said, that in our present Circumstances it is absolutely impossible for us to make *such* as are adequate to the Favour. I own it; but nevertheless let us do our Endeavour. 'Tis something to show a grateful Disposition.

In some of the uninhabited Parts of these Provinces, there are Numbers of these venomous Reptiles we call RATTLE-SNAKES; Felons-convict from the Beginning of the World: These, whenever we meet with them, we put to Death, by Virtue of an old Law, *Thou shalt bruise his Head*. But as this is a sanguinary Law, and may seem too cruel; and as however mischievous those Creatures are with us, they may possibly change their Natures, if they were to change the Climate; I would humbly propose, that this general Sentence of *Death* be changed for *Transportation*.

In the Spring of the Year, when they first creep out of their Holes, they are feeble, heavy, slow, and easily taken; and if a small Bounty were allow'd *per* Head, some Thousands might be collected annually, and *transported* to Britain. There I would propose to have them carefully distributed in St. James's Park, in the Spring-Gardens and other Places of Pleasure about London; in the Gardens of all the Nobility and Gentry throughout the Nation; but particularly in the Gardens of the *Prime Ministers*, the *Lords of Trade* and *Members of Parliament;* for to them we are *most particularly* obliged.

There is no human Scheme so perfect, but some Inconveniencies may be objected to it: Yet when the Conveniencies far exceed, the Scheme is judg'd rational, and fit to be executed. Thus Inconveniencies have been objected to that *good* and *wise* Act of Parliament, by virtue of which all the Newgates and Dungeons in Britain are emptied into the Colonies. It has been said, that these Thieves and Villains introduc'd among us, spoil the Morals of Youth in the Neighbourhoods that entertain them, and perpetrate many horrid Crimes: But let not *private Interests* obstruct *publick Utility*. Our *Mother* knows what is best for us. What is a little *Housebreaking, Shoplifting*, or *Highway Robbing;* what is a *Son* now and then *corrupted* and *hang'd*, a Daughter *debauch'd* and *pox'd*, a Wife *stabb'd*, a Husband's *Throat cut*, or a Child's *Brains beat out* with an Axe, compar'd with this "IMPROVEMENT and WELL PEOPLING of the Colonies!"

Thus it may perhaps be objected to my Scheme, that the *Rattle-Snake* is a mischievous Creature, and that his changing his Nature with the Clime is a mere Supposition, not yet confirm'd by sufficient Facts. What then? Is not Example more prevalent than Precept? And may not the honest rough British Gentry, by a Familiarity with these Reptiles, learn to *creep*, and to *insinuate*, and to *slaver*, and to *wriggle* into Place (and perhaps to *poison* such as stand in their Way) Qualities of no small Advantage to Courtiers! In comparison of which "*Improvement* and *Publick Utility*," what is a *Child* now and then kill'd by their venomous Bite,—or even a favourite *Lap-Dog?*

I would only add, That this Exporting of Felons to the Colonies, may be consider'd as a *Trade*, as well as in the Light of a *Favour*. Now all Commerce implies *Returns:* Justice requires them: There can be no Trade without them. And *Rattle-Snakes* seem the most *suitable Returns* for the *Human Serpents* sent us by our *Mother* Country. In this, however, as in every other Branch of Trade, she will have the Advantage of us. She will reap *equal* Benefits without equal Risque of the Inconveniencies and Dangers. For the *Rattle-Snake* gives Warning before he attempts his Mischief; which the Convict does not. I am Yours, &c.

AMERICANUS[1]

1. Franklin composed this essay largely in response to the Transportation Act of 1717. This Act led to the sentencing and transportation of more than 50,000 criminals to America by 1775. After the Revolutionary War, Britain transported criminals to Australia from 1787–1868. (4 Geo. i. C. 11)

Part V

6 June, 1753 – 1758

Letters to Joseph Huey

A Parable on Brotherly Love

The Albany Plan of Union

A Dialogue between X, Y, and Z

A Letter from Father Abraham to His Beloved Son

The Way to Wealth

Letter to Joseph Huey

6 June, 1753

Sir,

I received your kind Letter of the 2d Inst. and am glad to hear that you increase in Strength; I hope you will continue mending till you recover your former Health and Firmness. Let me know whether you still use the cold Bath, and what Effect it has.

As to the Kindness you mention, I wish it could have been of more Service to you. But if it had, the only Thanks I should desire is, that you would always be equally ready to serve any other Person that may need your Assistance, and so let good Offices go round, for Mankind are all of a Family.

For my own Part, when I am employed in serving others, I do not look upon my self as conferring Favours, but as paying Debts. In my Travels and since my Settlement I have received much Kindness from Men, to whom I shall never have any Opportunity of making the least direct Return. And numberless Mercies from God, who is infinitely above being benefited by our Services. These Kindnesses from Men I can therefore only return on their Fellow-Men; and I can only show my Gratitude for those Mercies from God, by a Readiness to help his other Children and my Brethren. For I do not think that Thanks, and Compliments, tho' repeated Weekly, can discharge our real Obligations to each other, and much less those to our Creator.

You will see in this my Notion of Good Works, that I am far from expecting (as you suppose) that I shall merit Heaven by them. By Heaven we understand, a State of Happiness, infinite in Degree, and eternal in Duration: I can do nothing to deserve such Reward: He that for giving a Draught of Water to a thirsty Person should expect to be paid with a good Plantation, would be modest in his Demands, compar'd with those who think they deserve Heaven for the little Good they do on Earth. Even the mix'd imperfect Pleasures we enjoy in this World are rather from God's Goodness than our Merit; how much more such Happiness of Heaven. For my own part, I have not the Vanity to think I deserve it, the Folly to expect it, nor the Ambition to desire it; but content myself in submitting to the Will and Disposal of that God who made me, who has hitherto preserv'd and bless'd me, and in whose fatherly Goodness I may well confide, that he will never make me miserable, and that even the Afflictions I may at any time suffer shall tend to my Benefit.

The Faith you mention has doubtless its use in the World; I do not desire to see it diminished, nor would I endeavour to lessen it in any Man. But I wish it were more productive of Good Works than I have generally seen it: I mean real good Works, Works of Kindness, Charity, Mercy, and Publick Spirit; not Holiday-keeping, Sermon-Reading or Hearing, performing Church Ceremonies, or making long Prayers, fill'd with Flatteries and Compliments, despis'd even by wise Men, and much less capable of pleasing the Deity. The Worship of God is a Duty, the hearing and reading of Sermons may be useful; but if Men rest in Hearing and Praying, as too many do, it is as if a Tree should value itself on being water'd and putting forth Leaves, tho' it never produc'd any Fruit.

Your great Master tho't much less of these outward Appearances and Professions than many of his modern Disciples. He prefer'd the Doers of the Word to the meer Hearers; the Son that seemingly refus'd to obey his Father and yet perform'd his Commands, to him that profess'd his Readiness but neglected the Works; the heretical but charitable Samaritan, to the uncharitable tho' orthodox Priest and sanctified Levite: and those who gave Food to the hungry, Drink to the Thirsty, Raiment to the Naked, Entertainment to the Stranger, and Relief to the Sick, &c. tho' they never heard of his Name, he declares shall in the last Day be accepted, when those who cry Lord, Lord; who value themselves on their Faith tho' great enough to perform Miracles but have neglected good Works shall be rejected. He profess'd that he came not to call the Righteous but Sinners to Repentance; which imply'd his modest Opinion that there were some in his Time so good that they need not hear even him for Improvement; but now a days we have scarce a little Parson, that does not think it the Duty of every Man within his Reach to sit under his petty Ministrations, and that whoever omits them offends God. I wish to such more Humility, and to you Health and Happiness, being Your Friend and Servant

B Franklin

A Parable on Brotherly Love

July, 1755

1 In those days there was no Worker of Iron in all the Land, And the Merchants of Midian passed by with their Camels, bearing Spices, and Myrrh, and Balm, and Wares of Iron. And Reuben bought an Ax from the Ishmaelite Merchants, which he prized highly, for there were none in his Father's house.[1]

2 And Simeon said unto Reuben his Brother, lend me I pray thee, thine Ax: But he refused, and would not.

3 And Levi also said unto him, My Brother, lend me thine Ax. And he refused him also.

4 Then came Judah unto Reuben and entreated him, saying, Lo, thou lovest me, and I have always loved thee do not refuse me the use of thine Ax, for I desire it earnestly.

5 But Reuben turned from him, and refused him Likewise.

---

1. *I Sam. 13:19–20* Now there was no smith found throughout all the land of Israel: for the Philistines said, Lest the Hebrews make them swords or spears: But all the Israelites went down to the Philistines, to sharpen every man his share, and his coulter, and his axe, and his mattock.

6 Now it came to pass that Reuben hewed Timber on the Bank of the River, and the Ax fell therein[2], and he could by no means find it.

7 But Simeon, Levi and Judah, had sent a Mesenger after the Ishmaelites with money and had bought for each of them an Ax also.

8 Then came Reuben unto Simeon, and said unto him, Lo, I have lost mine Ax, and my work is unfinished, lend me thine I pray thee.

9 And Simeon answered, saying, Thou wouldst not lend me thine Ax, therefore will I not lend thee mine.

10 Then went he unto Levi, and said unto him, My Brother, thou knowest my Loss and my Necessity; lend me, I pray thee, thine Ax.

11 And Levi reproached him, saying, Thou wouldest not lend me thine when I desired it, but I will be better than thee, and will lend thee mine.

12 And Reuben was grieved at the Rebuke of Levi; and being ashamed, turned from him, and took not the Ax; but sought his Brother Judah.

13 And as he drew near, Judah beheld his Countenance as it were confusedn with Grief and shame[3]; and he prevented him, saying, My Brother, I know thy Loss, but why should it grieve thee? Lo, have I not an Ax that will serve both thee and me? take it I pray thee, and use it as thine own.

---

2. *Kings 6:5–6* But as one was felling a beam, the axe head fell into the water: and he cried, and said, Alas, master! for it was borrowed. And the man of God [Elisha] said, Where fell it? And he shewed him the place. And he cut down a stick, and cast it in thither; and the iron did swim.

3. *Jer. 51:51* We are confounded, because we have heard reproach. shame hath covered our faces: for strangers are come into the sanctuaries of the Lord's house.

14 And Reuben fell on his Neck, and kissed him with Tears[4], saying, Thy Kindness is great, but thy Goodness in forgiving me is greater. Lo thou art indeed a Brother, and whilst I live will I surely love thee.

15 And Judah said, Let us also love our other Brethren; Behold, are we not all of one Blood.[5]

16 And Joseph saw these Things, and reported them to his Father Jacob.

17 And Jacob said, Reuben did wrong but he repented, Simeon also did wrong, and Levi was not altogether blameless.

18 But the Heart of Judah is princely. Judah hath the Soul of a King. His Fathers Children shall bow down before him, and he shall rule over his Brethren, nor shall the Sceptre depart from his house, nor a Lawgiver from between his Feet, until Shiloh come.[6]

---

4. *Gen. 33:4* And Esau ran to meet him, and embraced him, and fell on his neck, and kissed him: and they wept.

5. *Gen. 37: 26–27* And Judah said unto his brethren, What profit is it if we slay our brother, and conceal his blood? Come and let us sell him to the Ishmaelites, and let not our hand be upon him; for he is our brother and our flesh. And his brethren were content.

6. *Gen. 49:8, 10* Judah, thou art he whom they brethren shall praise: thy hand shall be in the neck of thine enemies; thy father's children shall bow down before thee. The sceptre shall not depart from Judah, nor a lawgiver from between his feet, until Shiloh come.

A Parable Against Persecution

July 1755

Chap. XXVII

1. And it came to pass after these Things, that Abraham sat in the Door of his Tent, about the going down of the Sun.

2. And behold a Man, bowed with Age, came from the Way of the Wilderness, leaning on a Staff.

3. And Abraham arose and met him, and said unto him, Turn in, I pray thee, and wash thy Feet, and tarry all Night, and thou shalt arise early on the Morrow, and go on thy Way.

4. And the Man said, Nay, for I will abide under this Tree.

5. But Abraham pressed him greatly; so he turned, and they went into the Tent; and Abraham baked unleavend Bread, and they did eat.

6. And when Abraham saw that the Man blessed not God, he said unto him, Wherefore dost thou not worship the most high God, Creator of Heaven and Earth?

7. And the Man answered and said, I do not worship the God thou speakest of; neither do I call upon his Name; for I have made to myself a God, which abideth alway in mine House, and provideth me with all Things.

8. And Abraham's Zeal was kindled against the Man; and he arose, and fell upon him, and drove him forth with Blows into the Wilderness.

9. And at Midnight God called unto Abraham, saying, Abraham, where is the Stranger?

10. And Abraham answered and said, Lord, he would not worship thee, neither would he call upon thy Name; therefore have I driven him out from before my Face into the Wilderness.

11. And God said, Have I born with him these hundred ninety and eight Years, and nourished him, and cloathed him, notwithstanding his Rebellion against me, and couldst not thou, that art thyself a Sinner, bear with him one Night?

12. And Abraham said, Let not the Anger of my Lord wax hot against his Servant. Lo, I have sinned; forgive me, I pray Thee:

13. And Abraham arose and went forth into the Wilderness, and sought diligently for the Man, and found him, and returned with him to his Tent; and when he had entreated him kindly, he sent him away on the Morrow with Gifts.

14. And God spake again unto Abraham, saying, For this thy Sin shall thy Seed be afflicted four Hundred Years in a strange Land:

15. But for thy Repentance will I deliver them; and they shall come forth with Power, and with Gladness of Heart, and with much Substance.

The Albany Plan of Union

10 July, 1754

PLAN of a Proposed Union of the Several Colonies of Masachusets-bay, New Hampshire, Coneticut, Rhode Island, New York, New Jerseys, Pensilvania, Maryland, Virginia, North Carolina, and South Carolina, For their Mutual Defence and Security, and for Extending the British Settlements in North America.

THAT humble Application be made for an Act of the Parliament of Great Britain, by Virtue of which, one General Government may be formed in America, including all the said Colonies, within and under which Government, each Colony may retain its present Constitution, except in the Particulars wherein a Change may be directed by the said Act, as hereafter follows.

President General Grand Council.

That the said General Government be administred by a President General, To be appointed and Supported by the Crown, and a Grand Council to be Chosen by the Representatives of the People of the Several Colonies, met in their respective Assemblies.

Election of Members.

That within (unknown) Months after the passing of such Act, The House of Representatives in the Several Assemblies, that Happen to be Sitting within that time or that shall be Specially for that purpose Convened, may and Shall Choose Members for the Grand Council in the following Proportions, that is to say.

Masachusets-Bay 7.
New Hampshire 2.
Conecticut 5.
Rhode-Island 2.
New-York 4.
New-Jerseys 3.
Pensilvania 6.
Maryland 4.
Virginia 7.
North-Carolina 4.
South-Carolina 4.
48.

Place of first meeting.

Who shall meet for the first time at the City of Philadelphia, in Pensilvania, being called by the President General as soon as conveniently may be, after his Appointment.

New Election.

That there shall be a New Election of Members for the Grand Council every three years; And on the Death or Resignation of any Member his Place shall be Supplyed by a New Choice at the next Sitting of the Assembly of the Colony he represented.

Proportion of Members after first 3 years.

That after the first three years, when the Proportion of Money arising out of each Colony to the General Treasury can be known, The Number of Members to be Chosen, for each Colony shall from time to time in all ensuing Elections be regulated by that proportion (yet so as that the Number to be Chosen by any one Province be not more than Seven nor less than Two).

Meetings of Grand Council Call.

That the Grand Council shall meet once in every Year, and oftner if Occasion require, at such Time and place as they shall adjourn to at the last preceeding meeting, or as they shall be called to meet at by the President General, on any Emergency, he having first obtained in Writing the Consent of seven of the Members to such call, and sent due and timely Notice to the whole.

Speaker Continuance.

That the Grand Council have Power to Chuse their Speaker, and shall neither be Dissolved, prorogued nor Continue Sitting longer than Six Weeks at one Time without their own Consent, or the Special Command of the Crown.

Member's Allowance

That the Members of the Grand Council shall be Allowed for their Service ten shillings Sterling per Diem, during their Sessions or Journey to and from the Place of Meeting; Twenty miles to be reckoned a days Journey.

Assent of President General. His Duty.

That the Assent of the President General be requisite, to all Acts of the Grand Council, and that it be His Office, and Duty to cause them to be carried into Execution.

Power of President and Grand Council. Peace and War. Indian Purchases. New Settlements. Laws to Govern them.

That the President General with the Advice of the Grand Council, hold or Direct all Indian Treaties in which the General Interest or Welfare of the Colony's may be Concerned; And make Peace or Declare War with the Indian Nations. That they make such Laws as they Judge Necessary for regulating all Indian Trade. That they make all Purchases from Indians for the Crown, of Lands not within the Bounds of Particular Colonies, or that shall not be within their Bounds when some of them are reduced to more Convenient Dimensions. That they make New Settlements on such Purchases, by Granting Lands in the Kings Name, reserving a Quit Rent to the Crown, for the use of the General Treasury. That they make Laws for regulating and Governing such new Settlements, till the Crown shall think fit to form them into Particular Governments.

Raise Soldiers &c. Lakes. Not to Impress. Power to make Laws Duties &c.
Treasurer. Money how to Issue.

That they raise and pay Soldiers, and build Forts for the Defence of any of the Colonies, and equip Vessels of Force to Guard the Coasts and Protect the Trade on the Ocean, Lakes, or Great Rivers; But they shall not Impress Men in any Colonies, without the Consent of its Legislature. That for these purposes they have Power to make Laws And lay and Levy such General Duties, Imposts, or Taxes, as to them shall appear most equal and Just, Considering the Ability and other Circumstances of the Inhabitants in the Several Colonies, and such as may be Collected with the least Inconvenience to the People, rather discouraging Luxury, than Loading Industry with unnecessary Burthens. That they may a General Treasurer and a Particular Treasurer in each Government, when Necessary, And from Time to Time may Order the Sums in the Treasuries of each Government, into the General Treasury, or draw on them for Special payments as they find most Convenient; Yet no money to Issue, but by joint Orders of the President General and Grand Council Except where Sums have been Appropriated to particular Purposes, And the President General is previously impowered By an Act to draw for such Sums.

Accounts.

That the General Accounts shall be yearly Settled and Reported to the Several Assembly's.

Quorum. Laws to be Transmitted.

That a Quorum of the Grand Council impower'd to Act with the President General, do consist of Twenty-five Members, among whom there shall be one, or more from a Majority of the Colonies. That the Laws made by them for the Purposes aforesaid, shall not be repugnant but as near as may be agreeable to the Laws of England, and Shall be transmitted to the King in Council for Approbation, as Soon as may be after their Passing and if not disapproved within Three years after Presentation to remain in Force.

Death of President General.

That in case of the Death of the President General The Speaker of the Grand Council for the Time Being shall Succeed, and be Vested with the Same Powers, and Authority, to Continue until the King's Pleasure be known.

Officers how Appointed. Vacancies how Supplied. Each Colony may defend itself on Emergency.

That all Military Commission Officers Whether for Land or Sea Service, to Act under this General Constitution, shall be Nominated by the President General But the Approbation of the Grand Council, is to be Obtained before they receive their Commissions, And all Civil Officers are to be Nominated, by the Grand Council, and to receive the President General's Approbation, before they Officiate; But in Case of Vacancy by Death or removal of any Officer Civil or Military under this Constitution, The Governor of the Province, in which such Vacancy happens, may Appoint till the Pleasure of the President General and Grand Council can be known. That the Particular Military as well as Civil Establishments in each Colony remain in their present State, this General Constitution Notwithstanding. And that on Sudden Emergencies any Colony may Defend itself, and lay the Accounts of Expence thence Arisen, before the President General and Grand Council, who may allow and order payment of the same As far as they Judge such Accounts Just and reasonable.

A Dialogue between X, Y, and Z

18 December, 1755

A Dialogue between X, Y, and Z, concerning the present State of Affairs in Pennsylvania.

X. Your Servant, Gentlemen; I am glad to see you at my House. Is there any thing new To-day?

Y. We have been talking of the Militia Act; have you seen it?

X. Yes; I have read it in the Papers.

Z. And what do you think of it?

X. The more I consider it, the better I like it. It appears to me a very good Act, and I am persuaded will be of good Use, if heartily carried into Execution.

Z. Ay, that may be; but who is to carry it into Execution? It says the People may form themselves into Companies, and chuse their own Officers; but there is neither Time nor Place appointed for this Transaction, nor any Person directed or impowered to call them together.

X. 'Tis true; but methinks there are some Words that point out the Method pretty plain to willing Minds. And it seems to me that we who joined so sincerely in the Petitions for a Militia Law, and really thought one so absolutely necessary for the Safety of our Country, should, now we have obtained the Law, rather endeavour to *explain*, than *invent*, Difficulties in the Construction of it.

Y. What are those Words you mention?

X. Here is the Act itself, I'll read that Part of it. "From and after the Publication of this Act, it shall and may be lawful for the Freemen of this

Province to form themselves into Companies, *as heretofore they have used in time of War without Law*, and for each Company, by Majority of Votes, in the Way of Ballot, to chuse its own Officers, &c." The Words I meant are these, *as heretofore they have used in Time of War*. Now I suppose we have none of us forgot the Association in the Time of the last War; 'tis not so long since, but that we may well enough remember the Method we took to form ourselves into Companies, chuse our Officers, and present them to the Governor for Approbation and Commissions; and the Act in question says plainly, we may now *lawfully do* in this Affair, what we then did *without Law*.

Y. I did not before take so much Notice of those Words, but to be sure the Thing is easy enough; for I remember very well how we managed at that Time; and indeed 'tis easier to effect it now than it was then: For the Companies and Regiments, and their Districts, &c. were then all to form and settle; but now, why may not the Officers of the old Companies call the old Associators together, with such others in the District of each Company as incline to be concerned, and proceed immediately to a new Choice by Virtue of the Act? Other new Companies may in other Places be formed as the associated Companies were.

Z. You say right. And if this were all the Objection to the Act, no Doubt they would do so immediately. But 'tis said there are other Faults in it.

X. What are they?

Z. The Act is so loose, that Persons who never intend to engage in the Militia, even Quakers may meet and vote in the Choice of the Officers.

X. Possibly; but was any such thing observed in the Association Elections?

Z. Not that I remember.

X. Why should it be more apprehended now, than it was at that Time? Can they have any Motives to such a Conduct now, which they had not then?

Z. I cannot say.

X. Nor can I. If a Militia be necessary for the Safety of the Province, I hope we shall not boggle at this little Difficulty. What else is objected?

Z. I have heard this objected, That it were better the Governor should appoint the Officers; for the Choice being in the People, a Man very unworthy to be an Officer, may happen to be popular enough to get himself chosen by the undiscerning Mob.

X. 'Tis possible. And if all Officers appointed by Governors were always Men of Merit, and fully qualified for their Posts, it would be wrong ever to hazard a popular Election. It is reasonable, I allow, that the Commander in Chief should not have Officers absolutely forced upon him, in whom, from his Knowledge of their Incapacity, he can place no Confidence. And, on the other Hand, it seems likely that the People will engage more readily in the Service, and face Danger with more Intrepidity, when they are commanded by a Man they know and esteem, and on whose Prudence and Courage, as well as Good will and Integrity, they can have Reliance, than they would under a Man they either did not know, or did not like. For supposing Governors ever so judicious and upright in the Distribution of Offices, they cannot know every Body, in every Part of the Province, and are liable to be imposed on by partial Recommendations; but the People generally know their Neighbours. And to me, the Act in question seems to have hit a proper Medium, between the two Modes of appointing: The People chuse, and if the Governor approves, he grants the Commission; if not, they are to chuse a second, and even a third Time. Out of three Choices, 'tis probable one may be right; and where an Officer is approved both by Superiors and Inferiors, there is the greater Prospect of those Advantages that attend a good Agreement in the Service. This Mode of Choice is moreover agreeable to the Liberty and Genius of our Constitution. 'Tis similar to the Manner in which by our Laws Sheriffs and Coroners are chosen and approved. And yet it has more Regard to the Prerogative than the Mode of Choice in some Colonies, where the military Officers are either chosen absolutely by the Companies themselves, or by the House of Representatives, without any

Negative on that Choice, or any Approbation necessary from the Governor.

Y. But is that agreeable to the English Constitution?

X. Considered in this Light, I think it is; British Subjects, by removing into America, cultivating a Wilderness, extending the Dominion, and increasing the Wealth, Commerce and Power of their Mother Country, at the Hazard of their Lives and Fortunes, ought not, and in Fact do not thereby lose their native Rights. There is a Power in the Crown to grant a Continuance of those Rights to such Subjects, in any Part of the World, and to their Posterity born in such new Country; and for the farther Encouragement and Reward of such Merit, to grant *additional*Liberties and Privileges, not used in England, but suited to the different Circumstances of different Colonies. If then the Grants of those additional Liberties and Privileges may be regularly made under an English Constitution, they may be enjoyed agreeable to that Constitution.

Y. But the Act is very short, there are numberless Circumstances and Occasions pertaining to a Body of armed Men, which are not as they ought to have been expresly provided for in the Act.

X. 'Tis true, there are not express Provisions in the Act for all Circumstances; but there is a Power lodged by the Act in the Governor and Field Officers of the Regiments, to make all such Provisions, in the Articles of War, which they may form and establish.

Y. But can it be right in the Legislature by any Act to delegate their Power of making Laws to others?

X. I believe not, generally; but certainly in particular Cases it may. Legislatures may, and frequently do give to Corporations, Power to make By Laws for their own Government. And in this Case, the Act of Parliament gives the Power of making Articles of War for the Government of the Army to the King alone, and there is no Doubt but the Parliament understand the Rights of Government.

Y. Are you sure the Act of Parliament gives such Power?

X. This is the Act. The Power I mention is here in Section LV. "Provided always, That it shall and may be lawful to and for his Majesty, to form, make and establish Articles of War for the better Government of his Majesty's Forces, and for bringing Offenders against the same to Justice; and to erect and constitute Courts Martial, with Power to try, hear, and determine any Crimes or Offences by such Articles of War, and inflict Penalties by Sentence or Judgment of the same." And here you see bound up with the Act, the Articles of War, made by his Majesty in Pursuance of the Act, and providing for every Circumstance.

Z. It is so, sure enough. I had been told that our Act of Assembly was impertinently singular in this Particular.

X. The G——r himself, in a Message to the House, expresly recommended this Act of Parliament for their Imitation, in forming the Militia Bill.

Z. I never heard that before.

X. But it is true. The Assembly, however (considering that this Militia would consist chiefly of Freeholders) have varied a little from that Part of the Act of Parliament, in Favour of Liberty; they have not given the sole Power of making those Articles of War *to the Governor*, as that Act does *to the King;* but have joined with the Governor, for that Purpose, a Number of Officers to be chosen by the People. The Articles moreover are not to be general Laws, binding on all the Province, nor on any Man who has not first approved of them, and voluntarily engaged to observe them.

Z. Is there no Danger that the Governor and Officers may make those Articles too severe?

X. Not without you can suppose them Enemies to the Service, and to their Country: For if they should make such as are unfit for Freemen and Englishmen to be subjected to, they will get no Soldiers; no body will engage. In some Cases, however, if you and I were in actual Service, I believe we should both think it necessary for our own Safety that the Articles should be pretty severe.

Z. What Cases are they?

X. Suppose a Centinel should betray his Trust, give Intelligence to the Enemy, or conduct them into our Quarters.

Z. To be sure there should be severe Punishments for such Crimes, or we might all be ruined.

X. Chuse reasonable Men for your Officers, and you need not fear their making reasonable Laws; and if they make such, I hope reasonable Men will not refuse to engage under them.

Y. But here is a Thing I don't like. By this Act of Assembly, the Quakers are neither compelled to muster, nor to pay a Fine if they don't.

X. It is true; nor could they be compelled either to muster or pay a Fine of that Kind by any Militia Law made here. They are exempted by the Charter and fundamental Laws of the Province.

Y. How so?

X. See here; it is the first Clause in the Charter. I'll read it. "Because no People can be truly happy, though under the greatest Enjoyment of civil Liberties, if abridged of the Freedom of their Consciences, as to their *Religious Profession* and Worship: And Almighty God being the only Lord of Conscience, Father of Lights and Spirits, and the Author as well as Object of all divine Knowledge, Faith and Worship, who only doth enlighten the Minds, and persuade and convince the Understandings of People, I do hereby grant and declare, That no Person or Persons inhabiting in this Province or Territories, who shall confess and acknowledge one Almighty God, the Creator, Upholder and Ruler of the World; and profess him or themselves obliged to live quietly under the civil Government, shall be, IN ANY CASE, MOLESTED or PREJUDICED in his or their PERSONS or ESTATE, because of his or their *conscientious Persuasion* or Practice, nor be compelled to frequent or maintain any religious Worship, Place or Ministry, contrary to his or their Mind, or to DO or SUFFER any OTHER ACT or THING, contrary to their religious Persuasion." And in the eighth Section of the same Charter, you see a Declaration, that "neither the Proprietor, nor his Heirs or Assigns, shall procure or do any Thing or Things, whereby the Liberties in this Charter contained or expressed, nor any Part thereof, shall be infringed or broken; and if any Thing shall be procured or done by *any Person or Persons*, contrary to these Presents, it shall be held of NO FORCE OR EFFECT." This Liberty of Conscience granted by Charter, is also established by the first Law in our Book, and confirmed by the Crown. And moreover, the Governor has an express Instruction from the Proprietaries, that in case of making any Militia Law, he shall take especial Care that the Charter be not infringed in this Respect. Besides, most of our Petitions for a Militia from the moderate Part of the People, requested particularly that due Regard might be had to scrupulous and tender Consciences. When Taxes are raised however, for the King's Service, the Quakers and Menonists pay their Part of them, and a great Part; for as their Frugality and Industry makes them generally wealthy, their Proportion is the greater compared with their Numbers. And out of these Taxes those Men are paid who go into actual Service. As for Mustering and Training, no Militia are any where paid for that. It is by many justly delighted in as a manly Exercise. But those who are engaged in actual Service for any Time, ought undoubtedly to have Pay.

Y. There is no Provision in this Militia Act to pay them.

X. There is a Provision that no Regiment, Company, or Party, though engaged in the Militia, shall be obliged "to more than three Days March, &c. without an Express Engagement for that Purpose first voluntarily entred into and subscribed by every Man so to march or remain in Garrison." And 'tis to be supposed that no Man will subscribe such particular Engagement without reasonable Pay, or other Encouragement.

Y. But where is that Pay to come from?

X. From the Government to be sure; and out of the Money struck by the Act for granting £60,000.

Z. Yes; but those who serve must pay their Share of the Tax, as well as those who don't.

X. Perhaps not. 'Tis to be supposed that those who engage in the Service for any Time, upon Pay, will be chiefly single Men, and they are expresly exempted from the Tax by the £60,000 Act. Consequently those who do not serve, must pay the more; for the Sum granted must be made up.

Z. I never heard before that they were exempted by that Act.

X. It is so, I assure you.

Y. But there is no Provision in the Militia Act for the Maimed.

X. If they are poor, they are provided for by the Laws of their Country. There is no other Provision by any Militia Law that I know of. If they have behaved well, and suffered in their Country's Cause, they deserve moreover some grateful Notice of their Service, and some Assistance from the common Treasury; and if any particular Township should happen to be overburthened, they may, on Application to the Government, reasonably expect Relief.

Z. Though the Quakers and others conscientiously scrupulous of bearing Arms, are exempted, as you say, by Charter; they might, being a Majority in the Assembly, have made the Law compulsory on others. At present, 'tis so loose, that no body is obliged by it, who does not voluntarily engage.

X. They might indeed have made the Law compulsory on all others. But it seems they thought it more equitable and generous to leave to all as much Liberty as they enjoy themselves, and not lay even a seeming Hardship on others, which they themselves declined to bear. They have however granted all we asked of them. Our Petitions set forth, that "we were freely willing and ready to defend ourselves and Country, and all we wanted was legal Authority, Order and Discipline." These are now afforded by the Law, if we think fit to make use of them. And indeed I do not see the Advantage of compelling People of any Sect into martial Service merely for the Sake of raising Numbers. I have been myself in some Service of Danger, and I always thought Cowards rather *weakened*, than *strengthened*, the Party. Fear is contagious, and a Pannick once begun spreads like Wildfire, and infects the stoutest Heart. All Men are not by Nature brave: And a few who are so, will do more effectual Service by themselves, than when accompanied by, and mixed with, a Multitude of Poltroons, who only create Confusion, and give Advantage to the Enemy.

Z. What signifies what *you thought* or think? Others think differently. And all the wise Legislatures in the other Colonies have thought fit to compel all Sorts of Persons to bear Arms, or suffer heavy Penalties.

X. As you say, what I *thought* or *think* is not of much Consequence. But a wiser Legislator than all those you mention put together, and who better knew the Nature of Mankind, made his military Law very different from theirs in that Respect.

Z. What Legislator do you mean?

X. I mean God himself, who would have no Man led to Battle that might rather wish to be at home, either from Fear or other Causes.

Z. Where do you find that Law?

X. 'Tis in the 20th Chapter of Deuteronomy, where are these Words, "When thou goest out to Battle against thine Enemies, the Officers shall speak unto the People, saying, What Man is there that hath built a new House, and hath not dedicated it? let him go and return to his House, lest he die in the Battle, and another Man dedicate it. And what Man is he that hath planted a Vineyard, and hath not yet eaten of it? let him also go, and return unto his House, lest he die in the Battle, and another Man eat of it. And what Man is there that hath betrothed a Wife, and hath not taken her? let him go and return unto his House, lest he die in Battle, and another Man take her.—And—"

Z. These all together could not be many; and this has no Relation to Cowardice.

X. If you had not interrupted me, I was coming to that Part, Verse 8. "And the Officers shall speak farther unto the People, and they shall say, What Man is there that is FEARFUL and FAINT-HEARTED? let him go and return unto his House; lest his Brethrens Heart faint as well as his Heart"; that is, lest he communicate his Fears, and his brave Brethren catch the Contagion, to the Ruin of the whole Army. Accordingly we find, that under this military Law, no People in the World fought more gallantly, or performed greater Actions than the Hebrew Soldiery. And if you would be informed what Proportion of the People would be discharged by such a Proclamation, you will find that Matter determined by an actual Experiment made by General Gideon, as related in the seventh Chapter of Judges: For he having assembled 32,000 Men against the Midianites, proclaimed, according to Law (Verse the third) "Whosever is FEARFUL and AFRAID, let him return and depart early from Mount Gilead."

Z. And pray how many departed?

X. The Text says, there departed 22,000, and there remained but 10,000. A very great Sifting! and yet on that particular Occasion a farther Sifting was required. Now it seems to me, that this Militia Law of ours, which gives the Brave all the Advantages they can desire, of Order, Authority, Discipline, and the like, and compels no Cowards into their Company, is such a Kind of Sieve, as the Mosaic Proclamation. For with us, not only every Man who has built a House, or planted a Vineyard, or betrothed a Wife, or is afraid of his Flesh; but the narrow Bigot, filled with Sectarian Malice (if such there be) who hates Quakers more than he loves his Country, his Friends, his Wife or Family, may say: "I won't engage, for I don't like the Act"; or, "I don't like the Officers that are chosen"; or, "I don't like the Articles of War"; and so we shall not be troubled with them, but all that engage will be hearty.

Z. For my Part, I am no Coward; but hang me if I'll fight to save the Quakers.

X. That is to say, you won't pump Ship, because 'twill save the Rats, as well as yourself.

Y. You have answered most of the Objections I have heard against the Act, to my Satisfaction; but there is one remaining. The Method of carrying it into Execution seems so round-about, I am afraid we cannot have the Benefit of it in any reasonable Time.

X. I cannot see much in that Objection. The several Neighbourhoods out of which Companies are formed may meet and chuse their Company-Officers in one and the same Day; and the Regiments may be formed, and the Field Officers chosen in a Week or ten Days after, who may immediately proceed to consider the several Militia Laws of Britain and the

Colonies, and (with the Governor) form out of them such Articles, as will appear most suitable for the Freemen of this Province, who incline to bear Arms voluntarily; and the Whole may be in Order in a Month from the first Elections, if common Diligence be used. And indeed, as the Colonies are at present the Prize contended for between Britain and France, and the latter, by the last Advices, seems to be meditating some grand Blow, Part of which may probably fall on Pennsylvania, either by Land or Sea, or both, it behoves us, I think, to make the best Use we can of this Act, and carry it immediately into Execution both in Town and Country. If there are material Defects in it, Experience will best discover them, and show what is proper or necessary to amend them. The approaching Winter will afford us some Time to arm and prepare, and more Leisure than other Seasons for Exercising and Improving in good Discipline.

Z. But if this Act should be carried into Execution, prove a good One, and answer the End; what shall we have to say against the Quakers at the next Election?

X. O my Friends, let us on this Occasion cast from us all these little Party Views, and consider ourselves as Englishmen and Pennsylvanians. Let us think only of the Service of our King, the Honour and Safety of our Country, and Vengeance on its Murdering Enemies. If Good be done, what imports it by whom 'tis done? The Glory of serving and saving others, is superior to the Advantage of being served or secured. Let us resolutely and generously unite in our Country's Cause (in which to die is the sweetest of all Deaths) and may the God of Armies bless our honest Endeavours.

A Letter from Father Abraham to His Beloved Son

August, 1758

Dear Isaac,

You frequently desire me to give you some *Advice*, in Writing. There is, perhaps, no other valuable Thing in the World, of which so great a Quantity is *given*, and so little *taken*. Men do not generally err in their Conduct so much through Ignorance of their Duty, as through Inattention to their own Faults, or through strong Passions and bad Habits; and, therefore, till that Inattention is cured, or those Passions reduced under the Government of Reason, *Advice* is rather resented as a Reproach, than gratefully acknowledged and followed.

Supposing then, that from the many good Sermons you have heard, good Books read, and good Admonitions received from your Parents and others, your Conscience is by this Time pretty well informed, and capable of advising you, if you attentively listen to it, I shall not fill this Letter with Lessons or Precepts of Morality and Religion; but rather recommend to you, that in order to obtain a *clear* Sight and *constant* Sense of your Errors, you would set apart a Portion of every Day for the Purpose of *Self-Examination*, and trying your daily Actions by that Rule of Rectitude implanted by God in your Breast. The properest Time for this, is when you are retiring to Rest; then carefully review the Transactions of the past Day; and consider how far they have agreed with *what you know* of your Duty to God and to Man, in the several Relations you stand in of a Subject to the Government, Servant to your Master, a Son, a Neighbour, a Friend, &c. When, by this Means, you have discovered the Faults of the Day, acknowledge them to God, and humbly beg of him not only Pardon for what is past, but Strength to fulfil your solemn Resolutions of guarding against them for the Future. Observing this Course steadily for some Time, you will find (through God's Grace assisting) that your Faults are continually diminishing, and your Stock of Virtue encreasing; in Consequence of which you will grow in Favour both with God and Man.

I repeat it, that for the Acquirement of solid, uniform, steady Virtue, nothing contributes more, than a daily strict Self-Examination, by the Lights of Reason, Conscience, and the Word of God; joined with firm Resolutions of amending what you find amiss, and fervent Prayer for Grace and Strength to execute those Resolutions. This Method is very antient. 'Twas recommended by Pythagoras, in his truly *Golden Verses*, and practised since in every Age, with Success, by Men of all Religions. Those golden Verses, as translated by Rowe, are well worth your Reading, and even getting by Heart. The Part relating to this Matter I have transcribed, to give you a Taste of them, *viz.*

Let not the stealing God of Sleep surprize,
Nor creep in Slumbers on thy weary Eyes,
Ere ev'ry Action of the former Day,
Strictly thou dost, and *righteously* survey.
With Rev'rence at thy own Tribunal stand,
And answer justly to thy own Demand.
Where have I been? In what have I transgrest?
What Good or Ill has this Day's Life exprest?
Where have I fail'd in what I ought to do?
In what to God, to Man, or to myself I owe?
Inquire severe whate'er from first to last,
From Morning's Dawn till Ev'nings Gloom has past.
If Evil were thy Deeds, repenting mourn,
And let thy Soul with strong Remorse be torn:
If Good, the Good with Peace of Mind repay,
And to thy secret Self with Pleasure say,

Rejoice, my Heart, for all went well to Day.

And that no Passage to your Improvement in Virtue may be kept secret, it is not sufficient that you make Use of *Self-Examination* alone; therefore I have also added a *golden Extract* from *a favourite* OLD BOOK, to instruct you in the prudent and deliberate Choice of some disinterested Friend, to remind you of such Misconduct as must necessarily escape your severest Inquiry: Which is as follows;

Every prudent Man ought to be jealous and fearful of himself, lest he run away too hastily with a Likelihood instead of Truth; and abound too much in his own Understanding. All Conditions are equal, that is, Men may be contented in every Condition: For Security is equal to Splendor; Health to Pleasure, &c. Every Condition of Life has its Enemies, for *Deus posuit duo et duo, unum contra unum*[1] . A rich Man hath Enemies sometimes for no other Reason than because he is rich; the poor Man hath as poor Neighbours, or rich Ones that gape after that small Profit which he enjoys. The Poor very often subsist merely by Knavery and Rapine among each other. Beware, therefore, how you offend any Man, for he that is displeased at your Words or Actions, commonly joins against you, without putting the *best* Construction on (or endeavouring to find out a reasonable Excuse for) them. And be sure you *hate* no Man, though you think him a worthless or unjust Person. Never *envy* any one above you: You have Enemies enough by the common Course of Human Nature; be cautious not to encrease the Number; and rather procure as many Friends as you can, to countenance and strengthen you. Every Man has also an Enemy within himself. Every Man is choleric and covetous, or gentle and generous by Nature. Man is naturally a beneficent Creature: But there are many external Objects and Accidents, met with as we go through Life, which *seem* to make great Alterations in our natural Dispositions and Desires. A Man naturally passionate and greedy, may, to all Appearance,

1. *God has placed two and two, one against the other.*

become complaisant and hospitable, merely by Force of Instruction and Discipline; and so the Contrary. 'Tis in vain for a passionate Man to say, *I am pardonable* because *it is natural to me*, when we can perhaps point out to him an Example in his next Neighbour, who was *once* affected in the very same Manner, and could say as much to defend himself, who is now exceedingly *different* in his Behaviour, and quite free from those unhappy Affections which disturbed his Repose so often, not long ago, and became a chearful, facetious, and profitable Companion to his Friends, and a Pattern of Humility to all around him.

Nothing was ever well done or said *in a Passion*. One Man's Infirmities and bad Inclinations may be harder to conquer than another Man's, according to the various and *secret* Circumstances that attend them; but they are all capable of being conquered, or very much improved for the better, except they have been suffered to *take Root in* OLD *Age;* in this Case it is most convenient to let them have their own Way, as the Phrase is.

The strongest of our natural Passions are seldom perceived by us; a choleric Man does not always discover when he is angry, nor an envious Man when he is invidious; at most they think they commit no great Faults.

Therefore it is necessary that you should have a MONITOR. Most Men are very indifferent Judges of themselves, and often think they do well when they sin; and, imagine they commit only small Errors, when they are guilty of Crimes. It is in Human Life as in the Arts and Sciences; their Plainest Doctrines are easily comprehended, but the finest Points cannot be discovered without the closest Attention; of these Parts only the wise and skilful in the Art or Science, can be deemed competent Judges. Many Vices and Follies resemble their opposite Virtues and Prudence; they border upon, and seem to mix with each other; and therefore the exact Line of Division betwixt them is hard to ascertain. Pride resembles a generous Spirit; Superstition and Enthusiasm frequently resemble true Religion; a laudable worthy Ambition resembles an unworthy Self-Sufficiency; Government resembles Tyranny; Liberty resembles Licentiousness; Subjection resembles Slavery; Covetousness resembles Frugality; Prodigality resembles

Generosity; and so of the Rest. Prudence chiefly consists in that Excellence of Judgement, which is capable of discerning the MEDIUM; or of acting so as not to intermingle the one with the other; and in being able to assign to every Cause its *proper* Actions and Effects. It is therefore necessary for every Person who desires to be a wise Man, to *take particular Notice of* HIS OWN *Actions*, and of HIS OWN *Thoughts and Intentions* which are the Original of his actions; with great Care and Circumspection; otherwise he can never arrive to that Degree of Perfection which constitutes the amiable Character he aspires after. And, lest all this Diligence should be insufficient, as Partiality to himself will certainly render it, it is very requisite for him to *chuse a* FRIEND, or MONITOR, who must be allowed the greatest Freedom to advertise and remind him of his Failings, and to point out Remedies. Such a One, I mean, as is a discreet and virtuous Person; but especially One that does not creep after the Acquaintance of, or play the Spaniel to, *great* Men; One who does not covet Employments which are known to be scandalous for Opportunities of Injustice: One who can bridle his Tongue and curb his Wit; One that can converse with himself, and industriously attends upon his own Affairs whatever they be. Find out such a *Man;* insinuate yourself into a Confidence with him; and desire him to observe your Conversation and Behaviour; intreat him to admonish you of what he thinks amiss, in a serious and friendly Manner; importune his Modesty till he condescends to grant your Request. Do not imagine that you live one Day without Faults, or that those Faults are undiscovered. Most Men see that in another, which they can not or will not see in themselves: And he is happiest, who through the whole Course of his Life, can attain to a reasonable Freedom from Sin and Folly, even by the Help of *Old Age*, that great Mortifier and Extinguisher of our Lusts and Passions. If such a Monitor informs you of any Misconduct, whether you know his Interpretations to be true or false, take it not only *patiently*, but *thankfully;* and be careful to reform. Thus you get and keep a Friend, break the inordinate and mischievous Affection you bore towards your Frailities, and advance yourself in Wisdom and Virtue. When you consider that you must give an Account of your Actions to your vigilant Reprover; that other Men see the same Imperfections in you as he does; and that it is impossible for a good Man to enjoy the Advantages of Friendship, except he first puts off those Qualities which render him subject to Flattery, that is, except he first cease to flatter himself. A good, a generous Christian Minister, or worthy sensible Parents, may be suitable Persons for such a difficult Office; difficult, though it should be performed by *familiar* Conversation. And how much more meritorious of Entertainment are People of such a Character, than those who come to your Table to *make Faces*, talk Nonsense, devour your Substance, censure their Neighbours, flatter and deride you? Remember that if a Friend tells you of a Fault, always imagine that he does not tell you the whole, which is commonly the Truth; for he desires your Reformation, but is loth to offend you. And *nunquam sine querela ægra tanguntur.*[2]

I know, dear Son, *Ambition* fills your Mind,
And in Life's Voyage, is th' impelling Wind;
But, at the Helm, let sober Reason stand,
To steer the Bark with Heav'n directed Hand;
So shall you safe *Ambition's* Gales receive,
And ride securely, though the Billows heave;
So shall you shun the giddy Hero's Fate,
And by her Influence be both good and great.

She bids you first, in Life's soft vernal Hours,
With active Industry wake Nature's Pow'rs;
With rising Years still rising Arts display,
With new-born Graces mark each new-born Day.
'Tis now the Time *young Passion* to command,
While yet the pliant Stem obeys the Hand;

---

2. *Never are the sick touched without complaint.*

Guide now the Courser with a steady Rein,
E'er yet he bounds o'er Pleasure's flowry Plain;
In Passion's Strife no Medium you can have;
You rule, a Master; or submit, a Slave.

To conclude. You are just entering into the World: Beware of the *first Acts* of Dishonesty: They present themselves to the Mind under *specious Disguises*, and *plausible Reasons* of Right and Equity: But being admitted, they open the Way for admitting others, that are *but a little* more dishonest, which are followed by others *a little* more knavish than they, till by Degrees, however slow, a Man becomes an *habitual* Sharper, and at length a *consummate Rascal* and Villain. Then farewel all Peace of Mind, and inward Satisfaction; all Esteem, Confidence, and Reputation among Mankind. And indeed if *outward* Reputation could be preserved, what Pleasure can it afford to a Man that must *inwardly* despise himself, whose own Baseness will, in Spite of his Endeavours to forget it, be ever presenting itself to his View. If you have a *Sir-Reverence* in your Breeches, what signifies it if you *appear* to Others neat and clean and genteel, when you *know* and *feel* yourself to be b----t. I make no Apology for the Comparison, however coarse, since none can be too much so for a defiled and foul Conscience. But never flatter yourself with *Concealment;*'tis impossible to last long. One Man may be too cunning for another Man, but not for *all Men:*Some Body or other will smell you out, or some Accident will discover you; or who can be sure that he shall never be heard to talk in his Sleep, or be delirious in a Fever, when the working Mind usually throws out Hints of what has inwardly affected it? Of this there have been many Instances; some of which are within the Compass of your own Knowledge.

Whether you chuse to act in a public or a private Station, if you would maintain the personal Character of a Man of Sincerity, Integrity and Virtue, there is a Necessity of becoming *really good*, if you would *do good:* For the thin Disguises of *pretended* private Virtue and Public Spirit, are easily seen through; the Hypocrite detected and exposed. For this Reason then, *My dear* Isaac, as well as for many others, be sincere, candid, honest, well-meaning, and upright, in all you do and say; be *really* good, if you would *appear* so: Your Life then shall give Strength to your *Counsels;* and though you should be found but an indifferent *Speaker* or *Writer*, you shall not be without Praise for the Benevolence of your Intention.

But, again, suppose it possible for a Knave to preserve a fair Character among Men, and even to approve his own Actions, what is that to the Certainty of his being discovered and detested by the all-seeing Eye of *that righteous* BEING, who made and governs the World, whose just Hand never fails to do right and to punish Iniquity, and whose Approbation, Favour, and Friendship, is worth the Universe?

Heartily wishing you every Accomplishment that can make a Man amiable and valuable, to HIS Protection I commit you, being, with sincere Affection, *dear Son*, Your very loving Father,

ABRAHAM.

The Way to Wealth

1758

Courteous Reader,

I have heard that nothing gives an Author so great Pleasure, as to find his Works respectfully quoted by other learned Authors. This Pleasure I have seldom enjoyed; for tho' I have been, if I may say it without Vanity, an *eminent Author* of Almanacks annually now a full Quarter of a Century, my Brother Authors in the same Way, for what Reason I know not, have ever been very sparing in their Applauses; and no other Author has taken the least Notice of me, so that did not my Writings produce me some solid *Pudding*, the great Deficiency of *Praise* would have quite discouraged me.

I concluded at length, that the People were the best Judges of my Merit; for they buy my Works; and besides, in my Rambles, where I am not personally known, I have frequently heard one or other of my Adages repeated, with, *as Poor Richard says*, at the End on't; this gave me some Satisfaction, as it showed not only that my Instructions were regarded, but discovered likewise some Respect for my Authority; and I own, that to encourage the Practice of remembering and repeating those wise Sentences, I have sometimes *quoted myself* with great Gravity.

Judge then how much I must have been gratified by an Incident I am going to relate to you. I stopt my Horse lately where a great Number of People were collected at a Vendue of Merchant Goods. The Hour of Sale not being come, they were conversing on the Badness of the Times, and one of the Company call'd to a plain clean old Man, with white Locks, *Pray,*

Father Abraham, what think you of the Times? Won't these heavy Taxes quite ruin the Country? How shall we be ever able to pay them? What would you advise us to? ——Father Abraham stood up, and reply'd, If you'd have my Advice, I'll give it you in short, for a *Word to the Wise is enough*, and *many Words won't fill a Bushel*, as *Poor Richard says*. They join'd in desiring him to speak his Mind, and gathering round him, he proceeded as follows;

"Friends, says he, and Neighbours, the Taxes are indeed very heavy, and if those laid on by the Government were the only Ones we had to pay, we might more easily discharge them; but we have many others, and much more grievous to some of us. We are taxed twice as much by our *Idleness*, three times as much by our *Pride*, and four times as much by our *Folly*, and from these Taxes the Commissioners cannot ease or deliver us by allowing an Abatement. However let us hearken to good Advice, and something may be done for us; *God helps them that help themselves*, as Poor Richard says, in his Almanack of 1733.

It would be thought a hard Government that should tax its People one tenth Part of their *Time*, to be employed in its Service. But *Idleness* taxes many of us much more, if we reckon all that is spent in absolute *Sloth*, or doing of nothing, with that which is spent in idle Employments or Amusements, that amount to nothing. *Sloth*, by bringing on Diseases, absolutely shortens Life. *Sloth, like Rust, consumes faster than Labour wears, while the used Key is always bright*, as Poor Richard says. But *dost thou love Life, then do not squander Time, for that's the Stuff Life is made of*, as Poor Richard says. How much more than is necessary do we spend in Sleep! forgetting that *The sleeping Fox catches no Poultry*, and that *there will be sleeping enough in the Grave*, as Poor Richard says. If Time be of all Things the most precious, *wasting Time* must be, as Poor Richard says, *the greatest Prodigality*, since, as he elsewhere tells us, *Lost Time is never found again*; and what we call *Time-enough, always proves little enough*: Let us then be up and be doing, and doing to the Purpose; so by Diligence shall we do more with less Perplexity. *Sloth makes all Things difficult, but Industry all easy*, as Poor Richard says; and *He that riseth late, must trot all Day, and shall scarce overtake his Business at Night.* While *Laziness travels so slowly, that Poverty soon overtakes him,* as we read in Poor Richard, who adds, *Drive thy Business, let not that drive thee*; and *Early to Bed, and early to rise, makes a Man healthy, wealthy and wise.*

So what signifies *wishing* and *hoping* for better Times. We may make these Times better if we bestir ourselves. *Industry need not wish,* as Poor Richard says, and *He that lives upon Hope will die fasting. There are no Gains, without Pains*; then *Help Hands, for I have no Lands*, or if I have, they are smartly taxed. And, as Poor Richard likewise observes, *He that hath a Trade hath an Estate*, and *He that hath a Calling hath an Office of Profit and Honour*; but then the *Trade* must be worked at, and the *Calling* well followed, or neither the *Estate*, nor the *Office*, will enable us to pay our Taxes. If we are industrious we shall never starve; for, as Poor Richard says, *At the working Man's House Hunger looks in, but dares not enter.* Nor will the Bailiff nor the Constable enter, for *Industry pays Debts, while Despair encreaseth them*, says Poor Richard. What though you have found no Treasure, nor has any rich Relation left you a Legacy, *Diligence is the Mother of Good luck*, as Poor Richard says, and *God gives all Things to Industry.* Then *plough deep, while Sluggards sleep, and you shall have Corn to sell and to keep*, says Poor Dick. Work while it is called To-day, for you know not how much you may be hindered To-morrow, which makes Poor Richard say, *One To-day is worth two Tomorrows*; and farther, *Have you somewhat to do To-morrow, do it To-day.* If you were a Servant, would you not be ashamed that a good Master should catch you idle? Are you then your own Master, *be ashamed to catch yourself idle*, as Poor Dick says. When there is so much to be done for yourself, your Family, your Country, and your gracious King, be up by Peep of Day; *Let not the Sun look down and say, Inglorious here he lies.* Handle your Tools without Mittens; remember that *the Cat in Gloves catches no Mice*, as Poor Richard says. 'Tis true there is much to be done, and perhaps you are weak handed, but stick to it steadily, and you will see great Effects, for *constant Dropping wears away Stones*, and by *Diligence and Patience the Mouse ate in two the Cable*; and *little Strokes fell great Oaks* as Poor Richard says in his Almanack, the Year I cannot just now remember.

Methinks I hear some of you say, *Must a Man afford himself no Leisure?* I will tell thee, my Friend, what Poor Richard says, *Employ thy Time well if thou meanest to gain Leisure*; and, *since thou art not sure of a Minute, throw not away an Hour.* Leisure, is Time for doing something useful; this Leisure the diligent Man will obtain, but the lazy Man never; so that, as Poor Richard says, a *Life of Leisure and a Life of Laziness are two Things.* Do you imagine that Sloth will afford you more Comfort than Labour? No, for as Poor Richard says, *Trouble springs from Idleness, and grievous Toil from needless Ease. Many without Labour, would live by their* wits *only, but they break for want of Stock.* Whereas Industry gives Comfort, and Plenty, and Respect: *Fly Pleasures, and they'll follow you. The diligent Spinner has a large Shift*; and *now I have a Sheep and a Cow, every Body bids me Good morrow*; all which is well said by Poor Richard.

But with our Industry, we must likewise be *steady, settled* and *careful*, and oversee our own Affairs *with our own Eyes*, and not trust too much to others; for, as Poor Richard says,

I never saw an oft removed Tree,
Nor yet an oft removed Family,
That throve so well as those that settled be.

And again, *Three Removes is as bad as a Fire* and again, *Keep thy Shop, and thy Shop will keep thee*; and again, *If you would have your Business done, go; If not, send.* And again,

He that by the Plough would thrive,
Himself must either hold or drive.

And again, *The Eye of a Master will do more Work than both his Hands*; and again, *Want of Care does us more Damage than Want of Knowledge*; and again, *Not to oversee Workmen, is to leave them your Purse open.* Trusting too much to others Care is the Ruin of many; for, as the Almanack says, *In the Affairs of this World, Men are saved, not by Faith, but by the Want of it*; but a Man's own Care is profitable; for, saith Poor Dick, *Learning is to the Studious*, and *Riches to the Careful*, as well as *Power to the Bold*, and *Heaven to the Virtuous*. And farther, *If you would have a faithful Servant, and one that you like, serve yourself*. And again, he adviseth to Circumspection and Care, even in the smallest Matters, because sometimes *a little Neglect may breed great Mischief*; adding, *For want of a Nail the Shoe was lost; for want of a Shoe the Horse was lost; and for want of a Horse the Rider was lost*, being overtaken and slain by the Enemy, all for want of Care about a Horse-shoe Nail.

So much for Industry, my Friends, and Attention to one's own Business; but to these we must add *Frugality*, if we would make our *Industry* more certainly successful. A Man may, if he knows not how to save as he gets, *keep his Nose all his Life to the Grindstone*, and die not worth a *Groat* at last. *A fat Kitchen makes a lean Will*, as Poor Richard says; and,

Many Estates are spent in the Getting,
Since Women for Tea forsook Spinning and Knitting,
And Men for Punch forsook Hewing and Splitting.

If you would be wealthy, says he, in another Almanack, *think of Saving as well as of Getting: The Indies have not made Spain rich, because her* Outgoes *are greater than her* Incomes. Away then with your expensive Follies, and you will not have so much Cause to complain of hard Times, heavy Taxes, and chargeable Families; for, as Poor Dick says,

Women and Wine, Game and Deceit,
Make the Wealth small, and the Wants great.

And farther, *What maintains one Vice, would bring up two Children*. You may think perhaps, That a *little* Tea, or a *little* Punch now and then, Diet a *little* more costly, Clothes a *little* finer, and a *little* Entertainment now and then, can be no *great* Matter; but remember what Poor Richard says, *Many* a Little *makes a Mickle* and farther, *Beware of* little *Expences; a small Leak will sink a great Ship*; and again, *Who Dainties love, shall Beggars prove*; and moreover, *Fools make Feasts, and wise Men eat them*.

Here you are all got together at this Vendue of *Fineries* and *Knicknacks*. You call them *Goods*, but if you do not take Care, they will prove *Evils* to some of you. You expect they will be sold *cheap*, and perhaps they may for less than they cost; but if you have no Occasion for them, they must be *dear* to you. Remember what Poor Richard says, *Buy what thou hast no Need of, and ere long thou shalt sell thy Necessaries*. And again, *At a great Pennyworth pause a while:* He means, that perhaps the Cheapness is *apparent* only, and not *real*; or the Bargain, by straitning thee in thy Business, may do thee more Harm than Good. For in another Place he says, *Many have been ruined by buying good Pennyworths*. Again, Poor Richard says, *'Tis foolish to lay out Money in a Purchase of Repentance*; and yet this Folly is practised every Day at Vendues, for want of minding the Almanack. *Wise Men*, as Poor Dick says, *learn by others Harms, Fools scarcely by their own*; but, *Felix quem faciunt aliena Pericula cautum.*[1] Many a one, for the Sake of Finery on the Back, have gone with a hungry Belly, and half starved their Families; *Silks and Sattins, Scarlet and Velvets*, as Poor Richard says, *put out the Kitchen Fire*. These are not the *Necessaries* of Life; they can scarcely be called the *Conveniencies*, and yet only because they look pretty, how many *want* to *have* them. The *artificial* Wants of Mankind thus become more numerous than the *natural*; and, as Poor Dick says, *For one* poor *Person, there are an hundred* indigent. By these, and other Extravagancies, the Genteel are reduced to Poverty, and forced to borrow of those whom they formerly despised, but who through *Industry* and *Frugality* have maintained their Standing; in which Case it appears plainly, that a *Ploughman on his Legs is higher than a Gentleman on his Knees*, as Poor Richard says. Perhaps they have had a small Estate left them, which they knew not the Getting of; they think *'tis Day, and will never be Night*; that a little to be spent out of *so much*, is not worth minding; (*a Child and a Fool*, as Poor Richard says, *imagine Twenty Shillings and*

1. *Happy is he whom the dangers of others make cautious.*

Twenty Years can never be spent) but, *always taking out of the Meal-tub, and never putting in, soon comes to the Bottom*; then, as Poor Dick says, *When the Well's dry, they know the Worth of Water.* But this they might have known before, if they had taken his Advice; *If you would know the Value of Money, go and try to borrow some*; for, *he that goes a borrowing goes a sorrowing*; and indeed so does he that lends to such People, when he goes *to get it in again*. Poor Dick farther advises, and says,

Fond Pride of Dress, *is sure a very Curse*;
E'er Fancy *you consult, consult your Purse.*

And again, *Pride is as loud a Beggar as Want, and a great deal more saucy.* When you have bought one fine Thing you must buy ten more, that your Appearance may be all of a Piece; but Poor Dick says, *'Tis easier to* suppress *the first Desire, than to* satisfy *all that follow it*. And 'tis as truly Folly for the Poor to ape the Rich, as for the Frog to swell, in order to equal the Ox.

Great Estates may venture more,
But little Boats should keep near Shore.

'Tis however a Folly soon punished; for *Pride that dines on Vanity sups on Contempt*, as Poor Richard says. And in another Place, *Pride breakfasted with Plenty, dined with Poverty, and supped with Infamy*. And after all, of what Use is this *Pride of Appearance*, for which so much is risked, so much is suffered? It cannot promote Health, or ease Pain; it makes no Increase of Merit in the Person, it creates Envy, it hastens Misfortune.

What is a Butterfly? At best
He's but a Caterpillar drest.
The gaudy Fop's his Picture just,

as Poor Richard says.

But what Madness must it be to *run in Debt* for these Superfluities! We are offered, by the Terms of this Vendue, *Six Months Credit*; and that perhaps has induced some of us to attend it, because we cannot spare the ready Money, and hope now to be fine without it. But, ah, think what you do when you run in Debt; *You give to another Power over your Liberty*. If you cannot pay at the Time, you will be ashamed to see your Creditor; you will be in Fear when you speak to him; you will make poor pitiful sneaking Excuses, and by Degrees come to lose your Veracity, and sink into base downright lying; for, as Poor Richard says, *The second Vice is Lying, the first is running in Debt*. And again, to the same Purpose, *Lying rides upon Debt's Back*. Whereas a freeborn Englishman ought not to be ashamed or afraid to see or speak to any Man living. But Poverty often deprives a Man of all Spirit and Virtue: *'Tis hard for an empty Bag to stand upright*, as Poor Richard truly says. What would you think of that Prince, or that Government, who should issue an Edict forbidding you to dress like a Gentleman or a Gentlewoman, on Pain of Imprisonment or Servitude? Would you not say, that you are free, have a Right to dress as you please, and that such an Edict would be a Breach of your Privileges, and such a Government tyrannical? And yet you are about to put yourself under that Tyranny when you run in Debt for such Dress! Your Creditor has Authority at his Pleasure to deprive you of your Liberty, by confining you in Goal for Life, or to sell you for a Servant, if you should not be able to pay him! When you have got your Bargain, you may, perhaps, think little of Payment; but *Creditors*, Poor Richard tells us, *have better Memories than Debtors*; and in another Place says, *Creditors are a superstitious Sect, great Observers of set Days and Times*. The Day comes round before you are aware, and the Demand is made before you are prepared to satisfy it. Or if you bear your Debt in Mind, the Term which at first seemed so long, will, as it lessens, appear extreamly short. *Time*will seem to have added Wings to his Heels as well as Shoulders. *Those have a short Lent*, saith Poor Richard, *who owe Money to be paid at Easter*. Then since, as he says, *The Borrower is a Slave to the Lender, and the Debtor to the Creditor*, disdain the Chain, preserve your Freedom; and maintain your Independency: Be *industrious* and *free*; be *frugal* and *free*. At present, perhaps, you may think yourself in thriving Circumstances, and that you can bear a little Extravagance without Injury; but,

For Age and Want, save while you may;

No Morning Sun lasts a whole Day,

as Poor Richard says. Gain may be temporary and uncertain, but ever while you live, Expence is constant and certain; and *'tis easier to build two Chimnies than to keep one in Fuel*, as Poor Richard says. So *rather go to Bed supperless than rise in Debt.*

Get what you can, and what you get hold;
'Tis the Stone that will turn all your Lead into Gold,

as Poor Richard says. And when you have got the Philosopher's Stone, sure you will no longer complain of bad Times, or the Difficulty of paying Taxes.

This Doctrine, my Friends, is *Reason* and *Wisdom*; but after all, do not depend too much upon your own *Industry*, and *Frugality*, and *Prudence*, though excellent Things, for they may all be blasted without the Blessing of Heaven; and therefore ask that Blessing humbly, and be not uncharitable to those that at present seem to want it, but comfort and help them. Remember Job suffered, and was afterwards prosperous.

And now to conclude, *Experience keeps a dear School, but Fools will learn in no other, and scarce in that*; for it is true, *we may give Advice, but we cannot give Conduct*, as Poor Richard says: However, remember this, *They that won't be counselled, can't be helped,* as Poor Richard says: And farther, That *if you will not hear Reason, she'll surely rap your Knuckles.*

Thus the old Gentleman ended his Harangue. The People heard it, and approved the Doctrine, and immediately practised the contrary, just as if it had been a common Sermon; for the Vendue opened, and they began to buy extravagantly, notwithstanding all his Cautions, and their own Fear of Taxes. I found the good Man had thoroughly studied my Almanacks, and digested all I had dropt on those Topicks during the Course of Five-and-twenty Years. The frequent Mention he made of me must have tired any one else, but my Vanity was wonderfully delighted with it, though I was conscious that not a tenth Part of the Wisdom was my own which he ascribed to me, but rather the *Gleanings* I had made of the Sense of all Ages and Nations. However, I resolved to be the better for the Echo of it;

and though I had at first determined to buy Stuff for a new Coat, I went away resolved to wear my old One a little longer. *Reader*, if thou wilt do the same, thy Profit will be as great as mine. I am, as ever, Thine to serve thee,

RICHARD SAUNDERS.

Part VI

13 AUGUST, 1761 - 4 APRIL, 1769

Of the Meanes of Disposing the Enemie to Peace

Examination before the Committee of the Whole of the House of Commons

On the Price of Corn and Management of the Poor

On the Propriety of Taxing America

Of Lightning, and the Method (Now Used in America) of Securing Buildings and Persons from Its Mischievous Effects

On Smuggling

On Railing and Reviling

A New Version of the Lord's Prayer

Positions to Be Examined

Of the Meanes of Disposing the Enemie to Peace

13 August, 1761

To the Printer of the London Chronicle.

Sir,

I send you for your excellent Paper, an extract from the famous Jesuit Campanella's discourses address'd to the King of Spain, intituled, *Of the Meanes of extending the Greatnesse of the Spanish Monarchie.* The language is a little antiquated, being the old translation in the edition of 1629; but the matter contain'd is so *apropos* to our present situation (only changing *Spain* for *France*) that I think it well worth the attention of the Publick at this critical conjuncture, as it discovers the arts of our enemies, and may therefore help in some degree to put us on our guard against them. After discoursing largely on the wars to be made, particularly against England and Holland, the conquests to be attempted, and the various means of securing them when gained, he comes to his

CHAP. XIV.

Of the Meanes of disposing the Enemie to Peace.

"Warres, with whatsoever prudence undertaken and conducted, do not always succeed; many thinges out of mans power to governe, such as dearthe of provisions, tempests, pestilence, and the like, oftentimes interfering, and totally overthrowing the best designes; so that these enemies of our Monarchie, though apparentlie at first the weaker, may, by disastrous events of warre on our part, become the stronger; and though not in such degree as to endanger the bodie of this great kingdome, yet, by their greater power of shipping and aptness in sea-affaires, to be able to cut off, if I may so speak, some of its smaller limbes and members, that, being remote therefrom, are not easilie defended; to wit, our islands and colonies in the Indies; thereby however depriving the bodie of its wonted nourishment, so that it must thenceforthe languish and grow weake, if those parts be not recovered, which possibly may, by continuance of warre, be found unlikely to be done. And the enemie, puffed up with their successes, and hoping still for more, may not be disposed to peace on such termes as would be suitable to the honour of your Majestie, and to the welfare of your State and Subjectes. In such case, the following meanes may have good effect.

"It is well known, that these northerne people, though hardie of bodie, and bold in fight, be neverthelesse, through overmuch eating and other intemperance, slowe of wit and dull in understanding, so that they be oftimes more easilie to be governed and turned by skille than by force. There is therefore always hope, that by wise counsel and dextrous managemente, those advantages which through cross accidents in warre have been lost, may again with honour be recovered. In this place I shall say little of the power of money secretly distributed amongst grandees or their friends or mistresses, that method being in all ages known and practised. If the *minds* of enemies can be *changed*, they may, be brought to grant willingly and for nothing, what much golde would scarcelie have otherwise prevailed to obtaine. Yet as the procuring this change is to be by fitte instruments, some few doublones will not unprofitablie be disbursed by your Majestie; the manner whereof I shall now brieflie recite.

"In those countries, and particularly in England, there are not wanting men of learning, ingenious speakers and writers, who are neverthelesse in lowe estate and pinched by fortune; these being privatelie gained by proper meanes, must be instructed in their sermons, discourses, writings, poems and songs, to handle and specially inculcate points like these which followe. Let them magnify the blessings of peace and enlarge mightily thereon, which is not unbecoming grave Divines and other Christian men; let them expatiate on the miseries of warre, the waste of Christian bloode, the growing scarcitie of labourers and workmen, the dearness of all foreign wares and merchandises, the interruption of commerce by the captures or delay of ships, the increase and great burthen of taxes, and the impossibilitie of supplying much longer the expence of the contest; let them represent the warre as an unmeasurable advantage to particulars, and to particulars only (thereby to excite envie against those that manage and provide for the same) while so prejudicial to the Commonweale and people in general: let them represent the advantages gained against us as trivial and of little import; the places taken from us as of small trade or produce, inconvenient for situation, unwholesome for ayre and climate, useless to their nations, and greatly chargeable to keepe, draining the home Countries both of men and money: let them urge, that if a peace be forced on us, and those places withheld, it will nourishe secret griefe and malice in the King and Grandees of Spain, which will ere long breake for the in new warres, wherein those places may again be retaken, and lost without the merit and grace of restoring them willingly for peace-sake: let them represent the making and continuance of warres from view of gaine, to be base and unworthie a brave people; as those made from view of ambition are mad and wicked; and let them insinuate that the continuance of the present warre on their parte, when peace is offered, hath these ingredients strongly in its nature. Then let them magnifie the great power of your Majestie, and the strength of your kingdome, the inexhaustible wealthe of your mines, the greatness of your incomes, and thence your abilitie of continuing the warre; hinting withal, the new alliances you may possibly make; at the same time setting forth the sincere disposition you have for peace, and that it is only a concerne for your honour and the honour of your realme, that induceth you to insist on the restitution of the places taken. If with all this they shrewdly intimate and cause it to be understood by artfull words, and beleeved, that their own Prince is himself in heart for peace on your Majesties termes, and grieved at the obstinacie and perverseness of those among his people that be for continuing the warre, a marvellous effect shall by these discourses and writings be produced; and a wonderful strong party shall your Majestie raise among your enemies in favour of the peace you desire; insomuch that their own Princes and wisest Councellours will in a sort be constrained to yeeld thereto. For in this warre of words, the avarice and ambition, the hopes and fears, and all the croud of human passions, will, in the minds of your enemies, be raised, armed, and put in array, to fight for your interests, against the reall and substantiall interest of their own countries. The simple and undiscerning many, shall be carried away by the plausibilitie and well seeming of these discourses; and the opinions becoming popular, all the rich men, who have great possessions, and fear the continuance of taxes, and hope peace will end them, shall be imboldened thereby to cry aloud for peace; their dependents who are many, must do the same: all marchants, fearing loss of ships and greater burthens on trade by farther duties and subsidies, and hoping greater profittes by the ending of the warre, shall join in the cry for peace: All the usurers and lenders of monies to the state, who on a peace hope great profit from their bargaines, and fear if the warre be continued, the State shall become bankeroute, and unable to pay them: these who have no small weight, shall joine the cry for peace: All the gowne and booke statesmen, who maligne the bold conductors of the warre, and envie the glorie they may have thereby obtained; these shall cry aloud for peace; hoping, that when the Warre shall cease, such men becoming less necessarie shall be more lightelie esteemed, and themselves more sought after: All the officers of the enemies armies and fleets, who wish for repose, and to enjoy their spoiles, salaries, or rewards, in quietness, and without peril, these, and their friends and families, who desire their safetie, and the solace of their societie, shall all cry for peace: All those who be timorous by nature, amongst whom be reckoned men of learning that lead sedentarie lives, using little exercise of bodie, and thence obtaining but few and weake spirits; great Statesmen, whose natural spirits be exhausted by much thinking, or depress'd by over-much feasting; together with all women, whose power, weake as they are, is not a little among such men; these shall incessantly speake for peace: And finallie, all Courtiers, who suppose they conforme thereby to the inclinations of the Prince; all who are *in* places of profit, and fear to lose them, or hope for better; all who are *out* of places, and hope to obtain them; all the worldly-minded clergie, who seeke preferment; these, with all the weight of their character and influence, shall joine the cry for peace, till it becomes one universal clamour, and no sound but that of *Peace, Peace, Peace*, shall be heard from every quarter. Then shall your Majesties termes of peace be listened to with much readiness, the places taken from you be willingly restored, and your kingdome, recovering its strength, shall only need to waite, a few years for more favourable occasions, when the advantages to your power proposed by beginning the warre, but lost by its bad successe, shall, with better fortune, be finallie obtained."

What effect the artifices here recommended might have had in the times when this Jesuit wrote, I cannot pretend to say; but I believe, the present age being more enlightened, and our people better acquainted than formerly with our true national interests, such arts can now hardly prove so generally successful. For we may with pleasure observe, and to the honour of the British people, that though writings and discourses like these have lately not been wanting, yet few in any of the classes he particularises seem to be affected by them; but all ranks and degrees among us persist hitherto in declaring for a vigorous prosecution of the war, in preference to an unsafe, disadvantageous peace.

Yet, as a little change of fortune may make such writings more attended to, and give them greater weight, I think the publication of this piece, as it shows the spring from whence these scribblers draw their poisoned waters, may be of publick utility. I am, Sir, yours, &c.

A Briton.

Examination before the Committee of the Whole of the House of Commons

13 February, 1766

The EXAMINATION of Doctor BENJAMIN FRANKLIN, before an August Assembly, relating to the Repeal of the STAMP-ACT, &c.[1]

1 Q. What is your name, and place of abode?

A. Franklin, of Philadelphia.

[2] Q. Do the Americans pay any considerable taxes among themselves?

A. Certainly many, and very heavy taxes.

[3] Q. What are the present taxes in Pennsylvania, laid by the laws of the colony?

A. There are taxes on all estates real and personal, a poll tax, a tax on all offices, professions, trades and businesses, according to their profits; an excise on all wine, rum, and other spirits; and a duty of Ten Pounds per head on all Negroes imported, with some other duties.

[4] Q. For what purposes are those taxes laid?

A. For the support of the civil and military establishments of the country, and to discharge the heavy debt contracted in the last war.

[5] Q. How long are those taxes to continue?

A. Those for discharging the debt are to continue till 1772, and longer, if the debt should not be then all discharged. The others must always continue.

---

1. This testimony was recorded in the House of Commons by Nathaniel Ryder, 1st Baron Harrowby.

[6] Q. Was it not expected that the debt would have been sooner discharged?

A. It was, when the peace was made with France and Spain— But a fresh war breaking out with the Indians, a fresh load of debt was incurred, and the taxes, of course, continued longer by a new law.

[7] Q. Are not all the people very able to pay those taxes?

A. No. The frontier counties, all along the continent, having been frequently ravaged by the enemy, and greatly impoverished, are able to pay very little tax. And therefore, in consideration of their distresses, our late tax laws do expressly favour those counties, excusing the sufferers; and I suppose the same is done in other governments.

[8] Q. Are not you concerned in the management of the Post-Office in America?

A. Yes. I am Deputy Post-Master General of North-America.

[9] Q. Don't you think the distribution of stamps, by post, to all the inhabitants, very practicable, if there was no opposition?

A. The posts only go along the sea coasts; they do not, except in a few instances, go back into the country; and if they did, sending for stamps by post would occasion an expence of postage, amounting, in many cases, to much more than that of the stamps themselves.

[10] Q. Are you acquainted with Newfoundland?

A. I never was there.

[11] Q. Do you know whether there are any post roads on that island?

A. I have heard that there are no roads at all; but that the communication between one settlement and another is by sea only.

[12] Q. Can you disperse the stamps by post in Canada?

A. There is only a post between Montreal and Quebec. The inhabitants live so scattered and remote from each other, in that vast country, that posts cannot be supported among them, and therefore they cannot get stamps per post. The English Colonies too, along the frontiers, are very thinly settled.

[13] Q. From the thinness of the back settlements, would not the stamp-act be extreamly inconvenient to the inhabitants, if executed?

A. To be sure it would; as many of the inhabitants could not get stamps when they had occasion for them, without taking long journeys, and spending perhaps Three or Four Pounds, that the Crown might get Sixpence.

[14] Q. Are not the Colonies, from their circumstances, very able to pay the stamp duty?

A. In my opinion, there is not gold and silver enough in the Colonies to pay the stamp duty for one year.

[15] Q. Don't you know that the money arising from the stamps was all to be laid out in America?

A. I know it is appropriated by the act to the American service; but it will be spent in the conquered Colonies, where the soldiers are, not in the Colonies that pay it.

[16] Q. Is there not a ballance of trade due from the Colonies where the troops are posted, that will bring back the money to the old colonies?

A. I think not. I believe very little would come back. I know of no trade likely to bring it back. I think it would come from the Colonies where it was spent directly to England; for I have always observed, that in every Colony the more plenty the means of remittance to England, the more goods are sent for, and the more trade with England carried on.

[17] Q. What number of white inhabitants do you think there are in Pennsylvania?

A. I suppose there may be about 160,000.

[18] Q. What number of them are Quakers?

A. Perhaps a third.

[19] Q. What number of Germans?

A. Perhaps another third; but I cannot speak with certainty.

[20] Q. Have any number of the Germans seen service, as soldiers, in Europe?

A. Yes,—many of them, both in Europe and America.

[21] Q. Are they as much dissatisfied with the stamp duty as the English?

A. Yes, and more; and with reason, as their stamps are, in many cases, to be double.

[22] Q. How many white men do you suppose there are in North-America?

A. About 300,000, from sixteen to sixty years of age.

[23] Q. What may be the amount of one year's imports into Pennsylvania from Britain?

A. I have been informed that our merchants compute the imports from Britain to be above 500,000 Pounds.

[24] Q. What may be the amount of the produce of your province exported to Britain?

A. It must be small, as we produce little that is wanted in Britain. I suppose it cannot exceed 40,000 Pounds.

[25] Q. How then do you pay the ballance?

A. The Ballance is paid by our produce carried to the West-Indies, and sold in our own islands, or to the French, Spaniards, Danes and Dutch; by the same carried to other colonies in North-America, as to New-England, Nova-Scotia, Newfoundland, Carolina and Georgia; by the same carried to different parts of Europe, as Spain, Portugal and Italy. In all which places we receive either money, bills of exchange, or commodities that suit for remittance to Britain; which, together with all the profits on the industry of our merchants and mariners, arising in those circuitous voyages, and the freights made by their ships, center finally in Britain, to discharge the ballance, and pay for British manufactures continually used in the province, or sold to foreigners by our traders.

[26] Q. Have you heard of any difficulties lately laid on the Spanish trade?

A. Yes, I have heard that it has been greatly obstructed by some new regulations, and by the English men of war and cutters stationed all along the coast in America.

[27] Q. Do you think it right that America should be protected by this country, and pay no part of the expence?

A. That is not the case. The Colonies raised, cloathed and paid, during the last war, near 25000 men, and spent many millions.

[28] Q. Were you not reimbursed by parliament?

A. We were only reimbursed what, in your opinion, we had advanced beyond our proportion, or beyond what might reasonably be expected from us; and it was a very small part of what we spent. Pennsylvania, in particular, disbursed about 500,000 Pounds, and the reimbursements, in the whole, did not exceed 60,000 Pounds.

[29] Q. You have said that you pay heavy taxes in Pennsylvania; what do they amount to in the Pound?

A. The tax on all estates, real and personal, is Eighteen Pence in the Pound, fully rated; and the tax on the profits of trades and professions, with other taxes, do, I suppose, make full Half a Crown in the Pound.

[30] Q. Do you know any thing of the rate of exchange in Pennsylvania, and whether it has fallen lately?

A. It is commonly from 170 to 175. I have heard that it has fallen lately from 175 to 162 and a half, owing, I suppose, to their lessening their orders for goods; and when their debts to this country are paid, I think the exchange will probably be at par.

[31] Q. Do not you think the people of America would submit to pay the stamp duty, if it was moderated?

A. No, never, unless compelled by force of arms.

[32] Q. Are not the taxes in Pennsylvania laid on unequally, in order to burthen the English trade, particularly the tax on professions and business?

A. It is not more burthensome in proportion than the tax on lands. It is intended, and supposed to take an equal proportion of profits.

[33] Q. How is the assembly composed? Of what kinds of people are the members, landholders or traders?

A. It is composed of landholders, merchants and artificers.

[34] Q. Are not the majority landholders?

A. I believe they are.

[35] Q. Do not they, as much as possible, shift the tax off from the land, to ease that, and lay the burthen heavier on trade?

A. I have never understood it so. I never heard such a thing suggested. And indeed an attempt of that kind could answer no purpose. The merchant or trader is always skilled in figures, and ready with his pen and ink. If unequal burthens are laid on his trade, he puts an additional price on his goods; and the consumers, who are chiefly landholders, finally pay the greatest part, if not the whole.

[36] Q. What was the temper of America towards Great-Britain before the year 1763?

A. The best in the world. They submitted willingly to the government of the Crown, and paid, in all their courts, obedience to acts of parliament. Numerous as the people are in the several old provinces, they cost you nothing in forts, citadels, garrisons or armies, to keep them in subjection. They were governed by this country at the expence only of a little pen, ink and paper. They were led by a thread. They had not only a respect, but an affection, for Great-Britain, for its laws, its customs and manners, and even a fondness for its fashions, that greatly increased the commerce. Natives of Britain were always treated with particular regard; to be an Old England-man was, of itself, a character of some respect, and gave a kind of rank among us.

[37] Q. And what is their temper now?

A. O, very much altered.

[38] Q. Did you ever hear the authority of parliament to make laws for America questioned till lately?

A. The authority of parliament was allowed to be valid in all laws, except such as should lay internal taxes. It was never disputed in laying duties to regulate commerce.

[39] Q. In what proportion hath population increased in America?

A. I think the inhabitants of all the provinces together, taken at a medium, double in about 25 years. But their demand for British manufactures increases much faster, as the consumption is not merely in proportion to their numbers, but grows with the growing abilities of the same numbers to pay for them. In 1723, the whole importation from Britain to Pennsylvania, was but about 15,000 Pounds Sterling; it is now near Half a Million.

[40] Q. In what light did the people of America use to consider the parliament of Great-Britain?

A. They considered the parliament as the great bulwark and security of their liberties and privileges, and always spoke of it with the utmost respect and veneration. Arbitrary ministers, they thought, might possibly, at times, attempt to oppress them; but they relied on it, that the parliament, on application, would always give redress. They remembered, with gratitude, a strong instance of this, when a bill was brought into parliament, with a clause to make royal instructions laws in the Colonies, which the house of commons would not pass, and it was thrown out.

[41] Q. And have they not still the same respect for parliament?

A. No; it is greatly lessened.

[42] Q. To what causes is that owing?

A. To a concurrence of causes; the restraints lately laid on their trade, by which the bringing of foreign gold and silver into the Colonies was prevented; the prohibition of making paper money among themselves; and then demanding a new and heavy tax by stamps; taking away, at the same time, trials by juries, and refusing to receive and hear their humble petitions.

[43] Q. Don't you think they would submit to the stamp-act, if it was modified, the obnoxious parts taken out, and the duty reduced to some particulars, of small moment?

A. No; they will never submit to it.

[44] Q. What do you think is the reason that the people of America increase faster than in England?

A. Because they marry younger, and more generally.

[45] Q. Why so?

A. Because any young couple that are industrious, may easily obtain land of their own, on which they can raise a family.

[46] Q. Are not the lower rank of people more at their ease in America than in England?

A. They may be so, if they are sober and diligent, as they are better paid for their labour.

[47] Q. What is your opinion of a future tax, imposed on the same principle with that of the stamp-act; how would the Americans receive it?

A. Just as they do this. They would not pay it.

[48] Q. Have you not heard of the resolutions of this house, and of the house of lords, asserting the right of parliament relating to America, including a power to tax the people there?

A. Yes, I have heard of such resolutions.

[49] Q. What will be the opinion of the Americans on those resolutions?

A. They will think them unconstitutional, and unjust.

[50] Q. Was it an opinion in America before 1763, that the parliament had no right to lay taxes and duties there?

A. I never heard any objection to the right of laying duties to regulate commerce; but a right to lay internal taxes was never supposed to be in parliament, as we are not represented there.

[51] Q. On what do you found your opinion, that the people in America made any such distinction?

A. I know that whenever the subject has occurred in conversation where I have been present, it has appeared to be the opinion of every one, that we could not be taxed in a parliament where we were not represented. But the payment of duties laid by act of parliament, as regulations of commerce, was never disputed.

[52] Q. But can you name any act of assembly, or public act of any of your governments, that made such distinction?

A. I do not know that there was any; I think there was never an occasion to make any such act, till now that you have attempted to tax us; that has occasioned resolutions of assembly, declaring the distinction, in which I think every assembly on the continent, and every member in every assembly, have been unanimous.

[53] Q. What then could occasion conversations on that subject before that time?

A. There was in 1754 a proposition made (I think it came from hence) that in case of a war, which was then apprehended, the governors of the Colonies should meet, and order the levying of troops, building of forts, and taking every other necessary measure for the general defence; and should draw on the treasury here for the sums expended, which were afterwards to be raised in the Colonies by a general tax, to be laid on them by act of parliament. This occasioned a good deal of conversation on the subject, and the general opinion was, that the parliament neither would nor could lay any tax on us, till we were duly represented in parliament, because it was not just, nor agreeable to the nature of an English constitution.

[54] Q. Don't you know there was a time in New-York, when it was under consideration to make an application to parliament to lay taxes on that Colony, upon a deficiency arising from the assembly's refusing or neglecting to raise the necessary supplies for the support of the civil government?

A. I never heard of it.

[55] Q. There was such an application under consideration in New-York; and do you apprehend they could suppose the right of parliament to lay a tax in America was only local, and confined to the case of a deficiency in a particular Colony, by a refusal of its assembly to raise the necessary supplies?

A. They could not suppose such a case, as that the assembly would not raise the necessary supplies to support its own government. An assembly that would refuse it must want common sense, which cannot be supposed. I think there was never any such case at New-York, and that it must be a misrepresentation, or the fact must be misunderstood. I know there have been some attempts, by ministerial instructions from hence, to oblige the assemblies to settle permanent salaries on governors, which they wisely refused to do; but I believe no assembly of New-York, or any other Colony, ever refused duly to support government by proper allowances, from time to time, to public officers.

[56] Q. But in case a governor, acting by instruction, should call on an assembly to raise the necessary supplies, and the assembly should refuse to do it, do you not think it would then be for the good of the people of the colony, as well as necessary to government, that the parliament should tax them?

A. I do not think it would be necessary. If an assembly could possibly be so absurd as to refuse raising the supplies requisite for the maintenance of government among them, they could not long remain in such a situation; the disorders and confusion occasioned by it must soon bring them to reason.

[57] Q. If it should not, ought not the right to be in Great-Britain of applying a remedy?

A. A right only to be used in such a case, I should have no objection to, supposing it to be used merely for the good of the people of the Colony.

[58] Q. But who is to judge of that, Britain or the Colony?

A. Those that feel can best judge.

[59] Q. You say the Colonies have always submitted to external taxes, and object to the right of parliament only in laying internal taxes; now can you shew that there is any kind of difference between the two taxes to the Colony on which they may be laid?

A. I think the difference is very great. An external tax is a duty laid on commodities imported; that duty is added to the first cost, and other charges on the commodity, and when it is offered to sale, makes a part of the price. If the people do not like it at that price, they refuse it; they are not obliged to pay it. But an internal tax is forced from the people without their consent, if not laid by their own representatives. The stamp-act says, we shall have no commerce, make no exchange of property with each other, neither purchase nor grant, nor recover debts; we shall neither marry, nor make our wills, unless we pay such and such sums, and thus it is intended to extort our money from us, or ruin us by the consequences of refusing to pay it.

[60] Q. But supposing the external tax or duty to be laid on the necessaries of life imported into your Colony, will not that be the same thing in its effects as an internal tax?

A. I do not know a single article imported into the Northern Colonies, but what they can either do without, or make themselves.

[61] Q. Don't you think cloth from England absolutely necessary to them?

A. No, by no means absolutely necessary; with industry and good management, they may very well supply themselves with all they want.

[62] Q. Will it not take a long time to establish that manufacture among them? and must they not in the mean while suffer greatly?

A. I think not. They have made a surprising progress already. And I am of opinion, that before their old clothes are worn out, they will have new ones of their own making.

[63] Q. Can they possibly find wool enough in North-America?

A. They have taken steps to increase the wool. They entered into general combinations to eat no more lamb, and very few lambs were killed last year. This course persisted in, will soon make a prodigious difference in the quantity of wool. And the establishing of great manufactories, like those in the clothing towns here, is not necessary, as it is where the business is to be carried on for the purposes of trade. The people will all spin, and work for themselves, in their own houses.

[64] Q. Can there be wool and manufacture enough in one or two years?

A. In three years, I think, there may.

[65] Q. Does not the severity of the winter, in the Northern Colonies, occasion the wool to be of bad quality?

A. No; the wool is very fine and good.

[66] Q. In the more Southern Colonies, as in Virginia; don't you know that the wool is coarse, and only a kind of hair?

A. I don't know it. I never heard it. Yet I have been sometimes in Virginia. I cannot say I ever took particular notice of the wool there, but I believe it is good, though I cannot speak positively of it; but Virginia, and the Colonies south of it, have less occasion for wool; their winters are short, and not very severe, and they can very well clothe themselves with linen and cotton of their own raising for the rest of the year.

[67] Q. Are not the people, in the more Northern Colonies, obliged to fodder their sheep all the winter?

A. In some of the most Northern Colonies they may be obliged to do it some part of the winter.

[68] Q. Considering the resolutions of parliament, as to the right, do you think, if the stamp-act is repealed, that the North Americans will be satisfied?

A. I believe they will.

[69] Q. Why do you think so?

A. I think the resolutions of right will give them very little concern, if they are never attempted to be carried into practice. The Colonies will probably consider themselves in the same situation, in that respect, with Ireland; they know you claim the same right with regard to Ireland, but you never exercise it. And they may believe you never will exercise it in the Colonies, any more than in Ireland, unless on some very extraordinary occasion.

[70] Q. But who are to be the judges of that extraordinary occasion? Is it not the parliament?

A. Though the parliament may judge of the occasion, the people will think it can never exercise such right, till representatives from the Colonies are admitted into parliament, and that whenever the occasion arises, representatives will be ordered.

[71] Q. Did you never hear that Maryland, during the last war, had refused to furnish a quota towards the common defence?

A. Maryland has been much misrepresented in that matter. Maryland, to my knowledge, never refused to contribute, or grant aids to the Crown.

The assemblies every year, during the war, voted considerable sums, and formed bills to raise them. The bills were, according to the constitution of that province, sent up to the council, or upper house, for concurrence, that they might be presented to the governor, in order to be enacted into laws. Unhappy disputes between the two houses arising, from the defects of that constitution principally, rendered all the bills but one or two abortive. The proprietary's council rejected them. It is true Maryland did not contribute its proportion, but it was, in my opinion, the fault of the government, not of the people.

[72] Q. Was it not talked of in the other provinces as a proper measure to apply to parliament to compel them?

A. I have heard such discourse; but as it was well known, that the people were not to blame, no such application was ever made, nor any step taken towards it.

[73] Q. Was it not proposed at a public meeting?

A. Not that I know of.

[74] Q. Do you remember the abolishing of the paper currency in New England, by act of assembly?

A. I do remember its being abolished, in the Massachusett's Bay.

[75] Q. Was not Lieutenant Governor Hutchinson principally concerned in that transaction?

A. I have heard so.

[76] Q. Was it not at that time a very unpopular law?

A. I believe it might, though I can say little about it, as I lived at a distance from that province.

[77] Q. Was not the scarcity of gold and silver an argument used against abolishing the paper?

A. I suppose it was.

[78] Q. What is the present opinion there of that law? Is it as unpopular as it was at first?

A. I think it is not.

[79] Q. Have not instructions from hence been sometimes sent over to governors, highly oppressive and unpolitical?

A. Yes.

[80] Q. Have not some governors dispensed with them for that reason?

A. Yes, I have heard so.

[81] Q. Did the Americans ever dispute the controling power of parliament to regulate the commerce?

A. No.

[82] Q. Can any thing less than a military force carry the stamp-act into execution?

A. I do not see how a military force can be applied to that purpose.

[83] Q. Why may it not?

A. Suppose a military force sent into America, they will find nobody in arms; what are they then to do? They cannot force a man to take stamps who chooses to do without them. They will not find a rebellion; they may indeed make one.

[84] Q. If the act is not repealed, what do you think will be the consequences?

A. A total loss of the respect and affection the people of America bear to this country, and of all the commerce that depends on that respect and affection.

[85] Q. How can the commerce be affected?

A. You will find, that if the act is not repealed, they will take very little of your manufactures in a short time.

[86] Q. Is it in their power to do without them?

A. I think they may very well do without them.

[87] Q. Is it their interest not to take them?

A. The goods they take from Britain are either necessaries, mere conveniences, or superfluities. The first, as cloth, &c. with a little industry they can make at home; the second they can do without, till they are able to provide them among themselves; and the last, which are much the greatest part, they will strike off immediately. They are mere articles of fashion, purchased and consumed, because the fashion in a respected country, but will now be detested and rejected. The people have already struck off, by general agreement, the use of all goods fashionable in mournings, and many thousand pounds worth are sent back as unsaleable.

[88] Q. Is it their interest to make cloth at home?

A. I think they may at present get it cheaper from Britain, I mean of the same fineness and neatness of workmanship; but when one considers other circumstances, the restraints on their trade, and the difficulty of making remittances, it is their interest to make every thing.

[89] Q. Suppose an act of internal regulations, connected with a tax, how would they receive it?

A. I think it would be objected to.

[90] Q. Then no regulation with a tax would be submitted to?

A. Their opinion is, that when aids to the Crown are wanted, they are to be asked of the several assemblies, according to the old established usage, who will, as they always have done, grant them freely. And that their money ought not to be given away without their consent, by persons at a distance, unacquainted with their circumstances and abilities. The granting aids to the Crown, is the only means they have of recommending themselves to their sovereign, and they think it extremely hard and unjust, that a body of men, in which they have no representatives, should make a merit to itself of giving and granting what is not its own, but theirs, and deprive them of a right they esteem of the utmost value and importance, as it is the security of all their other rights.

[91] Q. But is not the post-office, which they have long received, a tax as well as a regulation?

A. No; the money paid for the postage of a letter is not of the nature of a tax; it is merely a quantum meruit for a service done; no person is compellable to pay the money, if he does not chuse to receive the service. A man may still, as before the act, send his letter by a servant, a special messenger, or a friend, if he thinks it cheaper and safer.

[92] Q. But do they not consider the regulations of the postoffice, by the act of last year, as a tax?

A. By the regulations of last year the rate of postage was generally abated near thirty per cent. through all America; they certainly cannot consider such abatement as a tax.

[93] Q. If an excise was laid by parliament, which they might likewise avoid paying, by not consuming the articles excised, would they then not object to it?

A. They would certainly object to it, as an excise is unconnected with any service done, and is merely an aid which they think ought to be asked of them, and granted by them, if they are to pay it, and can be granted for them by no others whatsoever, whom they have not impowered for that purpose.

[94] Q. You say they do not object to the right of parliament in laying duties on goods to be paid on their importation; now, is there any kind of difference between a duty on the importation of goods, and an excise on their consumption?

A. Yes; a very material one; an excise, for the reasons I have just mentioned, they think you can have no right to lay within their country. But the sea is yours; you maintain, by your fleets, the safety of navigation in it; and keep it clear of pirates; you may have therefore a natural and equitable right to some toll or duty on merchandizes carried through that part of your dominions, towards defraying the expence you are at in ships to maintain the safety of that carriage.

[95] Q. Does this reasoning hold in the case of a duty laid on the produce of their lands exported? And would they not then object to such a duty?

A. If it tended to make the produce so much dearer abroad as to lessen the demand for it, to be sure they would object to such a duty; not to your right of laying it, but they would complain of it as a burthen, and petition you to lighten it.

[96] Q. Is not the duty paid on the tobacco exported a duty of that kind?

A. That, I think, is only on tobacco carried coastwise from one Colony to another, and appropriated as a fund for supporting the college at Williamsburgh, in Virginia.

[97] Q. Have not the assemblies in the West-Indies the same natural rights with those in North America?

A. Undoubtedly.

[98] Q. And is there not a tax laid there on their sugars exported?

A. I am not much acquainted with the West-Indies, but the duty of four and a half per cent. on sugars exported, was, I believe, granted by their own assemblies.

[99] Q. How much is the poll-tax in your province laid on unmarried men?

A. It is, I think, Fifteen Shillings, to be paid by every single freeman, upwards of twenty-one years old.

[100] Q. What is the annual amount of all the taxes in Pennsylvania?

A. I suppose about 20,000 Pounds sterling.

[101] Q. Supposing the stamp-act continued, and enforced, do you imagine that ill humour will induce the Americans to give as much for worse manufactures of their own, and use them, preferably to better of ours?

A. Yes, I think so. People will pay as freely to gratify one passion as another, their resentment as their pride.

[102] Q. Would the people at Boston discontinue their trade?

A. The merchants are a very small number, compared with the body of the people, and must discontinue their trade, if nobody will buy their goods.

[103] Q. What are the body of the people in the Colonies?

A. They are farmers, husbandmen or planters.

[104] Q. Would they suffer the produce of their lands to rot?

A. No; but they would not raise so much. They would manufacture more, and plough less.

[105] Q. Would they live without the administration of justice in civil matters, and suffer all the inconveniences of such a situation for any considerable time, rather than take the stamps, supposing the stamps were protected by a sufficient force, where every one might have them?

A. I think the supposition impracticable, that the stamps should be so protected as that every one might have them. The act requires sub-distributors to be appointed in every county town, district and village, and they would be necessary. But the principal distributors, who were to have had a considerable profit on the whole, have not thought it worth while to continue in the office, and I think it impossible to find sub-distributors fit to be trusted, who, for the trifling profit that must come to their share, would incur the odium, and run the hazard that would attend it; and if they could be found, I think it impracticable to protect the stamps in so many distant and remote places.

[106] Q. But in places where they could be protected, would not the people use them rather than remain in such a situation, unable to obtain any right, or recover, by law, any debt?

A. It is hard to say what they would do. I can only judge what other people will think, and how they will act, by what I feel within myself. I have a great many debts due to me in America, and I had rather they should remain unrecoverable by any law, than submit to the stamp-act. They will be debts of honour. It is my opinion the people will either continue in that situation, or find some way to extricate themselves, perhaps by generally agreeing to proceed in the courts without stamps.

[107] Q. What do you think a sufficient military force to protect the distribution of the stamps in every part of America?

A. A very great force; I can't say what, if the disposition of America is for a general resistance.

[108] Q. What is the number of men in America able to bear arms, or of disciplined militia?

A. There are, I suppose, at least—[*Question objected to. He withdrew. Called in again.*]

[109] Q. Is the American stamp-act an equal tax on that country?

A. I think not.

[110] Q. Why so?

A. The greatest part of the money must arise from law suits for the recovery of debts, and be paid by the lower sort of people, who were too poor easily to pay their debts. It is therefore a heavy tax on the poor, and a tax upon them for being poor.

[111] Q. But will not this increase of expence be a means of lessening the number of law suits?

A. I think not; for as the costs all fall upon the debtor, and are to be paid by him, they would be no discouragement to the creditor to bring his action.

[112] Q. Would it not have the effect of excessive usury?

A. Yes, as an oppression of the debtor.

[113] Q. How many ships are there laden annually in North-America with flax-seed for Ireland?

A. I cannot speak to the number of ships, but I know that in 1752, 10,000 hogsheads of flax-seed, each containing 7 bushels, were exported from Philadelphia to Ireland. I suppose the quantity is greatly increased since that time; and it is understood that the exportation from New York is equal to that from Philadelphia.

[114] Q. What becomes of the flax that grows with that flax-seed?

A. They manufacture some into coarse, and some into a middling kind of linen.

[115] Q. Are there any slitting mills in America?

A. I think there are, but I believe only one at present employed. I suppose they will all be set to work, if the interruption of the trade continues.

[116] Q. Are there any fulling mills there?

A. A great many.

[117] Q. Did you never hear that a great quantity of stockings were contracted for for the army, during the war, and manufactured in Philadelphia?

A. I have heard so.

[118] Q. If the stamp act should be repealed, would not the Americans think they could oblige the parliament to repeal every external tax law now in force?

A. It is hard to answer questions of what people at such a distance will think.

[119] Q. But what do you imagine they will think were the motives of repealing the act?

A. I suppose they will think that it was repealed from a conviction of its inexpediency; and they will rely upon it, that while the same inexpediency subsists, you will never attempt to make such another.

[120] Q. What do you mean by its inexpediency?

A. I mean its inexpediency on several accounts; the poverty and inability of those who were to pay the tax; the general discontent it has occasioned; and the impracticability of enforcing it.

[121] Q. If the act should be repealed, and the legislature should shew its resentment to the opposers of the stamp-act, would the Colonies acquiesce in the authority of the legislature? What is your opinion they would do?

A. I don't doubt at all, that if the legislature repeal the stamp-act, the Colonies will acquiesce in the authority.

[122] Q. But if the legislature should think fit to ascertain its right to lay taxes, by any act laying a small tax, contrary to their opinion, would they submit to pay the tax?

A. The proceedings of the people in America have been considered too much together. The proceedings of the assemblies have been very different from those of the mobs, and should be distinguished, as having no connection with each other. The assemblies have only peaceably resolved what they take to be their rights; they have taken no measures for opposition by force; they have not built a fort, raised a man, or provided a grain of ammunition, in order to such opposition. The ringleaders of riots they think ought to be punished; they would punish them themselves, if they could. Every sober sensible man would wish to see rioters punished; as otherwise peaceable people have no security of person or estate. But as to any internal tax, how small soever, laid by the legislature here on the people there, while they have no representatives in this legislature, I think it will never be submitted to. They will oppose it to the last. They do not consider it as at all necessary for you to raise money on them by your taxes, because they are, and always have been, ready to raise money by taxes among themselves, and to grant large sums, equal to their abilities, upon requisition from the Crown. They have not only granted equal to their abilities, but, during all the last war, they granted far beyond their abilities, and beyond their proportion with this country, you yourselves being judges, to the amount of many hundred thousand pounds, and this they did freely and readily, only on a sort of promise from the secretary of state, that it should be recommended to parliament to make them compensation. It was accordingly recommended to parliament, in the most honourable manner, for them. America has been greatly misrepresented and abused here, in papers, and pamphlets, and speeches, as ungrateful, and unreasonable, and unjust, in having put this nation to immense expence for their defence, and refusing to bear any part of that expence. The Colonies raised, paid and clothed, near 25000 men during the last war, a number equal to those sent from Britain, and far beyond their proportion; they went deeply into debt in doing this, and all their taxes and estates are mortgaged, for many years to come, for discharging that debt. Government here was at that time very sensible of this. The Colonies were recommended to parliament. Every year the King sent down to the house a written message to this purpose, That his Majesty, being highly sensible of the zeal and vigour with which his faithful subjects in North-America had exerted themselves, in defence of his Majesty's just rights and possessions, recommended it to the house to take the same into consideration, and enable him to give them a proper compensation. You will find those messages on your own journals every year of the war to the very last, and you did accordingly give 200,000 Pounds annually to the Crown, to be distributed in such compensation to the Colonies. This is the strongest of all proofs that the Colonies, far from being unwilling to bear a share of the burthen, did exceed their proportion; for if they had done less, or had only equalled their proportion, there would have been no room or reason for compensation. Indeed the sums reimbursed them, were by no means adequate to the expence they incurred beyond their proportion; but they never murmured at that; they esteemed their Sovereign's approbation of their zeal and fidelity, and the approbation of this house, far beyond any other kind of compensation; therefore there was no occasion for this act, to force money from a willing people; they had not refused giving money for the purposes of the act; no requisition had been made; they were always willing and ready to do what could reasonably be expected from them, and in this light they wish to be considered.

[123] Q. But suppose Great-Britain should be engaged in a war in Europe, would North-America contribute to the support of it?

A. I do think they would, as far as their circumstances would permit. They consider themselves as a part of the British empire, and as having one common interest with it; they may be looked on here as foreigners, but they do not consider themselves as such. They are zealous for the honour and prosperity of this nation, and, while they are well used, will always be ready to support it, as far as their little power goes. In 1739 they were called upon to assist in the expedition against Carthagena, and they sent 3000 men to join your army. It is true Carthagena is in America, but as remote from the Northern Colonies, as if it had been in Europe. They make no distinction of wars, as to their duty of assisting in them. I know the last war is commonly spoke of here as entered into for the defence, or for the sake of the people of America. I think it is quite misunderstood. It began about the limits between Canada and Nova-Scotia, about territories to which the Crown indeed laid claim, but were not claimed by any British Colony; none of the lands had been granted to any Colonist; we had therefore no particular concern or interest in that dispute. As to the Ohio, the contest there began about your right of trading in the Indian country, a right you had by the treaty of Utrecht, which the French infringed; they seized the traders and their goods, which were your manufactures; they took a fort which a company of your merchants, and their factors and correspondents, had erected there, to secure that trade. Braddock was sent with an army to re-take that fort (which was looked on here as another incroachment on the King's territory) and to protect your trade. It was not till after his defeat that the Colonies were attacked. They were before in perfect peace with both French and Indians; the troops were not therefore sent for their defence. The trade with the Indians, though carried on in America, is not an American interest. The people of America are chiefly farmers and planters; scarce any thing that they raise or produce is an article of commerce with the Indians. The Indian trade is a British interest; it is carried on with British manufactures, for the profit of British merchants and manufacturers; therefore the war, as it commenced for the defence of territories of the Crown, the property of no American, and for the defence of a trade purely British, was really a British war—and yet the people of America made no scruple of contributing their utmost towards carrying it on, and bringing it to a happy conclusion.

[124] Q. Do you think then that the taking possession of the King's territorial rights, and strengthening the frontiers, is not an American interest?

A. Not particularly, but conjointly a British and an American interest.

[125] Q. You will not deny that the preceding war, the war with Spain, was entered into for the sake of America; was it not occasioned by captures made in the American seas?

A. Yes; captures of ships carrying on the British trade there, with British manufactures.

[126] Q. Was not the late war with the Indians, since the peace with France, a war for America only?

A. Yes; it was more particularly for America than the former, but it was rather a consequence or remains of the former war, the Indians not having been thoroughly pacified, and the Americans bore by much the greatest share of the expence. It was put an end to by the army under General Bouquet; there were not above 300 regulars in that army, and above 1000 Pennsylvanians.

[127] Q. Is it not necessary to send troops to America, to defend the Americans against the Indians?

A. No, by no means; it never was necessary. They defended themselves when they were but an handful, and the Indians much more numerous. They continually gained ground, and have driven the Indians over the mountains, without any troops sent to their assistance from this country. And can it be thought necessary now to send troops for their defence from those diminished Indian tribes, when the Colonies are become so populous, and so strong? There is not the least occasion for it; they are very able to defend themselves.

[128] Q. Do you say there were no more than 300 regular troops employed in the late Indian war?

A. Not on the Ohio, or the frontiers of Pennsylvania, which was the chief part of the war that affected the Colonies. There were garrisons at Niagara, Fort Detroit, and those remote posts kept for the sake of your trade; I did not reckon them, but I believe that on the whole the number of Americans, or provincial troops, employed in the war, was greater than that of the regulars. I am not certain, but I think so.

[129] Q. Do you think the assemblies have a right to levy money on the subject there, to grant to the Crown?

A. I certainly think so; they have always done it.

[130] Q. Are they acquainted with the declaration of rights? And do they know that, by that statute, money is not to be raised on the subject but by consent of parliament?

A. They are very well acquainted with it.

[131] Q. How then can they think they have a right to levy money for the Crown, or for any other than local purposes?

A. They understand that clause to relate to subjects only within the realm; that no money can be levied on them for the Crown, but by consent of parliament. The Colonies are not supposed to be within the realm; they have assemblies of their own, which are their parliaments, and they are in that respect, in the same situation with Ireland. When money is to be raised for the Crown upon the subject in Ireland, or in the Colonies, the consent is given in the parliament of Ireland, or in the assemblies of the Colonies. They think the parliament of Great-Britain cannot properly give that consent till it has representatives from America; for the petition of right expressly says, it is to be by common consent in parliament, and the people of America have no representatives in parliament, to make a part of that common consent.

[132] Q. If the stamp-act should be repealed, and an act should pass, ordering the assemblies of the Colonies to indemnify the sufferers by the riots, would they obey it?

A. That is a question I cannot answer.

[133] Q. Suppose the King should require the Colonies to grant a revenue, and the parliament should be against their doing it, do they think they can grant a revenue to the King, without the consent of the parliament of G. Britain?

A. That is a deep question. As to my own opinion, I should think myself at liberty to do it, and should do it, if I liked the occasion.

[134] Q. When money has been raised in the Colonies, upon requisitions, has it not been granted to the King?

A. Yes, always; but the requisitions have generally been for some service expressed, as to raise, clothe and pay troops, and not for money only.

[135] Q. If the act should pass, requiring the American assemblies to make compensation to the sufferers, and they should disobey it, and then the parliament should, by another act, lay an internal tax, would they then obey it?

A. The people will pay no internal tax; and I think an act to oblige the assemblies to make compensation is unnecessary, for I am of opinion, that as soon as the present heats are abated, they will take the matter into consideration, and, if it is right to be done, they will do it of themselves.

[136] Q. Do not letters often come into the post-offices in America, directed to some inland town where no post goes?

A. Yes.

[137] Q. Can any private person take up those letters, and carry them as directed?

A. Yes; any friend of the person may do it, paying the postage that has occurred.

[138] Q. But must he not pay an additional postage for the distance to such inland town?

A. No.

[139] Q. Can the post-master answer delivering the letter, without being paid such additional postage?

A. Certainly he can demand nothing, where he does no service.

[140] Q. Suppose a person, being far from home, finds a letter in a post-office directed to him, and he lives in a place to which the post generally goes, and the letter is directed to that place, will the post-master deliver him the letter, without his paying the postage receivable at the place to which the letter is directed?

A. Yes; the office cannot demand postage for a letter that it does not carry, or farther than it does carry it.

[141] Q. Are not ferrymen in America obliged, by act of parliament, to carry over the posts without pay?

A. Yes.

[142] Q. Is not this a tax on the ferrymen?

A. They do not consider it as such, as they have an advantage from persons travelling with the post.

[143] Q. If the stamp-act should be repealed, and the Crown should make a requisition to the Colonies for a sum of money, would they grant it?

A. I believe they would.

[144] Q. Why do you think so?

A. I can speak for the Colony I live in; I had it in instruction from the assembly to assure the ministry, that as they always had done, so they should always think it their duty to grant such aids to the Crown as were suitable to their circumstances and abilities, whenever called upon for the purpose, in the usual constitutional manner; and I had the honour of communicating this instruction to that honourable gentleman then minister.

[145] Q. Would they do this for a British concern; as suppose a war in some part of Europe, that did not affect them?

A. Yes, for any thing that concerned the general interest. They consider themselves as a part of the whole.

[146] Q. What is the usual constitutional manner of calling on the Colonies for aids?

A. A letter from the secretary of state.

[147] Q. Is this all you mean, a letter from the secretary of state?

A. I mean the usual way of requisition, in a circular letter from the secretary of state, by his Majesty's command, reciting the occasion, and recommending it to the Colonies to grant such aids as became their loyalty, and were suitable to their abilities.

[148] Q. Did the secretary of state ever write for money for the Crown?

A. The requisitions have been to raise, clothe and pay men, which cannot be done without money.

[149] Q. Would they grant money alone, if called on?

A. In my opinion they would, money as well as men, when they have money, or can make it.

[150] Q. If the parliament should repeal the stamp-act, will the assembly of Pennsylvania rescind their resolutions?

A. I think not.

[151] Q. Before there was any thought of the stamp-act, did they wish for a representation in parliament?

A. No.

[152] Q. Don't you know that there is, in the Pennsylvania charter, an express reservation of the right of parliament to lay taxes there?

A. I know there is a clause in the charter, by which the King grants that he will levy no taxes on the inhabitants, unless it be with the consent of the assembly, or by act of parliament.

[153] Q. How then could the assembly of Pennsylvania assert, that laying a tax on them by the stamp-act was an infringement of their rights?

A. They understand it thus; by the same charter, and otherwise, they are intitled to all the privileges and liberties of Englishmen; they find in the great charters, and the petition and declaration of rights, that one of the privileges of English subjects is, that they are not to be taxed but by their common consent; they have therefore relied upon it, from the first settlement of the province, that the parliament never would, nor could, by colour of that clause in the charter, assume a right of taxing them, till it had qualified itself to exercise such right, by admitting representatives from the people to be taxed, who ought to make a part of that common consent.

[154] Q. Are there any words in the charter that justify that construction?

A. The common rights of Englishmen, as declared by Magna Charta, and the petition of right, all justify it.

[155] Q. Does the distinction between internal and external taxes exist in the words of the charter?

A. No, I believe not.

[156] Q. Then may they not, by the same interpretation, object to the parliament's right of external taxation?

A. They never have hitherto. Many arguments have been lately used here to shew them that there is no difference, and that if you have no right to tax them internally, you have none to tax them externally, or make any other law to bind them. At present they do not reason so, but in time they may possibly be convinced by these arguments.

[157] Q. Do not the resolutions of the Pennsylvania assembly say all taxes?

A. If they do, they mean only internal taxes; the same words have not always the same meaning here and in the Colonies. By taxes they mean internal taxes; by duties they mean customs; these are their ideas of the language.

[158] Q. Have you not seen the resolutions of the Massachusett's Bay assembly?

A. I have.

[159] Q. Do they not say, that neither external nor internal taxes can be laid on them by parliament?

A. I don't know that they do; I believe not.

[160] Q. If the same Colony should say neither tax nor imposition could be laid, does not that province hold the power of parliament can hold neither?3

A. I suppose that by the word imposition, they do not intend to express duties to be laid on goods imported, as regulations of commerce.

[161] Q. What can the Colonies mean then by imposition as distinct from taxes?

A. They may mean many things, as impressing of men, or of carriages, quartering troops on private houses, and the like; there may be great impositions, that are not properly taxes.

[162] Q. Is not the post-office rate an internal tax laid by act of parliament?

A. I have answered that.

[163] Q. Are all parts of the Colonies equally able to pay taxes?

A. No, certainly; the frontier parts, which have been ravaged by the enemy, are greatly disabled by that means, and therefore, in such cases, are usually favoured in our tax-laws.

[164] Q. Can we, at this distance, be competent judges of what favours are necessary?

A. The Parliament have supposed it, by claiming a right to make tax laws for America; I think it impossible.

[165] Q. Would the repeal of the stamp-act be any discouragement of your manufactures? Will the people that have begun to manufacture decline it?

A. Yes, I think they will; especially if, at the same time, the trade is opened again, so that remittances can be easily made. I have known several instances that make it probable. In the war before last, tobacco being low, and making little remittance, the people of Virginia went generally into family manufactures. Afterwards, when tobacco bore a better price, they returned to the use of British manufactures. So fulling mills were very much disused in the last war in Pennsylvania, because bills were then plenty, and remittances could easily be made to Britain for English cloth and other goods.

[166] Q. If the stamp-act should be repealed, would it induce the assemblies of America to acknowledge the rights of parliament to tax them, and would they erase their resolutions?

A. No, never.

[167] Q. Is there no means of obliging them to erase those resolutions?

A. None that I know of; they will never do it unless compelled by force of arms.

[168] Q. Is there a power on earth that can force them to erase them?

A. No power, how great soever, can force men to change their opinions.

[169] Q. Do they consider the post-office as a tax, or as a regulation?

A. Not as a tax, but as a regulation and conveniency; every assembly encouraged it, and supported it in its infancy, by grants of money, which they would not otherwise have done; and the people have always paid the postage.

[170] Q. When did you receive the instructions you mentioned?

A. I brought them with me, when I came to England, about 15 months since.

[171] Q. When did you communicate that instruction to the minister?

A. Soon after my arrival, while the stamping of America was under consideration, and before the bill was brought in.

[172] Q. Would it be most for the interest of Great-Britain, to employ the hands of Virginia in tobacco, or in manufactures?

A. In tobacco to be sure.

[173] Q. What used to be the pride of the Americans?

A. To indulge in the fashions and manufactures of Great-Britain.

[174] Q. What is now their pride?

A. To wear their old cloaths over again, till they can make new ones.

Withdrew.

The END.

On the Price of Corn and Management of the Poor

29 November, 1766

To Messieurs the Public and Co.

I Am one of that class of people that feeds you all, and at present is abus'd by you all; in short I am a *Farmer*.

By your News-papers we are told, that God had sent a very short harvest to some other countries of Europe. I thought this might be in favour to Old England; and that now we should get a good price for our grain, which would bring in millions among us, and make us flow in money, that to be sure is scarce enough.

But the wisdom of Government forbad the exportation.

Well, says I, then we must be content with the market price at home.

No, says my Lords the mob, you sha'n't have that. Bring your corn to market if you dare; we'll sell it for you, for less money, or take it for nothing.

Being thus attack'd by both ends *of the Constitution*, the head and the tail *of Government*, what am I to do?

Must I keep my corn in barn to feed and increase the breed of rats? be it so; they cannot be less thankful than those I have been used to feed.

Are we Farmers the only people to be grudged the profits of honest labour? And why? One of the late scribblers against us gives a bill of fare of the provisions at my daughter's wedding, and proclaims to all the world that we had the insolence to eat beef and pudding! Has he never read that precept in the good book, *Thou shalt not muzzle the mouth of the ox that treadeth out the corn;* or does he think us less worthy of good living than our oxen?

O, but the Manufacturers! the Manufacturers! they are to be favour'd, and they must have bread at a cheap rate!

Hark-ye, Mr. Oaf; The Farmers live splendidly, you say. And pray, would you have them hoard the money they get? Their fine cloaths and furniture, do they make them themselves, or for one another, and so keep the money among them? Or do they employ these your darling Manufacturers, and so scatter it again all over the nation?

My wool would produce me a better price if it were suffer'd to go to foreign markets. But that, Messieurs the Public, your laws will not permit. It must be kept all at home, that our *dear* Manufacturers may have it the cheaper. And then, having yourselves thus lessened our encouragement for raising sheep, you curse us for the scarcity of mutton!

I have heard my grandfather say, that the Farmers submitted to the prohibition on the exportation of wool, being made to expect and believe, that when the Manufacturer bought his wool cheaper, they should have their cloth cheaper. But the deuce a bit. It has been growing dearer and dearer from that day to this. How so? why truly the cloth is exported; and that keeps up the price.

Now if it be a good principle, that the exportation of a commodity is to be restrain'd, that so our own people at home may have it the cheaper, stick to that principle, and go thorough stitch with it. Prohibit the exportation of your cloth, your leather and shoes, your iron ware, and your manufactures of all sorts, to make them all cheaper at home. And cheap enough they will be, I'll warrant you—till people leave off making them.

Some folks seem to think they ought never to be easy, till England becomes another *Lubberland*, where 'tis fancied the streets are paved with penny rolls, the houses tiled with pancakes, and chickens ready roasted cry, come eat me.

I say, when you are sure you have got a good principle, stick to it, and carry it thorough. I hear 'tis said, that though it was *necessary and right* for the M——y to advise a prohibition of the exportation of corn, yet it was *contrary to law;* and also, that though it was *contrary to law* for the mob to obstruct the waggons, yet it was *necessary and right*. Just the same thing, to a tittle. Now they tell me, an act of indemnity ought to pass in favour of the M——y, to secure them from the consequences of having acted illegally. If so, pass another in favour of the mob. Others say, some of the mob ought to be hanged, by way of example. If so, ——but I say no more than I have said before, *when you are sure that you have got a good principle, go thorough with it.*

You say, poor labourers cannot afford to buy bread at a high price, unless they had higher wages. Possibly. But how shall we Farmers be able to afford our labourers higher wages, if you will not allow us to get, when we might have it, a higher price for our corn?

By all I can learn, we should at least have had a guinea a quarter more if the exportation had been allowed. And this money England would have got from foreigners.

But, it seems, we Farmers must take so much less, that the poor may have it so much cheaper.

This operates then as a tax for the maintenance of the poor. A very good thing, you will say. But I ask, Why a partial tax? Why laid on us Farmers only? If it be a good thing, pray, Messrs. the Public, take your share of it, by indemnifying us a little out of your public treasury. In doing a good thing there is both honour and pleasure; you are welcome to your part of both.

For my own part, I am not so well satisfied of the goodness of this thing. I am for doing good to the poor, but I differ in opinion of the means. I think the best way of doing good to the poor, is not making them easy *in* poverty, but leading or driving them *out* of it. In my youth I travelled much, and I observed in different countries, that the more public provisions were made for the poor, the less they provided for themselves, and of course became poorer. And, on the contrary, the less was done for them, the more they did for themselves, and became richer. There is no country in the world where so many provisions are established for them; so many hospitals to receive them when they are sick or lame, founded and maintained by voluntary charities; so many alms-houses for the aged of both sexes, together with a solemn general law made by the rich to subject their estates to a heavy tax for the support of the poor. Under all these obligations, are our poor modest, humble, and thankful; and do they use their best endeavours to maintain themselves, and lighten our shoulders of this burthen? On the contrary, I affirm that there is no country in the world in which the poor are more idle, dissolute, drunken, and insolent. The day you passed that act, you took away from before their eyes the greatest of all inducements to industry, frugality, and sobriety, by giving them a dependance on somewhat else than a careful accumulation during youth and health, for support in age or sickness. In short, you offered a premium for the encouragement of idleness, and you should not now wonder that it has had its effect in the increase of poverty. Repeal that law, and you will soon see a change in their manners. St. Monday[1] , and St. Tuesday, will cease to be holidays. Six *days shalt thou labour*, though one of the old commandments long treated as out of date, will again be looked upon as a respectable precept; industry will increase, and with it plenty among the lower people; their circumstances will mend, and more will be done for their happiness by inuring them to provide for themselves, than could be done by dividing all your estates among them.

Excuse me, Messrs. the Public, if upon this *interesting* subject, I put you to the trouble of reading a little of *my* nonsense. I am sure I have lately read a great deal of *yours;* and therefore from you (at least from those of you who are writers) I deserve a little indulgence. I am, your's, &c.

Arator.

---

1. Franklin's reference to his younger years among the London printers in 1724–26 where the expression "making a St. Monday" represented a printer's absence from work due to weekend dissipation.

On the Propriety of Taxing America

April 11, 1767

To the Printer of the London Chronicle.

Sir,

The propriety of taxing America by laws made here, is frequently handled in public papers and pamphlets by writers, who seem not well acquainted with the circumstances of that country, or with the points in dispute. Will you give me leave, through your paper, to offer some information, that may be of use to them in their future discussions. The following positions are generally taken for granted;

1. That the colonies were settled at the expence of parliament.

2. That they received their constitutions from parliament, which could not be supposed to give away its own powers of taxing them.

3. That they have been constantly protected from the Indians, at the expence of money granted by parliament.

4. That the two last wars were entered into for their protection.

5. That they refused to contribute towards the expence of those wars.

6. That they are great gainers by the event of the last war.

7. That they pay no taxes.

8. That they contend the parliament of Great Britain has no authority over them.

Upon these positions assumed as facts, there has been much declamation, on the unreasonableness, selfishness, ingratitude of the Colonists, (some have even used the word *rebellion*) and government is urged to proceed against them by force of arms. Let us coolly consider these positions, one by one.

1. *That the colonies were settled at the expence of parliament.* If we examine our records, the journals of parliament, we shall not find that a farthing was ever granted for the settling any colonies before the last reign, and then only for Georgia and Nova Scotia, which are still of little value. But the colonies of New-Hampshire, Massachusetts, Rhode-Island, Connecticut, New-York, (as far as the English were concerned in it) New-Jersey, Pensylvania, Maryland, Virginia, North and South Carolina, &c. were settled at the private expence of the adventurers.

2. *That they received their constitutions from parliament, which could not be supposed to give away its own power of taxing them.* The charters themselves shew that they were granted by the King; and the truth is, that parliament had no participation in these grants, and was not so much as consulted upon them. The right to the territory in America, was supposed to be in the King, that is, so far as to exclude the claim of any other European Prince; but in reality was in the tribes of Indians who inhabited it, and from whom the settlers were obliged to purchase or conquer it at *their own expence*, without any expence to parliament. But they settled there with the King's leave, promising him their allegiance, which they hold faithfully to this day.

3. *That they have been constantly protected from the Indians at the expence of parliament.* No grants for that purpose appear on our records, and the fact is, that they protected themselves, at their own expence, for near 150 years after, the first settlement, and never thought of applying to parliament for any aid against the Indians.

4. *That the two last wars were entered into for their protection.* The truth is, that the war with Spain, 1739, was occasioned by the Spaniards interrupting with their guarda costas the British trade, carried on indeed in the American seas, but in British ships chiefly, and wholly with British manufactures. It was, therefore, a war for the protection of our commerce, and not for the protection of the people of America. The last war began

concerning the boundaries of Acadia, a country ceded to the crown by the treaty of Aix-la-Chapelle; the lands in dispute belonged to the crown only, and to no colony or Colonist whatever: Another motive was, the security of the Ohio trade with the Indians, a trade carried on chiefly for account of British merchants, members of that company, and wholly with the manufactures of Britain, which had also all the skins and furs produced by that trade. It was, therefore, a British interest, that was to be defended and secured by that war. The colonies were in peace, and the settlers had not been attacked or molested in the least, 'till after the miscarriage of Braddock's expedition to the Ohio.

5. *That the colonies refused to contribute their share towards the expence of those wars.* The fact is, that in the first war, upon requisitions from the crown, the colonies sent between 3 and 4000 men to join our army in the siege of Carthagena; and in the last war they raised and paid 25,000 men, a number equal to those sent from Britain; which was far beyond their proportion. If we examine the journals of the house of commons, we shall there find, that their conduct was approved of by government here; for every year during the war, a message came down from the crown to this purpose, "That his Majesty being highly sensible of the great zeal and vigour with which his faithful subjects in America had exerted themselves in defence of his rights and territories there, recommended it to parliament to enable him to make them some compensation, &c." The parliament did accordingly grant £200,000 yearly for that purpose, which his Majesty divided among the colonies in honorary gratuities; not to discharge their accounts, for they produced none, and their expence was ten times greater than the money returned to them. But if they had not in our own judgment done their share, and more, there could have been no room or reason for any payment, or any compensation.

6. *That the colonies are great gainers by the event of the last war.* There is to be sure a great extent of country conquered. It was however ceded not to the colonies, but to the crown, which is now granting it away in large tracts to British gentlemen. No colony has more landed property than it had

before the war; and though it may be supposed the land the colonists had in possession was increased in value by being rendered more secure, the fact is otherwise; for it is in land as in other commodities, the greater the quantity at market, the lower the price; so that the value of the old possessions is really diminished instead of being increased. Plenty of money was indeed circulated in the colonies by means of the war, but this was a temporary advantage only, and by introducing habits of luxury and expence before unknown there, the money is not only all returned already to Britain, and with it what money there was before in the colonies, but has left them under a load of debt to the British merchants, that they must now labour hard to discharge; besides the heavy public debt incurred by the war itself.

7. *That the colonies pay no taxes*. There cannot be a greater mistake than this. They have their own civil and military establishments to support, and the public debt just mentioned to discharge, for which heavy taxes are and must be levied among themselves. They are besides under great burthens that we are free from. Our ancestors in Britain have long since defrayed the expence of most of our publick buildings, churches, colleges, highways, bridges, and other conveniences, which are left to us as an inheritance: These our people who remove to America cannot enjoy, but as they extend their settlements, are obliged to tax themselves anew for all such publick works: And all who know their circumstances, and the taxes they really pay, are and must be satisfied, that those taxes in proportion to the property in the country, are not only equal but greater than the taxes paid in Britain compared with the property in Britain.

8. *That the colonies contend the parliament of Britain has no authority over them*. The truth is, that all acts of the British legislature, expressly extending to the colonies, have ever been received there as laws, and executed in their courts, the right of parliament to make them being never yet contested, acts to raise money upon the colonies by internal taxes only and alone excepted. In granting their money to the crown, they think their assent is constitutionally necessary; they say that voluntary grants by themselves of what is their own, are the only means they have of manifest-

ing their loyalty and duty, and recommending themselves to the favour of their sovereign. That they have always made such grants chearfully when required, in proportion to their abilities: And they think it hard that a parliament in which they have no representative, should make a merit to itself by granting *their money* to the crown without asking their consent, and deprive them of the privilege of granting it themselves, which they have always enjoyed, never abused, and are always ready and willing to exercise in behalf of the crown when occasion shall require, and the usual requisitions are made to their assemblies. This is the *sole point* that has been in dispute: It is now indeed determined here by an act of parliament, and therefore I say no more of it; and should not have said so much but to obviate mistakes of what the point really was. The colonies submit to pay all external taxes laid on them by way of duty on merchandizes imported into their country, and never disputed the authority of parliament to lay such duties. The distinction indeed between internal and external taxes is here looked upon as groundless and frivolous, and some are apt to wonder how a sensible people should ever advance it. But an American founds it thus; an internal tax to be raised in the colonies by authority of parliament, forces the money out of my purse without the consent of my representative in assembly: An external tax or duty is added to the first cost and other charges of the commodity on which it is laid, and makes a part of its price: If I do not like it, at that price I refuse it. If I do like it, I pay the price, and do not need to give my consent by my representative for the payment of this tax, because I can consent to it myself in person. However, whether there be validity in this distinction or not, seems to be immaterial; since if they are willing to pay *external* though not *internal* taxes, and we say they are the same, 'tis then the same thing to us, provided we get the same money from them, as much as they ought or are able to pay, and we may let them please themselves with their futile distinction as long as they think proper.

There is however another distinction of theirs, which will here appear less exceptionable. The colonies were originally chartered companies for the purposes of trade and settlement. They joined a more than equal number of troops with ours in the operations of the American war: Advantages were obtained by that war, to wit, greater security of trade and settlement free from the interruptions of the French, and a great extent of territory and dominion. In dividing these advantages they suppose, that the security of trade and settlement only belongs to them, and that the territory and dominion acquired appertain to the crown. They never pretended to lay claim to the least part of either of these latter advantages. Their adversaries, who think *another trading Company* (in exactly *similar* circumstances) have a right to both, must at least allow, on the same principle, that the colonies in this particular are modest, however silly it may have been in them to waive their pretentions in favour of government. And probably, whenever these Gentlemen come again into power, a regard to justice, and a noble disdain to take advantage of the simplicity and ignorance of the colonists, will induce them to give the colonies all the same advantages now claimed for that other company.

I hope, Mr. Printer, that your Readers will, on considering the premises, be a little less hasty in censuring their brethren in America, upon the groundless surmises, and mistaken facts, so frequently delivered as truths in our public papers; and that they will consider the importance of a firm union between the two countries, in affection as well as in government; and not suffer themselves to be exasperated by false insinuations against the *absent* and the *distant*. I am, yours, &c.

BENEVOLUS.

Of Lightning, and the Method (Now Used in America) of Securing Buildings and Persons from Its Mischievous Effects

September, 1767

Paris

Experiments made in electricity first gave philosophers a suspicion that the matter of lightning was the same with the electric matter. Experiments afterwards made on lightning obtained from the clouds by pointed rods, received into bottles, and subjected to every trial, have since proved this suspicion to be perfectly well founded; and that whatever properties we find in electricity, are also the properties of lightning.

This matter of lightning, or of electricity, is an extream subtile fluid, penetrating other bodies, and subsisting in them, equally diffused.

When by any operation of art or nature, there happens to be a greater proportion of this fluid in one body than in another, the body which has most, will communicate to that which has least, till the proportion becomes equal; provided the distance between them be not too great; or, if it is too great, till there be proper conductors to convey it from one to the other.

If the communication be through the air without any conductor, a bright light is seen between the bodies, and a sound is heard. In our small experiments we call this light and sound the electric spark and snap; but in the great operations of nature, the light is what we call *lightning*, and the sound (produced at the same time, tho' generally arriving later at our ears than the light does to our eyes) is, with its echoes, called *thunder*.

If the communication of this fluid is by a conductor, it may be without either light or sound, the subtle fluid passing in the substance of the conductor.

If the conductor be good and of sufficient bigness, the fluid passes through it without hurting it. If otherwise, it is damaged or destroyed.

All metals, and water, are good conductors. Other bodies may become conductors by having some quantity of water in them, as wood, and other materials used in building, but not having much water in them, they are not good conductors, and therefore are often damaged in the operation.

Glass, wax, silk, wool, hair; feathers, and even wood, perfectly dry are non-conductors: that is, they resist instead of facilitating the passage of this suble fluid.

When this fluid has an opportunity of passing through two conductors, one good, and sufficient, as of metal, the other not so good, it passes in the best, and will follow it in any direction.

The distance at which a body charged with this fluid will discharge itself suddenly, striking through the air into another body that is not charged, or not so highly charg'd, is different according to the quantity of the fluid, the dimensions and form of the bodies themselves, and the state of the air between them. This distance, whatever it happens to be between any two bodies, is called their *striking distance*, as till they come within that distance of each other, no stroke will be made.

The clouds have often more of this fluid in proportion than the earth; in which case as soon as they come near enough (that is, within the striking distance) or meet with a conductor, the fluid quits them and strikes into the earth. A cloud fully charged with this fluid, if so high as to be beyond the striking distance from the earth, passes quietly without making noise or giving light; unless it meets with other clouds that have less.

Tall trees, and lofty buildings, as the towers and spires of churches, become sometimes conductors between the clouds and the earth; but not being good ones, that is, not conveying the fluid freely, they are often damaged.

Buildings that have their roofs covered with lead, or other metal, and spouts of metal continued from the roof into the ground to carry off the water, are never hurt by lightning, as whenever it falls on such a building, it passes in the metals and not in the walls.

When other buildings happen to be within the striking distance from such clouds, the fluid passes in the walls whether of wood, brick or stone, quitting the walls only when it can find better conductors near them, as metal rods, bolts, and hinges of windows or doors, gilding on wainscot, or frames of pictures; the silvering on the backs of looking-glasses; the wires for bells; and the bodies of animals, as containing watry fluids. And in passing thro' the house it follows the direction of these conductors, taking as many in it's way as can assist it in its passage, whether in a strait or crooked line, leaping from one to the other, if not far distant from each other, only rending the wall in the spaces where these partial good conductors are too distant from each other.

An iron rod being placed on the outside of a building, from the highest part continued down into the moist earth, in any direction strait or crooked, following the form of the roof or other parts of the building, will receive the lightning at its upper end, attracting it so as to prevent its striking any other part; and, affording it a good conveyance into the earth, will prevent its damaging any part of the building.

A small quantity of metal is found able to conduct a great quantity of this fluid. A wire no bigger than a goose quill, has been known to conduct (with safety to the building as far as the wire was continued) a quantity of lightning that did prodigious damage both above and below it; and probably larger rods are not necessary, tho' it is common in America, to make them of half an inch, some of three quarters, or an inch diameter.

The rod may be fastened to the wall, chimney, &c. with staples of iron. The lightning will not leave the rod (a good conductor) to pass into the wall (a bad conductor), through those staples. It would rather, if any were in the wall, pass out of it into the rod to get more readily by that conductor into the earth.

If the building be very large and extensive, two or more rods may be placed at different parts, for greater security.

Small ragged parts of clouds suspended in the air between the great body of clouds and the earth (like leaf gold in electrical experiments), often serve as partial conductors for the lightning, which proceeds from one of them to another, and by their help comes within the striking distance to the earth or a building. It therefore strikes through those conductors a building that would otherwise be out of the striking distance.

Long sharp points communicating with the earth, and presented to such parts of clouds, drawing silently from them the fluid they are charged with, they are then attracted to the cloud, and may leave the distance so great as to be beyond the reach of striking.

It is therefore that we elevate the upper end of the rod six or eight feet above the highest part of the building, tapering it gradually to a fine sharp point, which is gilt to prevent its rusting.

Thus the pointed rod either prevents a stroke from the cloud, or, if a stroke is made, conducts it to the earth with safety to the building.

The lower end of the rod should enter the earth so deep as to come at the moist part, perhaps two or three feet; and if bent when under the surface so as to go in a horizontal line six or eight feet from the wall, and then bent again downwards three or four feet, it will prevent damage to any of the stones of the foundation.

A person apprehensive of danger from lightning, happening during the time of thunder to be in a house not so secured, will do well to avoid sitting near the chimney, near a looking glass, or any gilt pictures or wainscot; the safest place is in the middle of the room, (so it be not under a metal lustre suspended by a chain) sitting in one chair and laying the feet up in another. It is still safer to bring two or three mattrasses or beds into the middle of the room, and folding them up double, place the chair upon them; for they not being so good conductors as the walls, the lightning will not chuse an interrupted course through the air of the room and the bedding, when it can go thro' a continued better conductor the wall. But where it can be had, a hamock or swinging bed, suspended by silk cords equally distant from the walls on every side, and from the cieling and floor above and below, affords the safest situation a person can have in any room whatever; and what indeed may be deemed quite free from danger of any stroke by lightning.

B.F.

On Smuggling

24 November, 1767

To the Printer of the London Chronicle.

Sir,

There are many people that would be thought, and even think themselves *honest men*, who fail nevertheless in particular points of honesty, deviating from that character sometimes by the prevalence of mode or custom, and sometimes through mere inattention; so that their honesty is *partial* only, and not *general* or universal. Thus one who would scorn to over-reach you in a bargain, shall make no scruple of tricking you a little now and then at cards. Another, that plays with the utmost fairness, shall with great freedom cheat you in the sale of a horse. But there is no kind of dishonesty into which otherwise good people more easily and frequently fall, than that of defrauding government of its revenues, by smuggling when they have an opportunity, or encouraging smugglers by buying their goods.

I fell into these reflections the other day, on hearing two gentlemen of reputation discoursing about a small estate, which one of them was inclined to sell, and the other to buy; when the seller, in recommending the place, remarked, that its situation was very advantageous on this account, that being on the seacoast, in a smuggling country, one had frequent opportunities of buying many of the expensive articles used in a family, such as tea, coffee, chocolate, brandy, wines, cambricks, Brussels laces, French silks, and all kinds of India goods, 20, 30, and in some articles 50 per cent cheaper than they could be had in the more interior parts, of traders that paid duty. The other *honest* Gentleman allowed this to be an advantage, but insisted that the seller, in the advanced price he demanded on that account, rated the advantage much above its value. And neither of them seemed to think dealing with Smugglers a practice that an *honest* man (provided he got his goods cheaper) had the least reason to be ashamed of.

At a time when the load of our public debt and the heavy expence of maintaining our fleets and armies to be ready for our defence on occasion, makes it necessary not only to continue old taxes but often to look out for new ones perhaps it may not be unuseful to state this matter in a light that few seem to have considered it in.

The people of Great Britain under the happy constitution of this country, have a privilege few other Countries enjoy, that of chusing the third branch of the legislature, which branch has alone the power of regulating their taxes. Now whenever the government finds it necessary for the common benefit, advantage and safety of the nation, for the security of our liberties, property, religion, and every thing that is dear to us, that certain sums shall be yearly raised by taxes, duties, &c. and paid into the publick treasury, thence to be dispensed by government for those purposes, ought not every *honest man* freely and willingly to pay his just proportion of this necessary expence? Can he possibly preserve a right to that character, if by any fraud, stratagem, or contrivance, he avoids that payment in whole or in part.

What should we think of a companion, who having sup'd with his friends at a tavern, and partaken equally of the joys of the evening with the rest of us, would nevertheless contrive by some artifice to shift his share of the reckoning upon others, in order to go off scot-free? If a man who practis'd this would when detected, be deem'd and called a scoundrel; what ought he to be called, who can enjoy all the inestimable benefits of publick society, and yet by smuggling or dealing with smugglers, contrive to evade paying his just share of the expence, as settled by his own Representatives in Parliament, and wrongfully throw it upon his honester and perhaps much poorer neighbours? He will perhaps be ready to tell me, that he does not wrong his neighbours, he scorns the imputation; he only cheats the King a little, who is very able to bear it. This however is a mistake. The publick treasure is the treasure of the nation, to be apply'd for national purposes. And when a duty is laid for a particular publick and necessary purpose, if through smuggling that duty falls short of raising the sum required, and other duties must therefore be laid to make up the deficiency, all the additional sum laid by the new duties, and paid by other people, though it should amount to no more than a halfpenny or a farthing per head, is so much actually picked out of the pockets of those other people by the smugglers and their abettors and encourages. Are they then any better or other than pickpockets? And what mean, low, rascally pickpockets must those be that can pick pockets for half pence and for farthings?

I would not however be suppos'd to allow in what I have just said, that cheating the King is a less offence against honesty, than cheating the Publick. The King and the Publick in this case are different names for the same thing. But if we consider the King distinctly, it will not lessen the crime. It is no justification of a robbery that the person robbed was rich and able to bear it. The King has as much right to justice as the meanest of his subjects. And as He is truly the common *father* of his people, those that rob him fall under the scripture woe, pronounced against the son, *that robbeth his father, and saith it is no sin.*[1]

Mean as this practice is, do we not daily see people of character and fortune engaged in it for trifling advantages to themselves? Is any Lady ashamed to request of a Gentleman of her acquaintance, that when he returns from abroad, he would smuggle her home a piece of silk or lace from France or Flanders? Is any Gentleman ashamed to undertake and execute the commission? Not in the least. They will talk of it freely, even

---

1. *Proverbs 28:24* Whoso robbeth his father or his mother, and saith, It is no transgression; the same is the companion of a destroyer.

before others whose pockets they are thus contriving to pick by this piece of knavery!

Among other branches of the revenue, that of the Post-Office is by a late law, appropriated to the discharge of our publick debt, and to defray the expences of the State. None but members of parliament and a few publick officers have now a right to avoid by a frank, the payment of postage. Whenever any letter not written by them or on their business, is franked by any of them, 'tis a hurt to the revenue; an injury which they must now take the pains to conceal by writing the whole superscription themselves. And yet such is our insensibility to justice in this particular, that nothing is more common than to see, even in reputable company, a *very honest* Gentleman or Lady declare his or her Intention to cheat the nation of threepence by a frank, and without blushing apply to one of the very Legislators themselves, with a modest request that he would please to become an accomplice in the crime, and assist in the perpetration of it.

There are those who by these practices take a great deal in a year out of the publick purse, and put the money into their own private pockets. If passing through a room where publick treasure is deposited, a man takes the opportunity of clandestinely pocketing and carrying off a guinea, is he not truly and properly a thief? And if another evades paying into the Treasury a guinea that he ought to pay in, and applies it to his own use, when he knows it belongs to the publick as much as that which has been paid in, what difference is there in the nature of the crime, or the baseness of committing it?

Some laws make the receiving of stolen goods equally penal with stealing, and upon this principle, that if there were no receivers there would be few thieves. Our proverb too says truly, that *the receiver is as bad as the thief*. By the same reasoning, as there would be few smugglers, if there were none who knowingly encouraged them by buying their goods, we may say that the encouragers of smuggling are as bad as the smugglers; and that as smugglers are a kind of thieves, both equally deserve the punishments of thievery.

In this view of wronging the revenue, what must we think of those who can evade paying for their wheels and their plate, in defiance of law and justice, and yet declaim against corruption and peculation, as if their own hands and hearts were pure and unsullied? The Americans offend us grievously, when, contrary to our laws, they smuggle goods into their own country: and yet they had no hand in making those laws. I do not however pretend from thence to justify them. But I think the offence much greater in those who either directly or indirectly have been concerned in making the very laws they break. And when I hear them exclaiming against the Americans, and for every little infringement of the arts of trade, or obstruction given by a petty mob to an officer of our customs in that country, calling for vengeance against the whole people as Rebels and Traitors, I cannot help thinking there are still those in the world who can *see a mote in their brother's eye, while they do not discern a beam in their own*; and that the old saying is as true now as ever it was, *one man may better steal a horse, than another look over the hedge.*

F.B.

On Railing and Reviling

6 January, 1768

To the Printer of the Gazetteer

Instead of raving (with your correspondent of yesterday) against the Americans as "diggers of pits for this country," "lunaticks," "sworn enemies," "false," "ungrateful," "cut-throats," &c. which is a treatment of customers that I doubt is not like to bring them back to our shop; I would recommend to all writers on American affairs (however *hard* their *arguments* may be) *soft words*, civility, and good manners. It is only from a redress of grievances and equitable regulations of commerce, with mild and reasonable measures of government, permitting and securing to those people the full enjoyment of their privileges, that we may hope to recover the affection and respect of that great and valuable part of our fellow subjects, and restore and confirm the solid union between the two countries, that is so necessary to the strength and stability of the whole empire. Railing and reviling can answer no good end; it may make the breach wider; it can never heal it.

Old England *in its Senses.*[1]

1. The previous day the London-based *Gazetteer* published a scathing critique of the Boston Non-importation resolutions, a boycott by Boston merchants in response to the Stamp Act, signing their demeaning remonstration - Old England.

A New Version of the Lord's Prayer

1768

Old Version

1. Our Father which art in Heaven.
2. Hallowed be thy Name.
3. Thy Kingdom come.
4. May thy Laws be obeyed on Earth as perfectly as they are in Heaven.
5. Give us this Day our daily Bread.
6. Forgive us our Debts as we forgive our Debtors.
7. And lead us not into Temptation, but deliver us from Evil.

New Version, by B.F.

1. Heavenly Father,
2. May all revere thee,
3. And become thy dutiful Children and faithful Subjects.
4. May thy Laws be obeyed on Earth as perfectly as they are in Heaven.
5. Provide for us this Day as thou has hitherto daily done.
6. Forgive us our Trespasses, and enable us likewise to forgive those that offend us.
7. Keep us out of Temptation, and deliver us from Evil.

Reasons for the Change of Expression

Old Version. *Our Father which art in Heaven*

New V. *Heavenly Father*, is more concise, equally expressive, and better modern English.

Old. *Hallowed be thy Name.* This seems to relate to an Observance among the Jews not to pronounce the proper or peculiar Name of God, they deeming it a Profanation so to do. We have in our Language no *proper Name* for God; the Word *God* being a common or general Name, expressing all chief Objects of Worship, true or false. The Word *hallowed* is almost obsolete: People now have but an imperfect Conception of the Meaning of the Petition. It is therefore proposed to change the Expression into

New. *May all revere thee.*

Old V. *Thy Kingdom come.* This Petition seems suited to the then Condition of the Jewish Nation. Originally their State was a Theocracy: God was their King. Dissatisfied with that kind of Government, they desired a visible earthly King in the manner of the Nations round them. They had such King's accordingly; but their Happiness was not increas'd by the Change, and they had reason to wish and pray for a Return of the Theocracy, or Government of God. Christians in these Times have other Ideas when they speak of the Kingdom of God, such as are perhaps more adequately express'd by

New V. *And become thy dutiful Children and faithful Subjects.*

Old V. *Thy Will be done on Earth as it is in Heaven.* More explicitly,

New V. *May thy Laws be obeyed on Earth as perfectly as they are in Heaven.*

Old V. *Give us this Day* our *daily Bread.* Give us what is *ours*, seems to put in a Claim of Right, and to contain too little of the grateful Acknowledgment and Sense of Dependance that becomes Creatures who live on the daily Bounty of their Creator. Therefore it is changed to

New V. *Provide for us this Day, as thou hast hitherto daily done.*

Old V. *Forgive us our Debts as we forgive our Debtors.* Matthew. *Forgive us our Sins, for we also forgive every one that is indebted to us.* Luke.

Offerings were *due* to God on many Occasions by the Jewish Law, which when People could not pay, or had forgotten as Debtors are apt to do, it was proper to pray that those Debts might be forgiven. Our Liturgy uses neither the *Debtors* of Matthew, nor the *indebted* of Luke, but instead of them speaks of *those that trespass against us*. Perhaps the Considering it as a Christian Duty to forgive Debtors, was by the Compilers thought an inconvenient Idea in a trading Nation. There seems however something presumptious in this Mode of Expression, which has the Air of proposing ourselves as an Example of Goodness fit for God to imitate. *We hope you will at least be as good as we are*; you see we forgive one another, and therefore we pray that you would forgive us. Some have considered it in another Sense, *Forgive us* as *we forgive others*; i.e. If we do not forgive others we pray that thou wouldst not forgive us. But this being a kind of conditional *Imprecation* against ourselves, seems improper in such a Prayer; and therefore it may be better to say humbly and modestly

New V. *Forgive us our Trespasses, and enable us likewise to forgive those that offend us.* This instead of assuming that we have already in and of ourselves the Grace of Forgiveness, acknowledges our Dependance on God, the Fountain of Mercy, for any Share we may have of it, praying that he would communicate of it to us.

Old V. *And lead us not into Temptation.* The Jews had a Notion, that God sometimes tempted, or directed or permitted the Tempting of People. Thus it was said he tempted Pharaoh; directed Satan to tempt Job; and a false Prophet to tempt Ahab, &c. Under this Persuasion it was natural for them to pray that he would not put them to such severe Trials. We now suppose that Temptation, so far as it is supernatural, comes from the Devil only; and this Petition continued, conveys a Suspicion which in our present Conceptions seems unworthy of God, therefore might be altered to

New V. Keep *us* out of *Temptation*.

Endorsed: Lord's Prayer

B. Franklin's Version of
The Lord's Prayer.

Heavenly Father, may all revere thee, and become thy dutiful Children and faithful Subjects; may thy Laws be obeyed on Earth as perfectly as they are in Heaven: Provide for us this Day as thou hast hitherto daily done: Forgive us our Trespasses, and enable us likewise to forgive those that offend us. Keep us out of Temptation, and deliver us from Evil.

Endorsed: New Version of the Lord's Prayer with Notes.

Positions to Be Examined

4 April, 1769

1 All Food or Subsistence for Mankind arise from the Earth or Waters.

2 Necessaries of Life that are not Foods, and all other Conveniencies, have their Values estimated by the Proportion of Food consumed while we are employed in procuring them.

3 A small People with a large Territory may subsist on the Productions of Nature, with no other Labour than that of gathering the Vegetables and catching the Animals.

4 A large People with a small Territory finds these insufficient, and, to subsist, must labour the Earth to make it produce greater Quantities of vegetable Food, suitable for the Nourishment of Men, and of the Animals they intend to eat.

5 From the Labour arises a *great Increase* of vegetable and animal Food, and of Materials for Clothing, as Flax, Wool, Silk, &c. The Superfluity of these is Wealth. With this Wealth we pay for the Labour employed in building our Houses, Cities, &c. which are therefore only Subsistence thus metamorphosed.

6 *Manufactures* are only *another Shape* into which so much Provisions and Subsistence are turned as were *equal in Value* to the Manufactures produced. This appears from hence, that the Manufacturer does not in fact, obtain from the Employer, for his Labour, *more* than a mere Subsistence, including Raiment Fuel and Shelter; all which derive their Value from the Provisions consumed in procuring them.

7 The Produce of the Earth, thus converted into Manufactures, may be more easily carried to distant Markets than before such Conversion.

8 *Fair* Commerce is where equal Values are exchanged for equal the Expence of Transport included. Thus if it costs A. in England as much Labour and Charge to raise a Bushel of Wheat as it costs B. in France to produce four Gallons of Wine then are four Gallons of Wine the fair Exchange for a Bushel of Wheat. A and B meeting at half Distance with their Commodities to make the Exchange. The Advantage of this fair Commerce is, that each Party increases the Number of his Enjoyments, having, instead of Wheat alone or Wine alone, the Use of both Wheat and Wine.

9 Where the Labour and Expence of producing both Commodities are known to both Parties Bargains will generally be fair and equal. Where they are known to one Party only, Bargains will often be unequal, Knowledge taking its Advantage of Ignorance.

10 Thus he that carries 1000 Bushels of Wheat abroad to sell, may not probably obtain so great a Profit thereon as if he had first turned the Wheat into Manufactures by subsisting therewith the Workmen while producing those Manufactures: since there are many expediting and facilitating Methods of working, not generally known; and Strangers to the Manufactures, though they know pretty well the Expences of raising Wheat, are unacquainted with those short Methods of working, and thence being apt to suppose more Labour employed in the Manufactures than there really is, are more easily imposed on in their Value, and induced to allow more for them than they are honestly worth.

11 Thus the Advantage of having Manufactures in a Country, does not consist as is commonly supposed, in their highly advancing the Value of rough Materials, of which they are formed; since, though sixpenny worth of Flax may be worth twenty shillings when worked into Lace, yet the very Cause of it's being worth twenty shillings is, that besides the Flax, it has cost nineteen shillings and sixpence in Subsistence to the Manufacturer. But the Advantage of Manufactures is, that under their shape Provisions may

be more easily carried to a foreign Market; and by their means our Traders may more easily cheat Strangers. Few, where it is not made are Judges of the Value of Lace. The importer may demand Forty, and perhaps get Thirty shillings for that which cost him but twenty.

12 Finally, there seem to be but three Ways for a Nation to acquire Wealth. The first is by *War*as the Romans did in plundering their conquered Neighbours. This is *Robbery*. The second by *Commerce* which is generally *Cheating*. The third by *Agriculture* the only *honest Way*; wherein Man receives a real Increase of the Seed thrown into the Ground, in a kind of continual Miracle wrought by the Hand of God in his Favour, as a Reward for his innocent Life, and virtuous Industry.

B F

Part VII

3 NOVEMBER, 1770 - 8 SEPTEMBER, 1777

An Expostulation

The Rise and Present State of Our Misunderstanding

On Claims to the Soil of America

Rules by Which a Great Empire May Be Reduced to a Small One

An Edict by the King of Prussia

The Declaration of Independence

Comparison of Great Britain and America as to Credit, in 1777

An Expostulation

3 November, 1770

For the Public Advertiser

An American, *to those* Englishmen *who virulently write and talk against his* Countrymen, *sends this Expostulation:*

If it be true, as some of you say it is, that our Non-Importation Agreements are not observed, but that we clandestinely import and consume as much British Goods as ever, why are you so angry with us, and why do you propose compelling us to trade with you by Force?

If, as others of you say, we do indeed generally forbear importing at present, but must soon from Necessity be obliged to break our Agreements, can't you have a little Patience?

Can you Englishmen think your abusing us in all the British Papers as Rebels, Knaves, Fools, Traitors, &c. &c. will put us into a better Humour, make us more inclined to come to your Shop, buy your Superfluities, and follow your Fashions?

Are you absolutely certain that there are no possible Means whereby we may supply ourselves with Conveniences and Necessaries without importing them from Britain?

If through the high Price of Labour, Manufactures are, as you assert, impracticable in America, cannot you be quiet, and let us convince ourselves of our own Folly by Experience, since that will make our future Commercial Connexions with you still stronger, and discourage future Attempts when perhaps become more practicable? Is it mere Good-will to us, and Fear of our hurting ourselves by such Attempts, that you take such

Pains to prove they cannot succeed? Or is it to convince Government that we may be used very ill, without the least Danger of Prejudice to your Trade and Manufactures?

If those Colonies, that entered into the Non-Importation Agreement, have done it, as some of you assert, because they are in bad Circumstances, deep in Debt to your Merchants, and on the Verge of Bankruptcy, can their refusing to take more of your Goods, and get deeper into your Debt, be so heinous a Crime as to provoke your calling down upon them National Vengeance?

If the Colonists are indeed generally such bad Paymasters; if your Factors and Agents among them find such infinite Difficulties in getting in your Debts; if the People of America are such a set of Hypocrites, Knaves and Cheats as you represent them to be, why, in the Name of Common-sense, are you so desirous of continuing the Commerce with them? Why in such Rage at their refusing it? Why in such Raptures when you heard that a few in New York had broken through the Agreement?

If the American Trade is of so little Consequence to this Nation, as others of you tell us, that your Merchants and Manufacturers do not miss it, that additional Demands from other Countries more than supply the Loss of it, and that it is not therefore of the smallest Importance whether the Americans are pleased or displeased with any Treatment they may receive from Britain, would you then punish them for doing you no Injury? If the Trade be only advantageous to them, cannot you leave them (like froward Children that quarrel with their Bread and Butter) to punish themselves by going without it?

On the other Hand, if our Commerce and Friendship are of some Advantage to you, while you are exasperating this Country against the Colonies by Misrepresentations and Falsehoods, if you are at the same Time by your Abuses so exasperating that Country against this, as that they will from Resentment exert themselves more earnestly to give Encouragement, and finally should succeed in every Manufacture, as they have already in several, will your Country then think that you have been doing it Service?

Don't you suppose it possible that civil Dissentions may encourage foreign Insults? Can you conceive the least Use in destroying all mutual Regard and Affection between Britain and America? Can you imagine a more diabolical Employment than that of fomenting Mischief, sowing the Seeds of Civil War, provoking a Prince against his Subjects, Fathers against their Children, and promoting deadly Feuds between different Branches of the same Family?

Do you think it impossible that England may ever need Assistance from the Colonies? Do you think it quite out of the Course of human Affairs that Britons should ever have Occasion to seek an Asylum in America? Would it not be more comfortable to you and your Children to find there LIBERTY and Friends, than SLAVERY and Enemies?

The Rise and Present State of Our Misunderstanding

8 November, 1770

To the Printer *of the* London Chronicle,

Sir,

Much abuse has lately been thrown out against the Colonies, by the Writers for the American part of our Administration. Our Fellow Subjects there are continually represented as Rebels to their Sovereign, and inimical to the British nation; in order to create a dislike of them here, that the harsh measures which have been taken, and are intended against them, may not be blamed by the People of England. Therefore to prevent our being led into mistakes in so important a business, it is fit that a full and particular account of the rise and present state of our misunderstanding with the Colonies should be laid before the Public. This, from the opportunities I have had, and the pains I have taken to inform myself, I think I am enabled to do, and I hope I shall do it with truth and candor.

The fact then is, that there is not nor has been any rebellion in America. If the rescue of a seizure by Smugglers, or the drubbing an Informer or low Custom-house Officer, were rebellion, England, Scotland, and Ireland, might be said to be in rebellion almost every week in the year; and instances of that kind are much fewer in America than here. The Americans were ever attached to the House of Hanover, and honour their present gracious Sovereign sincerely. This is therefore a groundless calumny. Nor have they any enmity to Britain: they love and honour the name of Englishman; they were fond of English manners, fashions, and manufactures; they had no desire of breaking the connection between the two countries, but wished a perpetual intercourse of good offices, commerce, and friendship. They are always willing to give aids to the Crown in proportion to their abilities: They think, however, and have always thought, that they themselves have alone the right of granting their own money, by their own Representatives in Assembly met, and that the Parliament of Britain hath no right to raise a revenue from them without their consent.

The Parliament hath, nevertheless, of late made several attempts to raise such a revenue among them.

Heretofore, whenever the Colonies thought themselves aggrieved by British government, they applied for redress by humble petition; and it was usual to receive and consider their petitions, and give them a reasonable answer.

They proceeded in the same manner on the late occasions. They sent over petitions after petitions to the House of Commons, and some to the House of Lords. These were scarce any of them received. Some (offered while the acts were under consideration) were refused on this reason, that it was against an order of the House to receive petitions against money bills; others, because they contained expressions that called the right of Parliament in question; and therefore, it was said, no Member dared to present them. Finding the petitions of separate Colonies were not attended to, they thought to give them more weight by petitioning jointly. To this end a congress of Committees from all the Assemblies was held at New York, when petitions to the King and both Houses of Parliament were agreed to and sent hither. But these could not be received, or were rejected, on the pretence that the congress was an illegal assembly which had no right to petition. Lastly, on occasion of the Duty Act, the Assemblies proposed by a correspondence with each other to obtain attention, by sending at the same time similar petitions. These were intended to the King their Sovereign, requesting his gracious influence with his Parliament to procure them redress. But this they were told by the American Minister was a FLAGITIOUS attempt! All the Governors were by him directed to prevent it, or to dissolve the Assemblies that persisted in it; and several of them were accordingly dissolved. And of those petitions that nevertheless came hither and were presented, it is said that no notice was ever taken, or any answer given to them.

By this management the ancient well contrived channel of communication between the head and members of this great Empire, thro' which the notice of grievances could be received that remedies might be applied, hath been cut off. How wisely, the Publick will judge. History of a similar conduct in the Ministry of Spain with regard to the Low Countries, makes one doubt a little the prudence (in any Government how great soever) of discouraging Petitions, and treating Petitioners (how mean soever) with contempt.

Instead of *preventing* complaints by removing the causes, it has been thought best that Soldiers should be sent to *silence* them.

The Soldiers have behaved in such a manner as to occasion more complaints.

They took possession of the publick building in which the Assembly or Parliament of New England usually convenes, obliged the Members to pass through lanes of men in arms to get to their Chamber, disturbing them in their debates by drumming and piping in and round the House, and pointed the cannon against the doors, treating the Province and People with every indignity and insult, proper to provoke their resentment, and produce some rash action that might justify making a massacre among them. And they have fired upon and murdered several of the inhabitants.

The Americans, upon the treatment their Petitions had repeatedly received, determined to petition no more: But said to one another, "We are too remote from Britain to have our complaints regarded by the Parliament there, especially as we have no share in their Election, nor any Representatives among them. They will not hear *us*, but perhaps they will hear *their own people*, their Merchants and Manufacturers, who are maintained and enriched in some degree by the commerce with our country. Let us agree to with-hold that commerce till our grievances are redressed. This will afford those people a foundation for petitioning, and they will be attended to as they were on a former occasion, and meet with success." This reasoning and expectation were the sole foundation of the Non-Importation agreements in America, and *not any enmity to Britain.*

In this expectation it seems they were mistaken. The Merchants trading to North America not well liking the Ministry, unwilling to solicit or be obliged to them for any thing, and hoping soon to see a change for others more to their mind, were backward in petitioning the Parliament. And when they did petition, the City being out of favour at Court, their Petition was very little attended to, and produced no effect. To prevent the Manufacturers from taking any part in the affair, they have been artfully amused with assurances that the Colonies could not long subsist without the trade, that manufactures among themselves were impossible, that they might depend there would be an extraordinary demand for goods as soon as the total want of conveniencies should compel the Americans to resume the commerce; and therefore they would do well to be quiet, mind their business, and get a great stock of goods beforehand to be ready for that demand, when the advanced price would make them ample amends for the delay.

In the mean time the Merchants in America have reaped great advantages. They have sold off most of the old goods that lay upon their hands; they have got in most of their debts from the people, and have in a great measure discharged their debt to England, that bore a heavy interest; this they have done at an advantage of near 20 per cent. in most of the Colonies, by the lowness of exchange, occasioned by the non-importation; and this nation has lost near that proportion (if I am rightly informed) on all the money drawn for these by British Agents, to pay and provide for the troops and ships of war, and to discharge other expences of contingent service. This loss must amount to a very great sum, besides the loss in commerce.

Many of these Merchants in America, however, having nearly compleated these points, and seeing the main end of their agreement, (the total abolition of the duties) not likely to be so soon obtained as they expected, begin to grow uneasy under the delay, and are rather desirous of altering the agreement made against general importation, and reducing it to the exclusion of those commercial articles only, on which the duties are, or shall be imposed. But the generality of the people in America, the artizans in the towns, and the farmers throughout the country, finding the non-importation advantageous to them all; to the artisans, as it occasions fuller employment, and encourages the beginners that introduce new arts; and to the farmers, as it prevents much useless expence in their families, and thereby enables them more expeditiously to improve their plantations to the raising a greater produce, at the same time that it is a spur to domestic industry, in such manufactures as though not fine, are now become fashionable and reputable, and from their superior strength are much more serviceable than the flimsy fineries that used to be made for them in Britain; and all feeling the advantage of having had money returned into the country for its produce, from Spain, Portugal, Italy, (and even from England since the balance of trade has turned against her) instead of those British superfluities for which all that cash was formerly remitted, or ordered into England. I say, the generality of the people in America, pleased with this situation of things, and relishing the sweets of it, have now taken the lead in a great degree, out of the hands of the Merchants, and in town and county meetings are entering into solemn resolutions not to purchase or consume British commodities, if they are imported, till the acts they esteem injurious to their privileges are repealed: and that if any Merchants do import before that time, they will mark them as enemies to their country, and never deal with them when the trade shall be opened. This is now become a restraint upon the Merchants. A party, however, of those at New-York, have broken through the agreement, and ordered goods; and the Merchants here, who had long lain idle, being rejoiced at this opening, have sent them over immense quantities, expecting a quick sale and speedy returns. But the event is yet very uncertain. The trade of New-York was chiefly with East New Jersey and Connecticut, their two neighbouring Colonies, and these have resolved to have no farther dealings with that city. Several counties, too, of the Province of New-York, and the greatest part of the inhabitants of the city itself, have protested against the infraction of the agreement, and determined not to buy or use the goods when they arrive. So that the exporters begin now to apprehend that their sanguine hopes will be disappointed. And as Rhode Island has returned to the agreement, some think it not unlikely that New-York may do the same.

What remedy, if any, the wisdom of Parliament shall think fit to apply to these disorders, a little time will shew. Mean while, I cannot but think that those writers, who busily employ their talents in endeavouring to exasperate this nation against the Colonies, are doing it a very ill office: For their virulent writings being dispersed among the inhabitants of the Plantations (who read all our papers and pamphlets, and imagine them of greater estimation here than they really are) do in some degree irritate the Colonists against a country which treats them, as they imagine, think so injuriously: And on our side, as nothing is likely to be well done that is done in anger; as customers are not naturally brought back to a shop by unkind usage; as the Americans are growing, and soon will be, a great people, and their friendship or enmity become daily of more and more consequence; as their fisheries, their coasting trade, their West-Indian and European Trades, greatly increase the numbers of English seamen, and thereby augment our naval power; as their joint operations with our's in time of war must make the whole national effort more weighty and more effectual; as enmities between countries, fostered and promoted till they have taken root, are scarce ever to be eradicated; and, when those countries are under the same Prince, such enmities are of the most mischievous consequence, encouraging foreign enemies, weakening the whole empire, and tending to its dissolution; therefore I cannot but wish, that no steps may be taken against the Colonists, tending to abridge their privileges, alter their charters, or inflict punishments on them, at the instance of *angry Governors, discarded Agents, or rash indiscreet Officers of the Customs*, who, having quarrelled with them, are their enemies, and are daily irritating Government here against them, by misrepresentations of their actions, and aggravations of their faults, with much malice: I hope the great principle of common justice, that *no man should be condemned unheard*, will not by us be violated in the case of a whole people; and that lenient measures will be adopted as most likely to heal the wound effectually: For harsh treatment may increase the inflammation, make the cure less practicable, and in time bring on the necessity of an amputation; death indeed to the severed limb, weakness and lameness to the mutilated body.

N.N.

On Claims to the Soil of America

16 March, 1773

To the Printer of the Public Advertiser.

SIR,

YOUR anonymous Correspondent in last Tuesday's Paper calls it *Arrogance* to place the Subjects in America and the Subjects in Great Britain upon a Level; and to prove it, asks and answers "from whom do the People of Great Britain hold their Lands? From no People under Heaven. From whom do most of the Inhabitants in North America hold their Lands? NOT FROM THEMSELVES, but from Great Britain. Does one Foot of Land on the Banks of the Missisippi belong to the American Colonists? No, the Lands on the Eastern Bank of the Mississippi, for the Extent of 1000 Miles, *are the* PROPERTY of the People of Great Britain, or of the King, as Trustee for the People of Great Britain." Thus far your positive Correspondent. To me, however it seems, that the Subjects in the two Countries are more upon a Level than he imagines. Britain was formerly the America of the Germans. They came hither in their Ships; found the *Cream* of the Land possessed by a Parcel of Welsh Caribbs, whom they judged unworthy of it, and therefore drove them into the Mountains, and sat down in their Places. These Anglo-Saxons, our Ancestors, came *at their own Expence*, and therefore supposed that when they had secured the new Country, they held it of themselves, and of no other People under Heaven. Accordingly we do not find that their Mother Country, Germany, ever pretended to tax them; nor is it likely, if she had, that they would have paid it. So far then the Level is clear; for unless Great Britain had a Property in the Lands of America before the Colonists went thither, it does not appear how they could take Lands of her to hold on any Terms. Now the Fact is well known, that Britain had not a Foot of Land in New-England; and that when the first Settlers went into that Country, they found it possessed by various Tribes of Indians, from whom they either purchased or conquered what they now enjoy. European Nations have indeed pretended, some, that the Pope could give them a Right to the Lands of America; others, that, sailing along a Coast there, landing on some Beach unseen by the Natives, and branding a Post with the Arms of their own Country, created a Right to as much of the internal Territory as they should afterwards think proper to claim. But "one would hardly imagine" as your Writer says, "that such Nonsense could find Advocates." And yet he himself tells us, "the Lands on the Eastern Bank of the Mississippi are *the Property* of the People of Great Britain." That is, the French claimed them because one of their Nation discovered them by sailing down that River in a Canoe, and at the End of the last War gave up that Claim to the English. Whatever Right this Conquest conferred, give me Leave to say, is as much a Right of the Colonies as of Great Britain; for they had Man for Man with her in the Armies that fought for it.

But if Englishmen should come with this Parchment Right in their Hands, and bid an Indian Nation, settled there, remove in Consequence of it, I believe they would say, what your Correspondent says on the other Side of the Question, "that it is directly contrary to the Nature of Things and to Common-sense." Thus, Cassini, the French Astronomer, discovered with his Telescope that District in the Moon, which, in Honour of his Sovereign, he called Louisiana. By a successful War, perhaps, we might oblige Louis to give it up, and agree that it should henceforth, in all Maps of the Moon be called Nova Britannia, and be held by King George as Trustee for the People of Great Britain. But if Englishmen could *fly* as well as *sail*, and arriving there should claim the Country upon that Right, the native Inhabitants, to acknowledge and submit to it must be *Lunatics* indeed.

In Fact, neither the Grantor nor the Grantees of these chimerical Rights, ever understood more by them than that they were an Exclusion of other Englishmen from the respective Boundaries of each Grant. The Grantees, to obtain some Title, were obliged to purchase of the Indians, or conquer them *at their own Charges*. And if they had insisted that the Crown should put them in Possession of what it granted, the Grant would probably never have been made. This Purchase and Conquest, with the Expence of settling and clearing the Lands, have occasioned many of the Grants to be relinquished, as not worth holding. And most of those who went thro' with their Undertakings find they have dearly earned or paid for what they now possess. And yet, notwithstanding what this Writer says, I believe he cannot produce an Instance since the Settlement of the Country, of any one Colonist's Refusal to pay the stipulated Quit-rent to the Crown, on any Pretence whatever. His Accusation, therefore, in this Point is injurious and quite without Foundation.

Since a good Understanding between the Parts of a great Empire is the Strength of the Whole, what beneficial End can it answer to represent the Colonists here as unreasonable and unjust, if they object to a Compliance with Exactions they think unconstitutional? Perpetual Abuse and false Representation, may exasperate and alienate on both Sides. It may divide. It can never unite. This Writer says, "The Colonists will most graciously accept of Land from Great Britain for nothing; but should Great Britain *ask for* a small Part of the Produce of those Lands to help to defray the Public Expence, the Colonist immediately cries out he is treated as a Slave, and robbed of his Property." Now it happens that Facts shew this Charge also to be groundless; and that the Writer does not, in his own Phrase, use "the Words of *Truth* and Soberness." The Grant of Lands *for nothing*, I have already spoken to; and I here add, that Great Britain never *asked for* a small or any Part of the Produce of those Lands to help defray the Public Expence, but it was immediately, voluntarily and freely *given*, in Proportion to the Abilities of the People. But there is some Difference between *asking* and *taking by Force*. The *old* Way, and the best, in my humble

Opinion, was for the Crown to *ask* Supplies, and then they were granted to an Extent beyond its Expectations. The new Way is to make an Act of Parliament to levy Duties on the Colonies without asking, and send a Fleet and Army to enforce it. A Landlord engaged in an expensive Law-suit may borrow Money of his Tenants who respect him, or by shewing them that their Interest in the Event is the same with his, he may receive their voluntary Contributions towards the Support of his Litigation; but if he should declare that he has a Right to take from them whatever he thinks proper, and should go from House to House among them with a Parcel of armed Servants, extorting Money Sword in Hand, perhaps it might be justly called *Robbery*; at least it would be manifest that the Want of Money was not his only Want—that he wanted Honesty—and it would be found in the End that he also wanted Understanding.

As a Friend to both Countries, being connected with both, I wish Governor Hutchinson had thought of some other Subject for his Speech, and not revived needlessly a Dispute that can end in nothing but Mischief. I am sure he could not expect to convince an Individual there by such known false Facts and sophistical Reasoning. Here the Discourse appears plausible by chiming in with national and ministerial Prejudices, and therefore I think it written to recommend himself here, and not to do Service there. It has been industriously printed and circulated here before the Assembly's Answer could come over. To that however I leave it, only reminding its Readers of the equitable Rule, *Audi et alteram partem*.[1]

The hacknied Argument of your Correspondent, that all the Freeholders in America ought to be taxed by Parliament, though they have no Share in the Choice of its Members, because many People in England are so taxed without having any Share in that Choice, seems to be arguing from bad to worse. If any here are unjustly deprived of that Privilege, restore it. Do right at home, if you please, and then make that a Precedent for doing

1. *Hear the other side.*

right abroad: But never think that doing wrong at home will justify your doing wrong all the World over. The Argument is a Confession indeed, but contains not the least Shadow of a Justification. I am, Sir,

A NEW ENGLAND-MAN

Rules by Which a Great Empire May Be Reduced to a Small One

11 September, 1773

For the Public Advertiser.

Rules *by which a* great Empire *may be reduced to a* small one. [Presented privately to a *late Minister*, when he entered upon his Administration; and now first published.]

An ancient Sage valued himself upon this, that tho' he could not fiddle, he knew how to make a *great City* of a *little one*. The Science that I, a modern Simpleton, am about to communicate is the very reverse.

I address myself to all Ministers who have the Management of extensive Dominions, which from their very Greatness are become troublesome to govern, because the Multiplicity of their Affairs leaves no Time for *fiddling*.

I. In the first Place, Gentlemen, you are to consider, that a great Empire, like a great Cake, is most easily diminished at the Edges. Turn your Attention therefore first to your remotest Provinces; that as you get rid of them, the next may follow in Order.

II. That the Possibility of this Separation may always exist, take special Care the Provinces are never incorporated with the Mother Country, that they do not enjoy the same common Rights, the same Privileges in Commerce, and that they are governed by *severer* Laws, all of *your enacting*, without allowing them any Share in the Choice of the Legislators. By carefully making and preserving such Distinctions, you will (to keep to my Simile of the Cake) act like a wise Gingerbread Baker, who, to facilitate a

Division, cuts his Dough half through in those Places, where, when bak'd, he would have it *broken to Pieces.*

III. These remote Provinces have perhaps been acquired, purchas'd, or conquer'd, at the *sole Expence* of the Settlers or their Ancestors, without the Aid of the Mother Country. If this should happen to increase her *Strength* by their growing Numbers ready to join in her Wars, her *Commerce* by their growing Demand for her Manufactures, or her *Naval Power* by greater Employment for her Ships and Seamen, they may probably suppose some Merit in this, and that it entitles them to some Favour; you are therefore to *forget it all*, or resent it as if they had done you Injury. If they happen to be zealous Whigs, Friends of Liberty, nurtur'd in Revolution Principles, *remember all that* to their Prejudice, and contrive to punish it: For such Principles, after a Revolution is thoroughly established, are of *no more Use*, they are even *odious* and *abominable.*

IV. However peaceably your Colonies have submitted to your Government, shewn their Affection to your Interest, and patiently borne their Grievances, you are to *suppose* them always inclined to revolt, and treat them accordingly. Quarter Troops among them, who by their Insolence may *provoke* the rising of Mobs, and by their Bullets and Bayonets *suppress* them. By this Means, like the Husband who uses his Wife ill *from Suspicion*, you may in Time convert your *Suspicions* into *Realities.*

V. Remote Provinces must have *Governors*, and *Judges*, to represent the Royal Person, and execute every where the delegated Parts of his Office and Authority. You Ministers know, that much of the Strength of Government depends on the *Opinion* of the People; and much of that Opinion on the Choice of Rulers placed immediately over them. If you send them wise and good Men for Governors, who study the Interest of the Colonists, and advance their Prosperity, they will think their King wise and good, and that he wishes the Welfare of his Subjects. If you send them learned and upright Men for judges, they will think him a Lover of Justice. This may attach your Provinces more to his Government. You are therefore to be careful who you recommend for those Offices. If you can find Prodigals who have ruined their Fortunes, broken Gamesters or Stock-Jobbers, these may do well as *Governors;* for they will probably be rapacious, and provoke the People by their Extortions. Wrangling Proctors and petty-fogging Lawyers too are not amiss, for they will be for ever disputing and quarrelling with their little Parliaments, if withal they should be ignorant, wrong-headed and insolent, so much the better. Attorneys Clerks and Newgate Solicitors will do for *Chief-Justices*, especially if they hold their Places *during your Pleasure*: And all will contribute to impress those ideas of your Government that are proper for a People *you would wish to renounce it*.

VI. To confirm these Impressions, and strike them deeper, whenever the Injured come to the Capital with Complaints of Mal-administration, Oppression, or Injustice, punish such Suitors with long Delay, enormous Expence, and a final Judgment in Favour of the Oppressor. This will have an admirable Effect every Way. The Trouble of future Complaints will be prevented, and Governors and Judges will be encouraged to farther Acts of Oppression and Injustice; and thence the People may become more disaffected, *and at length desperate*.

VII. When such Governors have crammed their Coffers, and made themselves so odious to the People that they can no longer remain among them with Safety to their Persons, recall and *reward* them with Pensions. You may make them *Baronets* too, if that respectable Order should not think fit to resent it. All will contribute to encourage new Governors in the same Practices, and make the supreme Government *detestable*.

VIII. If when you are engaged in War, your Colonies should vie in liberal Aids of Men and Money against the common Enemy, upon your simple Requisition, and give far beyond their Abilities, reflect, that a Penny taken from them by your Power is more honourable to you than a Pound presented by their Benevolence. Despise therefore their voluntary Grants, and resolve to harrass them with novel Taxes. They will probably complain to your Parliaments that they are taxed by a Body in which they have no Representative, and that this is contrary to common Right. They will petition for Redress. Let the Parliaments flout their Claims, reject their

Petitions, refuse even to suffer the reading of them, and treat the Petitioners with the utmost Contempt. Nothing can have a better Effect, in producing the Alienation proposed; for though many can forgive Injuries, *none ever forgave Contempt.*

IX. In laying these Taxes, never regard the heavy Burthens those remote People already undergo, in defending their own Frontiers, supporting their own provincial Governments, making new Roads, building Bridges, Churches and other public Edifices, which in old Countries have been done to your Hands by your Ancestors, but which occasion constant Calls and Demands on the Purses of a new People. Forget the *Restraints* you lay on their Trade for *your own* Benefit, and the Advantage a *Monopoly* of this Trade gives your exacting Merchants. Think nothing of the Wealth those Merchants and your Manufacturers acquire by the Colony Commerce; their encreased Ability thereby to pay Taxes at home; their accumulating, in the Price of their Commodities, most of those Taxes, and so levying them from their consuming Customers: All this, and the Employment and Support of thousands of your Poor by the Colonists, you are *intirely to forget.* But remember to make your arbitrary Tax more grievous to your Provinces, by public Declarations importing that your Power of taxing them has *no limits*, so that when you take from them without their Consent a Shilling in the Pound, you have a clear Right to the other nineteen. This will probably weaken every Idea of *Security in their Property*, and convince them that under such a Government *they have nothing they can call their own;* which can scarce fail of producing *the happiest Consequences*!

X. Possibly indeed some of them might still comfort themselves, and say, "Though we have no Property, we have yet *something* left that is valuable; we have constitutional *Liberty* both of Person and of Conscience. This King, these Lords, and these Commons, who it seems are too remote from us to know us and feel for us, cannot take from us our *Habeas Corpus* Right, or our Right of Trial *by a Jury of our Neighbours:* They cannot deprive us of the Exercise of our Religion, alter our ecclesiastical Constitutions, and compel us to be Papists if they please, or Mahometans." To annihilate this Comfort, begin by Laws to perplex their Commerce with infinite Regulations impossible to be remembered and observed; ordain Seizures of their Property for every Failure; take away the Trial of such Property by Jury, and give it to arbitrary Judges of your own appointing, and of the lowest Characters in the Country, whose Salaries and Emoluments are to arise out of the Duties or Condemnations, and whose Appointments are *during Pleasure*. Then let there be a formal Declaration of both Houses, that Opposition to your Edicts is *Treason*, and that Persons suspected of Treason in the Provinces may, according to some obsolete Law, be seized and sent to the Metropolis of the Empire for Trial; and pass an Act that those there charged with certain other Offences shall be sent away in Chains from their Friends and Country to be tried in the same Manner for Felony. Then erect a new Court of Inquisition among them, accompanied by an armed Force, with Instructions to transport all such suspected Persons, to be ruined by the Expence if they bring over Evidences to prove their Innocence, or be found guilty and hanged if they can't afford it. And lest the People should think you cannot possibly go any farther, pass another solemn declaratory Act, that "King, Lords, and Commons had, hath, and of Right ought to have, full Power and Authority to make Statutes of sufficient Force and Validity to bind the unrepresented Provinces IN ALL CASES WHATSOEVER." This will include *Spiritual* with temporal; and taken together, must operate wonderfully to your Purpose, by convincing them, that they are at present under a Power something like that spoken of in the Scriptures, which can not only *kill their Bodies*, but *damn their Souls* to all Eternity, by compelling them, if it pleases, *to worship the Devil*.

XI. To make your Taxes more odious, and more likely to procure Resistance, send from the Capital a Board of Officers to superintend the Collection, composed of the most *indiscreet, ill-bred* and *insolent* you can find. Let these have large Salaries out of the extorted Revenue, and live in open grating Luxury upon the Sweat and Blood of the Industrious, whom they are to worry continually with groundless and expensive Prosecutions before the above-mentioned arbitrary Revenue-Judges, all *at the Cost of the Party prosecuted* tho' acquitted, because *the King is to pay no Costs*. Let these Men *by your Order* be exempted from all the common Taxes and Burthens of the Province, though they and their Property are protected by its Laws. If any Revenue Officers are *suspected* of the least Tenderness for the People, discard them. If others are justly complained of, protect and reward them. If any of the Under-officers behave so as to provoke the People to drub them, promote those to better Offices: This will encourage others to procure for themselves such profitable Drubbings, by multiplying and enlarging such Provocations, and *all with work towards the End you aim at*.

XII. Another Way to make your Tax odious, is to misapply the Produce of it. If it was originally appropriated for the *Defence* of the Provinces and the better Support of Government, and the Administration of Justice where it may be *necessary*, then apply none of it to that *Defence*, but bestow it where it is *not necessary*, in augmented Salaries or Pensions to every Governor who has distinguished himself by his Enmity to the People, and by calumniating them to their Sovereign. This will make them pay it more unwillingly, and be more apt to quarrel with those that collect it, and those that imposed it, who will quarrel again with them, and all shall contribute to your *main Purpose* of making them *weary of your Government*.

XIII. If the People of any Province have been accustomed to support their own Governors and Judges to Satisfaction, you are to apprehend that such Governors and Judges may be thereby influenced to treat the People kindly, and to do them Justice. This is another Reason for applying Part of that Revenue in larger Salaries to such Governors and Judges, given, as their Commissions are, *during your Pleasure* only, forbidding them to take any Salaries from their Provinces; that thus the People may no longer hope any Kindness from their Governors, or (in Crown Cases) any Justice from their Judges. And as the Money thus mis-applied in one Province is extorted from all, probably *all will resent the Misapplication*.

XIV. If the Parliaments of your Provinces should dare to claim Rights or complain of your Administration, order them to be harass'd with repeated *Dissolutions*. If the same Men are continually return'd by new Elections, adjourn their Meetings to some Country Village where they cannot be accommodated, and there keep them *during Pleasure;* for this, you know, is your Prerogative; and an excellent one it is, as you may manage it, to promote Discontents among the People, diminish their Respect, and *increase their Disaffection*.

XV. Convert the brave honest Officers of your Navy into pimping Tide-waiters and Colony Officers of the Customs. Let those who in Time of War fought gallantly in Defence of the Commerce of their Countrymen, in Peace be taught to prey upon it. Let them learn to be corrupted by great and real Smugglers; but (to shew their Diligence) scour with armed Boats every Bay, Harbour, River, Creek, Cove or Nook throughout the Coast of your Colonies, stop and detain every Coaster, every Wood-boat, every Fisherman, tumble their Cargoes, and even their Ballast, inside out and upside down; and if a Penn'orth of Pins is found un-entered, let the Whole be seized and confiscated. Thus shall the Trade of your Colonists suffer more from their Friends in Time of Peace, than it did from their Enemies in War. Then let these Boats Crews land upon every Farm in their Way, rob the Orchards, steal the Pigs and Poultry, and insult the Inhabitants. If the injured and exasperated Farmers, unable to procure other Justice, should attack the Agressors, drub them and burn their Boats, you are to call this *High Treason* and *Rebellion*, order Fleets and Armies into their Country, and threaten to carry all the Offenders three thousand Miles to be hang'd, drawn and quartered. *O! this will work admirably!*

XVI. If you are told of Discontents in your Colonies, never believe that they are general, or that you have given Occasion for them; therefore do not think of applying any Remedy, or of changing any offensive Measure. Redress no Grievance, lest they should be encouraged to demand the Redress of some other Grievance. Grant no Request that is just and reasonable, lest they should make another that is unreasonable. Take all your Informations of the State of the Colonies from your Governors and Officers in Enmity with them. Encourage and reward these *Leasing-makers;* secrete their lying Accusations lest they should be confuted; but act upon them as the clearest Evidence, and believe nothing you hear from the Friends of the People. Suppose all *their* Complaints to be invented and promoted by a few factious Demagogues, whom if you could catch and hang, all would be quiet. Catch and hang a few of them accordingly; and the *Blood of the Martyrs* shall *work Miracles* in favour of your Purpose.

XVII. If you see *rival Nations* rejoicing at the Prospect of your Disunion with your Provinces, and endeavouring to promote it: If they translate, publish and applaud all the Complaints of your discontented Colonists, at the same Time privately stimulating you to severer Measures; let not that *alarm* or offend you. Why should it? since you all mean *the same Thing*.

XVIII. If any Colony should at their own Charge erect a Fortress to secure their Port against the Fleets of a foreign Enemy, get your Governor to betray that Fortress into your Hands. Never think of paying what it cost the Country, for that would *look*, at least, like some Regard for Justice; but turn it into a Citadel to awe the Inhabitants and curb their Commerce. If they should have lodged in such Fortress the very Arms they bought and used to aid you in your Conquests, seize them all, 'twill provoke like *Ingratitude* added to *Robbery*. One admirable Effect of these Operations will be, to discourage every other Colony from erecting such Defences, and so their and your Enemies may more easily invade them, to the great Disgrace of your Government, and of course *the Furtherance of your Project*.

XIX. Send Armies into their Country under Pretence of protecting the Inhabitants; but instead of garrisoning the Forts on their Frontiers with those Troops, to prevent Incursions, demolish those Forts, and order the Troops into the Heart of the Country, that the Savages may be encouraged to attack the Frontiers, and that the Troops may be protected by the Inhabitants: This will seem to proceed from your Ill will or your Ignorance, and contribute farther to produce and strengthen an Opinion among them, *that you are no longer fit to govern them*.

XX. Lastly, Invest the General of your Army in the Provinces with great and unconstitutional Powers, and free him from the Controul of even your own Civil Governors. Let him have Troops enow under his Command, with all the Fortresses in his Possession; and who knows but (like some provincial Generals in the Roman Empire, and encouraged by the universal Discontent you have produced) he may take it into his Head to set up for himself. If he should, and you have carefully practised these few *excellent Rules* of mine, take my Word for it, all the Provinces will immediately join him, and you will that Day (if you have not done it sooner) get rid of the Trouble of governing them, and all the *Plagues* attending their *Commerce* and Connection from thenceforth and for ever.

Q.E.D.

An Edict by the King of Prussia

22 September, 1773

For the Public Advertiser.

The Subject of the following Article of Foreign Intelligence being exceeding extraordinary, is the Reason of its being separated from the usual Articles of *Foreign News.*

Dantzick, September 5.

We have long wondered here at the Supineness of the English Nation, under the Prussian Impositions upon its Trade entering our Port. We did not till lately know the *Claims,* antient and modern, that hang over that Nation, and therefore could not suspect that it might submit to those Impositions from a Sense of *Duty,* or from Principles of *Equity.* The following *Edict,* just made public, may, if serious, throw some Light upon this Matter.

"Frederick, by the Grace of God, King of Prussia, &c. &c. &c. to all present and to come, Health. The Peace now enjoyed throughout our Dominions, having afforded us Leisure to apply ourselves to the Regulation of Commerce, the Improvement of our Finances, and at the same Time the easing our *Domestic Subjects* in their Taxes: For these Causes, and other good Considerations us thereunto moving, We hereby make known, that after having deliberated these Affairs in our Council, present our dear Brothers, and other great Officers of the State, Members of the same, We, of our certain Knowledge, full Power and Authority Royal, have made and issued this present Edict, viz.

Whereas it is well known to all the World, that the first German Settlements made in the Island of Britain, were by Colonies of People, Subjects to our renowned Ducal Ancestors, and drawn from *their* Dominions, under the Conduct of Hengist, Horsa, Hella, Uffa, Cerdicus, Ida, and others; and that the said Colonies have flourished under the Protection of our august House, for Ages past, have never been *emancipated* therefrom, and yet have hitherto yielded little Profit to the same. And whereas We Ourself have in the last War fought for and defended the said Colonies against the Power of France, and thereby enabled them to make Conquests from the said Power in America, for which we have not yet received adequate Compensation. And whereas it is just and expedient that a Revenue should be raised from the said Colonies in Britain towards our Indemnification; and that those who are Descendants of our antient Subjects, and thence still owe us due Obedience, should contribute to the replenishing of our Royal Coffers, as they must have done had their Ancestors remained in the Territories now to us appertaining: We do therefore hereby ordain and command, That from and after the Date of these Presents, there shall be levied and paid to our Officers of the Customs, on all Goods, Wares and Merchandizes, and on all Grain and other Produce of the Earth exported from the said Island of Britain, and on all Goods of whatever Kind imported into the same, a *Duty* of *Four and an Half* per Cent. *ad Valorem*, for the Use of us and our Successors. And that the said Duty may more effectually be collected, We do hereby ordain, that all Ships or Vessels bound from Great Britain to any other Part of the World, or from any other Part of the World to Great Britain, shall in their respective Voyages touch at our Port of Koningsberg, there to be unladen, searched, and charged with the said Duties.

And whereas there have been from Time to Time discovered in the said Island of Great Britain by our Colonists there, many Mines or Beds of Iron Stone; and sundry Subjects of our antient Dominion, skilful in converting the said Stone into Metal, have in Times past transported themselves thither, carrying with them and communicating that Art; and the

Inhabitants of the said Island, *presuming* that they had a natural Right to make the best Use they could of the natural Productions of their Country for their own Benefit, have not only built Furnaces for smelting the said Stone into Iron, but have erected Plating Forges, Slitting Mills, and Steel Furnaces, for the more convenient manufacturing of the same, thereby endangering a Diminution of the said Manufacture in our antient Dominion. WE *do therefore* hereby farther ordain, that from and after the Date hereof, no Mill or other Engine for Slitting or Rolling of Iron, or any Plating Forge to work with a Tilt-Hammer, or any Furnace for making Steel, shall be erected or continued in the said Island of Great Britain: And the Lord Lieutenant of every County in the said Island is hereby commanded, on Information of any such Erection within his County, to order and by Force to cause the same to be abated and destroyed, as he shall answer the Neglect thereof to Us at his Peril. But We are nevertheless graciously pleased to permit the Inhabitants of the said Island to transport their Iron into Prussia, there to be manufactured, and to them returned, they paying our Prussian Subjects for the Workmanship, with all the Costs of Commission, Freight and Risque coming and returning, any Thing herein contained to the contrary notwithstanding.

WE do not however think fit to extend this our Indulgence to the Article of *Wool*, but meaning to encourage not only the manufacturing of woollen Cloth, but also the raising of Wool in our antient Dominions, and to prevent *both*, as much as may be, in our said Island, We do hereby absolutely forbid the Transportation of Wool from thence even to the Mother Country Prussia; and that those Islanders may be farther and more effectually restrained in making any Advantage of their own Wool in the Way of Manufacture, We command that none shall be carried *out of oneCounty into another*, nor shall any Worsted-Bay, or Woollen-Yarn, Cloth, Says, Bays, Kerseys, Serges, Frizes, Druggets, Cloth-Serges, Shalloons, or any other Drapery Stuffs, or Woollen Manufactures whatsoever, made up or mixt with Wool in any of the said Counties, be carried into any other County, or be Waterborne even across the smallest River or Creek, on Penalty of

Forfeiture of the same, together with the Boats, Carriages, Horses, &c. that shall be employed in removing them. *Nevertheless* Our loving Subjects there are hereby permitted, (if they think proper) to use all their Wool as *Manure for the Improvement of their Lands.*

AND WHEREAS the Art and Mystery of making *Hats* hath arrived at great Perfection in Prussia, and the making of Hats by our remote Subjects ought to be as much as possible restrained. And forasmuch as the Islanders before-mentioned, being in Possession of Wool, Beaver, and other Furs, have *presumptuously* conceived they had a Right to make some Advantage thereof, by manufacturing the same into Hats, to the Prejudice of our domestic Manufacture, WE do therefore hereby strictly command and ordain, that no Hats or Felts whatsoever, dyed or undyed, finished or unfinished, shall be loaden or put into or upon any Vessel, Cart, Carriage or Horse, to be transported or conveyed *out of one County* in the said Island *into another County*, or to *any other Place whatsoever*, by any Person or Persons whatsoever, on Pain of forfeiting the same, with a Penalty of *Five Hundred Pounds* Sterling for every Offence. Nor shall any Hat-maker in any of the said Counties employ more than two Apprentices, on Penalty of *Five Pounds* Sterling per Month: We intending hereby that such Hat-makers, being so restrained both in the Production and Sale of their Commodity, may find no Advantage in continuing their Business. But lest the said Islanders should suffer Inconveniency by the Want of Hats, We are farther graciously pleased to permit them to send their Beaver Furs to Prussia; and We also permit Hats made thereof to be exported from Prussia to Britain, the People thus favoured to pay all Costs and Charges of Manufacturing, Interest, Commission to Our Merchants, Insurance and Freight going and returning, as in the Case of Iron.

And lastly, Being willing farther to favour Our said Colonies in Britain, We do hereby also ordain and command, that all the Thieves, Highway and Street-Robbers, House-breakers, Forgerers, Murderers, So[domi]tes, and Villains of every Denomination, who have forfeited their Lives to the Law in Prussia, but whom We, in Our great Clemency, do not think fit here to hang, shall be emptied out of our Gaols into the said Island of Great Britain *for the* BETTER PEOPLING *of that Country.*

We flatter Ourselves that these Our Royal Regulations and Commands will be thought *just* and *reasonable* by Our much-favoured Colonists in England, the said Regulations being copied from their own Statutes of 10 and 11 Will. iii. C. 10[1], 5 Geo. ii. C. 22[2], 23 Geo. ii. C. 29[3], 4 Geo. i. C. 11[4], and from other equitable Laws made by their Parliaments, or from Instructions given by their Princes, or from Resolutions of both Houses entered into for the GOOD *Government* of their own Colonies in Ireland and America.

---

1. Wool Act of 1699: Prohibited American colonists from exporting wool or wool products outside of the colony in which it was produced. Banned the export of sheep to the colonies in order to protect England's wool industry.

2. Hat Act of 1732: Intended to protect the British hat-making industry by prohibiting the export of hats from one colony to another or to foreign markets, and by limiting the number of apprentices that could be trained by colonial hat makers.

3. Iron Act of 1750: Intended to suppress the development of colonial manufacturing in competition with home industry by restricting the growth of the American iron industry to the supply of raw metals. See *Observations Concerning the Increase of Mankind, Peopling of Countries, &c.*

4. Transportation Act of 1717: Led to the sentencing and transportation of more than 50,000 criminals to America by 1775. After the Revolutionary War, Britain transported criminals to Australia from 1787–1868. See *Felons and Rattlesnakes.*

And all Persons in the said Island are hereby cautioned not to oppose in any wise the Execution of this Our Edict, or any Part thereof, such Opposition being HIGH TREASON, of which all who are *suspected* shall be transported in Fetters from Britain to Prussia, there to be tried and executed according to the *Prussian Law.*

Such is our Pleasure.

Given at Potsdam this twenty-fifth Day of the Month of August, One Thousand Seven Hundred and Seventy-three, and in the Thirty-third Year of our Reign.

By the King in his Council

RECHTMAESSIG, *Secr.*"

Some take this Edict to be merely one of the King's *Jeux d'Esprit*[5] *:* Others suppose it serious, and that he means a Quarrel with England: But all here think the Assertion it concludes with, "that these Regulations are copied from Acts of the English Parliament respecting their Colonies," a very *injurious* one: it being impossible to believe, that a People distinguish'd for their *Love of Liberty*, a Nation so *wise*, so *liberal in its Sentiments*, so *just and equitable* towards its *Neighbours*, should, from mean and *injudicious* Views of *petty immediate Profit*, treat *its own Children* in a Manner so *arbitrary* and TYRANNICAL!

5. *Games of Wit*

The Declaration of Independence

4 July, 1776

In CONGRESS, July 4, 1776.

The Unanimous Declaration of the thirteen United States of America

When in the Course of human events, it becomes necessary for one people to dissolve the political bands which have connected them with another, and to assume among the powers of the earth, the separate and equal station to which the Laws of Nature and of Nature's God entitle them, a decent respect to the opinions of mankind requires that they should declare the causes which impel them to the separation. We hold these truths to be self-evident, that all men are created equal, that they are endowed by their Creator with certain unalienable Rights, that among these are Life, Liberty and the pursuit of Happiness. That to secure these rights, Governments are instituted among Men, deriving their just powers from the consent of the governed, That whenever any Form of Government becomes destructive of these ends, it is the Right of the People to alter or to abolish it, and to institute new Government, laying its foundation on such principles and organizing its powers in such form, as to them shall seem most likely to effect their Safety and Happiness. Prudence, indeed, will dictate that Governments long established should not be changed for light and transient causes; and accordingly all experience hath shewn, that mankind are more disposed to suffer, while evils are sufferable, than to right themselves by abolishing the forms to which they are accustomed. But when a long train of abuses and usurpations, pursuing invariably the same Object evinces a design to reduce them under absolute Despotism, it is their right, it is their duty, to throw off such Government, and to provide new Guards for their future security. Such has been the patient sufferance of these Colonies; and such is now the necessity which constrains them to alter their former Systems of Government. The history of the present King of Great Britain is a history of repeated injuries and usurpations, all having in direct object the establishment of an absolute Tyranny over these States. To prove this, let Facts be submitted to a candid world. He has refused his Assent to Laws, the most wholesome and necessary for the public good.

He has forbidden his Governors to pass Laws of immediate and pressing importance, unless suspended in their operation till his Assent should be obtained; and when so suspended, he has utterly neglected to attend to them.

He has refused to pass other Laws for the accommodation of large districts of people, unless those people would relinquish the right of Representation in the Legislature, a right inestimable to them and formidable to tyrants only.

He has called together legislative bodies at places unusual, uncomfortable, and distant from the depository of their public Records, for the sole purpose of fatiguing them into compliance with his measures.

He has dissolved Representative Houses repeatedly, for opposing with manly firmness his invasions on the rights of the people.

He has refused for a long time, after such dissolutions, to cause others to be elected; whereby the Legislative powers, incapable of Annihilation, have returned to the People at large for their exercise; the State remaining in the mean time exposed to all the dangers of invasion from without, and convulsions within.

He has endeavoured to prevent the population of these States; for that purpose obstructing the Laws for Naturalization of Foreigners; refusing to pass others to encourage their migrations hither, and raising the conditions of new Appropriations of Lands.

He has obstructed the Administration of Justice, by refusing his Assent to Laws for establishing Judiciary powers.

He has made Judges dependent on his Will alone, for the tenure of their offices, and the amount and payment of their salaries.

He has erected a multitude of New Offices, and sent hither swarms of Officers to harrass our people, and eat out their substance.

He has kept among us, in times of peace, standing Armies without the Consent of our legislatures.

He has affected to render the Military independent of and superior to the Civil power.

He has combined with others to subject us to a jurisdiction foreign to our constitution, and unacknowledged by our laws; giving his Assent to their Acts of pretended Legislation: For Quartering large bodies of armed troops among us: For protecting them, by a mock Trial, from punishment for any Murders which they should commit on the Inhabitants of these States: For cutting off our Trade with all parts of the world: For imposing Taxes on us without our Consent: For depriving us in many cases of the benefits of Trial by Jury: For transporting us beyond Seas to be tried for pretended offences: For abolishing the free System of English Laws in a neighbouring Province, establishing therein an Arbitrary government, and enlarging its Boundaries so as to render it at once an example and fit instrument for introducing the same absolute rule into these Colonies: For taking away our Charters, abolishing our most valuable Laws, and altering fundamentally the Forms of our Governments: For suspending our own Legislatures, and declaring themselves invested with power to legislate for us in all cases whatsoever.

He has abdicated Government here, by declaring us out of his Protection and waging War against us.

He has plundered our seas, ravaged our Coasts, burnt our towns, and destroyed the Lives of our people.

He is at this time transporting large Armies of foreign Mercenaries to compleat the works of death, desolation and tyranny, already begun with circumstances of Cruelty & perfidy scarcely paralleled in the most barbarous ages, and totally unworthy the Head of a civilized nation.

He has constrained our fellow Citizens taken Captive on the high Seas to bear Arms against their Country, to become the executioners of their friends and Brethren, or to fall themselves by their Hands.

He has excited domestic insurrections amongst us, and has endeavoured to bring on the inhabitants of our frontiers, the merciless Indian Savages, whose known rule of warfare, is an undistinguished destruction of all ages, sexes and conditions.

In every stage of these Oppressions We have Petitioned for Redress in the most humble terms: Our repeated Petitions have been answered only by repeated injury. A Prince, whose character is thus marked by every act which may define a Tyrant, is unfit to be the ruler of a free people. Nor have We been wanting in attentions to our Brittish brethren. We have warned them from time to time of attempts by their legislature to extend an unwarrantable jurisdiction over us. We have reminded them of the circumstances of our emigration and settlement here. We have appealed to their native justice and magnanimity, and we have conjured them by the ties of our common kindred to disavow these usurpations, which, would inevitably interrupt our connections and correspondence. They too have been deaf to the voice of justice and of consanguinity. We must, therefore, acquiesce in the necessity, which denounces our Separation, and hold them, as we hold the rest of mankind, Enemies in War, in Peace Friends.

We, therefore, the Representatives of the united States of America, in General Congress, Assembled, appealing to the Supreme Judge of the world for the rectitude of our intentions, do, in the Name, and by Authority of the good People of these Colonies, solemnly publish and declare, That these United Colonies are, and of Right ought to be Free and Independent States; that they are Absolved from all Allegiance to the British Crown, and that all political connection between them and the State of Great Britain, is and ought to be totally dissolved; and that as Free and Independent States, they have full Power to levy War, conclude Peace, contract Alliances, establish Commerce, and to do all other Acts and Things which Independent States may of right do. And for the support of this Declaration, with a firm reliance on the protection of divine Providence, we mutually pledge to each other our Lives, our Fortunes and our sacred Honor.

John Hancock
Button Gwinnett Thos. Nelson jr. Richd. Stockton
Lyman Hall Francis Lightfoot Lee Jno Witherspoon
Geo Walton. Carter Braxton Fras. Hopkinson
Wm. Hooper Robt. Morris John Hart
Joseph Hewes, Benjamin Rush Abra Clark
John Penn Benja. Franklin Josiah Bartlett
Edward Rutledge. John Morton Wm: Whipple
Thos. Heyward Junr. Geo Clymer Sami. Adams
Thomas Lynch Junr. Jag. Smith. John Adams
Arthur Middleton Geo. Taylor Robt. Treat Paine
Samuel Chase James Wilson Elbridge Gerry
Wm. Paca Geo. Ross Step. Hopkins
Thos. Stone Cesar Rodney William Ellery
Charles Carroll of Carrollton Geo Read Roger Sherman
Tho McKean Sami. Huntington
George Wythe Wm. Floyd Wm. Williams
Richard Henry Lee Phil. Livingston Oliver Wolcott
Th Jefferson Frans. Lewis Matthew Thornton
Benja. Harrison Lewis Morris
[1]

1. *Authors: Thomas Jefferson, John Adams, Benjamin Franklin, Roger Sherman, Robert Livingston*

Comparison of Great Britain and America as to Credit, in 1777

8 September, 1777

In the Affair of Borrowing Money, a Man's Credit depends on some or all of the following Particulars:

1. His known Conduct with regard to former Loans, in the Punctuality with which he discharg'd them.

2. His Industry in his Business.

3. His Frugality in his Expences.

4. The Solidity of his Funds, his Estate being good, and free of prior Debts, whence his undoubted Ability of Paying.

5. His well-founded Prospects of greater future Ability, by the Improvement of his Estate in Value, and by Aids from others.

6. His known Prudence in Managing his general Affairs, and the Advantage they will probably receive from the present Loan he desires.

7. His known Virtue, and honest Character manifested by his voluntary Discharge of Debts that he could not otherwise have been oblig'd to pay.

The same Circumstances that give a private Man Credit, ought to have and will have their Weight with Lenders of Money to publick Bodies or to Nations.

If then we consider and compare Britain and America in those several Lights, upon the Question to which it is safest to lend Money we shall find

1. *With Regard to former Loans*; that America which borrowed Ten Millions Sterling during the last War for the Maintenance of her Army of 25,000 Men and other Charges, had faithfully *discharg'd* and *paid* that

Debt and all her other Debts, in 1772: whereas Britain during those ten years of Peace and profitable Commerce had made little or no Reduction of her Debt, but on the contrary from time to time diminish'd the Hopes of her Creditors by a wanton Diversion and Misapplication of the Sinking Fund which had been destin'd for the Discharge of it.

2. *With regard to Industry in Business.* Every Man in America is employ'd. The greatest Number in cultivating their own Lands; the rest in Handicrafts, Navigation and Commerce. An idle Man is a Rarity. Idleness and Inutility is a Character of Disgrace. In England the Quantity of that Character is immense. Fashion has spread it far and wide. Hence the Embarassment of private Fortunes and the daily Bankrupcies, arising from the universal fondness for Appearance and expensive Pleasures. And hence in some degree the Mismanagement of their publick Business: For Habits of Business and Ability in it are acquired only by Practice; and where universal Dissipation and the perpetual Pursuit of Amusement are the Mode, the Youth who are educated in it, can rarely afterward acquire that patient Attention and close Application to Affairs, which are so necessary to a Statesman charg'd with the Care of National Welfare. Hence their frequent Errors in Policy. Hence the Weariness at Publick Councils and the Backwardness in going to them; the constant Unwillingness to engage in any Measure that requires Thought and Consideration; and the Readiness for postponing every new Proposition, which postponing is therefore the only Part of Business that they come to be expert in, an Expertness produc'd necessarily by so much daily Practice. Whereas in America, Men bred to close Employment, in their private Affairs, attend with habitual Ease to those of the Publick when engag'd in them, and nothing fails through Negligence.

3. *With regard to Frugality in Expences.* The Manner of Living in America, is in general more simple, and less Expensive than that in England. Plain Tables, plain Clothing, plain Furniture in Houses, few Carriages of Pleasure. In America an expensive Appearance hurts Credit, and is therefore avoided. In England it is often put on with a View of gaining Credit,

and continued to Ruin. In publick Affairs the Difference is still greater. In England Salaries of Officers and Emoluments of Office are enormous. A King has a Million Sterling per Annum, and yet cannot maintain his Family free of Debt, Secretaries of State, Lords of Treasury, Admiralty, &c. have vast Appointments, an Auditor of the Exchequer has, tis Said, 6 pence the Pound or a Fortieth Part of all publick Money expended by the Nation, so that when a War costs 40,000,000 there is a Million for him: an Inspector of the Mint in the last new Coinage received as his Fees £65,000 Sterling a Year, to which Rewards no Service these Gentlemen can render the Public is by any means equivalent. This is all paid by the People, who are oppress'd by the Taxes so occasion'd, and thereby render'd less able to contribute to the Payment of necessary national Debts. In America, Salaries where indispensible are extreamly low, but much of publick Business is done gratis. The Honour of serving the publick ably and faithfully is deemed sufficient. *Public Spirit*really exists there, and has great Effects. In England it is universally deem'd a Non-Entity, and whoever pretends to it, is laugh'd at as a Fool, or suspected as a Knave. The Committees of Congress which form the Board of War, the Board of Treasury, the Naval Board, the Committee for Accounts, the Board of foreign Transactions for procuring Arms Ammunition, Clothing, &c. all attend the Business of their respective Functions without any Salary or Emolument whatever tho' they spend in it much more of their Time than any Lord of Treasury or Admiralty in England can afford from his Amusements. A late British Minister computed that the whole Expence of the Americans in their civil Government of 3,000,000 of People amounted to but £70,000 Sterling per Annum, and drew from thence a Conclusion that they ought to be taxed till their Expence equalled in proportion to what it cost Britain to govern Eight Millions: He had no Idea of a contrary Conclusion, that if 3,000,000 may be well governed for £70,000, Eight Millions may be as well governed for 3 times that Sum, and therefore the Expence of his own Government should be diminished. In that corrupted Nation, no Man is ashamed of being concern'd in lucrative Government Jobbs, in which the public Money is egregiously misapplied, and squandered; the Treasury pillaged; and more numerous and heavier Taxes are called for to the great Oppression of the People; while the Prospect of a greater Number of these Jobbs to be occasion'd by a War is an Inducement with many to cry out for War on all Occasions, and to oppose every Proposition of Peace. Hence the constant Increase of the National Debt, and the absolute Improbability of its ever being discharged.

4. *With Regard to the Solidity of Funds.* The whole 13 States of America are engag'd for the Payment of every Debt contracted by the Congress, and The Debt to be contracted by the present War is the only Debt they will have to pay, all or nearly all the former Debts of particular Colonies being already discharged. Whereas England will have to pay not only the enormous Debt this War must occasion, but all their vast preceding Debt on the Interest of it; and while America is enriching itself by Prizes made upon the British Commerce, more than it ever did by any Commerce of its own, under the Restraints of a British Monopoly, Britain is growing poorer by the Loss of that Monopoly, the Diminution of its Revenues, and of course less able to discharge the present indiscreet Encrease of its Expences.

5. *With Regard to Prospects of greater future Ability.* Britain has none such. Her islands are circumscrib'd by the Ocean. Excepting a few Parks or Forests she has no new Land to cultivate, and cannot therefore extend her Improvements. Her Numbers of People too, instead of Increasing from increas'd Subsistence, are continually diminishing from growing Luxury and the greater Difficulty of maintaining Families, which of course discourages early Marriage. Thus she will have fewer People to assist in paying her Debt, and that diminish'd Number will be poorer. America, on the contrary has besides her Lands already improved, a vast Territory yet to improve: The Lands cultivated continually increase in Value with the Encrease of People, and the People who double themselves by natural Propagation in 25 Years, will double yet faster by the Accession of Strangers as long as Lands are to be had for new Families; so that every 20 years there will be a double Number

of Inhabitants oblig'd to discharge publick Debts, and those Inhabitants being more opulent may pay their Share with greater Ease.

6. *With Regard to Prudence in general Affairs and the Advantages they expect from the Loan desired.* The Americans are Cultivators of Land, those engag'd in Fishery and Commerce are a small Number compar'd with the Body of the People. They have ever conducted their several Governments with Wisdom, avoiding Wars and vain expensive Projects, delighting only in their peaceable Occupations, which must considering the Extent of their yet uncultivated Territory, find them Employment still for Ages: Whereas England ever unquiet, ambitious, avaritious, imprudent, and quarrelsome, is half her time engag'd in some War or other, always at an Expence infinitely greater than the Advantage proposed if it could be obtained. Thus she made a War against Spain in 1739 for a Claim of Debt of about £95,000 (scarce a Groat a Head for the Nation) spent £40,000,000 Sterling in the War, and 50,000 Men, and made Peace without obtaining the Satisfaction demanded. Indeed there is scarce a Nation in Europe against which she has not made War on some frivolous Pretext or other, and by this means has imprudently accumulated a Debt that has brought her on the Verge of Bankrupcy. But the most indiscrete of all her Wars is the present against America, with which she might for Ages have preserv'd her profitable Connection by only a just and equitable Conduct. She is now acting like a mad Shopkeeper who should attempt by beating those that pass his Door to make them come in and be his Customers. America cannot submit to such Treatment without being first ruined, and being ruined her Custom will be worth nothing. And England to bring this to pass is adding to her Debt, and ruining herself effectually. America on the other Hand aims only at establishing her Liberty, and that Freedom of Commerce, which will be advantageous to all Europe, while the Abolishing of the Monopoly she has hitherto labour'd under will be an Advantage sufficiently ample to repay the Debt she may contract to accomplish it.

7. *With regard to Character in the honest Payment of Debts.* The Punctuality of America in Discharge of *Public Debts* is shown under the first

head; the general Character of the People in that respect appears from their faithful Payment of *private Debts* to England since the Commencement of the War. These were not indeed wanting some half Politicians who propos'd stopping that Payment till Peace should be restor'd alledging that in the usual Course of Commerce and of the Credit given there was always a Debt existing equal to the Trade of 18 Months. That the Trade being for 5 Millions Sterling per Annum, the Debt must be Seven Million and an half. That this Sum paid to the British Merchants would operate to prevent the Distress intended to be brought on Britain by our Stoppage of Commerce with her: For the Merchants receiving this Money and no Orders with it for farther Supplies would either lay it out in the Funds, or in employing Manufacturers to accumulate Goods for a future hungry Market in America, upon an expected Accommodation, by which Means the Funds would be kept up and the Manufacturers prevented from Murmuring. But in Answer it was alledged that Injuries from Ministers should not be reveng'd on Merchants who were our Friends; that the Credit was in consequence of private Contracts made in Confidence of good Faith; that these ought to be held sacred and faithfully comply'd with; for that whatever publick Utility might be suppos'd to arise from a Breach of private Faith, it was unjust, and would in the End be found unwise, *Honesty* being in truth *the best Policy*. On this Principle the Proposition was universally rejected: And tho' the English prosecuted the War against us with unexampled Barbarity, burning our defenceless Towns in the midst of Winter and arming Savages against us, the Debt was punctually paid; and the Merchants of London have testify'd to the Parliament and will testify to all the World that from their Experience in dealing with us they had before the War no Apprehensions of our Unfairness, and that since the War they have been convinc'd that their good Opinion of us was wellfounded. England on the Contrary, an old, corrupt, extravagant and profligate Nation, sees herself deep in Debt which she is in no Condition to pay, and yet is madly and dishonestly running deeper; despairing ever to satisfy her Creditors; and having no Prospect of discharging her Debts but by a Publick Bankrupcy.

On the whole it appears, that from the general Industry, Frugality, Ability, Prudence and Virtue of America, she is a much safer Debtor than Britain. To say nothing of the Satisfaction generous Minds must have in reflecting, that by Loans to America they are opposing Tyranny and aiding the Cause of Liberty which is the Cause of all Mankind.

Rough Draft of Affair of borrowing Money

Part VIII

The Ephemera

20 September, 1778

Passy.
To Madame Brillon.

You may remember, my dear Friend, that when we lately spent that happy Day in the delightful garden and sweet Society of the *Moulin-Joli*, I stopt a little in one of our Walks, and staid some time behind the Company. We had been shewn numberless Skeletons of a kind of little Fly, called an Ephemere, all whose successive Generations we were told were bred and expired within the Day. I happen'd to see a living Company of them on a Leaf, who appear'd to be engag'd in Conversation. You know I understand all the inferior Animal Tongues: my too great Application to the Study of them is the best Excuse I can give for the little Progress I have made in your charming Language. I listned thro' Curiosity to the Discourse of these little Creatures, but as they in their national Vivacity spoke three or four together, I could make but little of their Discourse. I found however, by some broken Expressions that I caught now and then, they were disputing warmly the Merit of two foreign Musicians, one a *Cousin*, the other a *Musketo*; in which Dispute they spent their time seemingly as regardless of the Shortness of Life, as if they had been sure of living a Month. Happy People! thought I, you live certainly under a wise, just and mild Government, since you have no public Grievances to complain of, nor any Subject of Contention but the Perfections or Imperfections of foreign Music. I turned from them to an old greyheaded one, who was single on another Leaf, and talking to himself. Being amus'd with his Soliloquy, I have put it down in writing, in hopes it will likewise amuse her to whom I am so much indebted for the most pleasing of all Amusements, her delicious Company, and her heavenly Harmony.

"It was," says he, "the Opinion of learned Philosophers of our Race, who lived and flourished long before my time, that this vast World, the *Moulin Joli*, could not itself subsist more than 18 Hours; and I think there was some Foundation for that Opinion, since by the apparent Motion of the great Luminary that gives Life to all Nature, and which in my time has evidently declin'd considerably towards the Ocean at the End of our Earth, it must then finish its Course, be extinguish'd in the Waters that surround us, and leave the World in Cold and Darkness, necessarily producing universal Death and Destruction. I have lived seven of those Hours; a great Age, being no less than 420 minutes of Time. How very few of us continue so long! I have seen Generations born, flourish, and expire. My present Friends are the Children and Grandchildren of the Friends of my Youth, who are now, alas, no more! And I must soon follow them; for by the Course of Nature, tho' still in Health, I cannot expect to live above 7 or 8 Minutes longer. What now avails all my Toil and Labour in amassing Honey-Dew on this Leaf, which I cannot live to enjoy! What the political Struggles I have been engag'd in for the Good of my *Compatriotes*, Inhabitants of this Bush; or my philosophical Studies for the Benefit of our Race in general! For in Politics, *what can Laws do without Morals!* Our present Race of Ephemeres will in a Course of Minutes, become corrupt like those of other and older Bushes, and consequently as wretched. And in Philosophy how small our Progress! Alas, *Art is long, and Life short!* My Friends would comfort me with the Idea of a Name they say I shall leave behind me; and they tell me I have *lived long enough, to Nature and to Glory:* But what will Fame be to an *Ephemere* who no longer exists? And what will become of all History, in the 18th Hour, when the World itself, even the whole *Moulin Joli*, shall come to its End, and be buried in universal Ruin?" To me, after all my eager Pursuits, no solid Pleasures now remain, but the Reflection of a long Life spent in meaning well, the sensible Conversation of a few good Lady-Ephemeres, and now and then a kind Smile, and a Tune from the ever-amiable *Brillante*.

The Whistle

10 November, 1779

Passy.
To Madame Brillon.

I Received my dear Friend's two Letters, one for Wednesday & one for Saturday. This is again Wednesday. I do not deserve one for to day, because I have not answered the former. But indolent as I am, and averse to Writing, the Fear of having no more of your pleasing Epistles, if I do not contribute to the Correspondance, obliges me to take up my Pen: And as M. B. has kindly sent me Word, that he sets out to-morrow to see you; instead of spending this Wednesday Evening as I have long done its Name-sakes, in your delightful Company, I sit down to spend it in thinking of you, in writing to you, & in reading over & over again your Letters.

I am charm'd with your Description of Paradise, & with your Plan of living there. And I approve much of your Conclusion, that in the mean time we should draw all the Good we can from this World. In my Opinion we might all draw more Good, from it than we do, & suffer less Evil, if we would but take care *not to give too much for our Whistles*. For to me it seems that most of the unhappy People we meet with, are become so by Neglect of that Caution.

You ask what I mean? —You love Stories, and will excuse my telling you one of my self. When I was a Child of seven Years old, my Friends on a Holiday fill'd my little Pocket with Halfpence. I went directly to a Shop where they sold Toys for Children; and being charm'd with the Sound of a Whistle that I met by the way, in the hands of another Boy, I voluntarily offer'd and gave all my Money for it. When I came home, whistling all over the House, much pleas'd with my Whistle, but disturbing all the Family, my Brothers, Sisters & Cousins, understanding the Bargain I had made, told me I had given four times as much for it as it was worth, put me in mind what good Things I might have bought with the rest of the Money, & laught at me so much for my Folly that I cry'd with Vexation; and the Reflection gave me more Chagrin than the Whistle gave me Pleasure.

This however was afterwards of use to me, the Impression continuing on my Mind; so that often when I was tempted to buy some unnecessary thing, I said to my self, *Do not give too much for the Whistle;* and I sav'd my Money.

As I grew up, came into the World, and observed the Actions of Men, I thought I met many *who gave too much for the Whistle.* —When I saw one ambitious of Court Favour, sacrificing his Time in Attendance at Levees, his Repose, his Liberty, his Virtue and perhaps his Friend, to obtain it; I have said to my self, *This Man gives too much for his Whistle.* —When I saw another fond of Popularity, constantly employing himself in political Bustles, neglecting his own Affairs, and ruining them by that Neglect, *He pays*, says I, *too much for his Whistle.* —If I knew a Miser, who gave up every kind of comfortable Living, all the Pleasure of doing Good to others, all the Esteem of his Fellow Citizens, & the Joys of benevolent Friendship, for the sake of Accumulating Wealth, *Poor Man*, says I, *you pay too much for your Whistle.* —When I met with a Man of Pleasure, sacrificing every laudable Improvement of his Mind or of his Fortune, to mere corporeal Satisfactions, & ruining his Health in their Pursuit, *Mistaken Man*, says I, *you are providing Pain for your self instead of Pleasure, you pay too much for your Whistle.* —If I see one fond of Appearance, of fine Cloaths, fine Houses, fine Furniture, fine Equipages, all above his Fortune, for which he contracts Debts, and ends his Career in a Prison; *Alas*, says I, *he has paid too much for his Whistle.* —When I saw a beautiful sweet-temper'd Girl, marry'd to an ill-natured Brute of a Husband; *What a Pity*, says I, *that she should pay so much for a Whistle!* —In short, I conceiv'd that great Part of the Miseries of Mankind, were brought upon them by the false Estimates they had made of the Value of Things, and by their *giving too much for the Whistle.*

Yet I ought to have Charity for these unhappy People, when I consider that with all this Wisdom of which I am boasting, there are certain things in the World so tempting; for Example the Apples of King John, which happily are not to be bought, for if they were put to sale by Auction, I might very easily be led to ruin my self in the Purchase, and find that I had once more *given too much for the Whistle.*

Adieu, my dearest Friend, and believe me ever yours very sincerely and with unalterable Affection.

à Passy, ce 10 Nov. 1779

J' AI reçu les deux Lettres de ma chere Amie, l'une pour Mercredi, l'autre pour le Sammedi. C'est aujourd'hui encore Mercredi. Je ne mérite pas d'en avoir encore, parce que je n'ai pas fait Réponse aux précédentes. Mais, tout indolent que je suis, & quelque Aversion que j'aie d'écrire, la Crainte de n'avoir plus de vos charmantes Epitres, si je ne contribue aussi ma part pour soutenir la Correspondance, me force de prendre la Plume. Et comme M. B. m'a mandé si obligeamment qu'il part demain matin pour vous voir, moi, au lieu de passer ce Mercredi au soir, comme je l'ai fait si long-temps de ses Prédécesseurs du même Nom, en votre douce Société, je me suis mis à mon Ecritoire, pour le passer à penser à vous, à vous écrire, & à lire & relire ce que vous m'avez si délicieusement écrit.

Je suis charmé de votre Description du Paradis, & de vos Plans pour y vivre. J'approuve aussi très-fortement la Conclusion que vous faites, qu'en attendant il faut tirer de ce bas monde tout le Bien qu'on en peut tirer. A mon Avis il est trèspossible pour nous d'en tirer beaucoup plus de Bien, que nous n'en tirons, & d'en souffrir moins de mal, si nous voulions seulement prendre garde de *ne donner pas trop pour nos Sifflets.* Car il me semble que la plupart des Malheureux qu'on trouve dans le Monde, sont devenus tels par leur Négligence de cette Précaution.

Vous demandez ce que je veux dire? —Vous aimez les Histoires, & vous m'excuserez si je vous en donne qui regarde moi-même. Quand j'étois un Enfant de cinq ou six ans, mes Amis, un Jour de Fête, remplirent ma petite Poche de Sols. J'allai tout de suite à une Boutique où on vendoit des Babioles; mais étant charmé du Son d'un Sifflet, que je rencontrai en Chemin dans les mains d'un autre petit Garçon, je lui offris & donnai volontiers pour cela tout mon Argent. Revenu chez moi, sifflant par toute la Maison, fort content de mon Achat, mais fatiguant les Oreilles de toute la Famille, mes Freres, mes Soeurs, mes Cousines, entendant que j'avois tant donné pour ce mauvais Bruit, me dirent que c'étoit dix fois plus que la Valeur; alors ils me firent penser au Nombre de bonnes Choses, que je pouvois acheter avec le Reste de ma Monnoie, si j'avois été plus prudent; & ils me ridiculiserent tant de ma Follie, que je pleurois de cette Vexation; & la Réflexion me donnoit plus de Chagrin, que le Sifflet de Plaisir.

Cet Accident fut cependant dans la Suite, de quelque Utilité pour moi, l'Impression restant sur mon Ame; de sorte que, tant lorsque j'étois tenté d'acheter quelque chose qui ne m'étoit pas nécessaire, je disois en moi-même, *Ne donnons pas trop pour le Sifflet:* & j'épargnois mon Argent.

Devenant grand Garçon, entrant dans le Monde & observant les Actions des Hommes, je vis que je rencontrois Nombre de Gens *qui donnoient trop pour le Sifflet.*

Quand j'ai vu quelqu'un, qui, ambitieux de la Faveur de la Cour, consumoit son Temps en les Assiduités aux Levers; son Repos, sa Liberté, sa Vertu, & peut-être ses vrais Amis, pour obtenir quelque petite Distinction; j'ai dis en moi-même, *Cet homme donne trop pour son Sifflet.* —Quand j'en ai vu une autre, avide de se rendre populaire, & pour cela s'occupant toujours de Contestations publiques, négligeant ses Affaires particulieres, & les ruinant par cette Négligence; *Il paye trop*, ai-je dit, *pour son Sifflet.* —Si j'ai connu un Avare, qui renonçoit à toute Maniere de vivre commodement, à tout le Plaisir de faire le bien aux autres, à toute l'Estime de ses Compatriotes, & à tous les Charmes de l'Amitié, pour avoir un Morçeau de Métal jaune: *Pauvre homme*, disois-je; *vous donnez trop pour votre Sifflet.* —Quand j'ai rencontré un Homme de Plaisir, sacrifiant tout louable Perfectionnement de son Ame, & toute Amélioration de son Etat, aux Voluptés du Sens purement corporel, & détruisant sa Santé dans leur Poursuite, *Homme trompé*, ai-je dit, *vous vous procurez des Peines au lieu des Plaisirs; vous payez trop pour votre Sifflet.* —Si j'en ai vu un autre, entété de beaux Habillemens, belles Maisons, beaux Meubles, beaux Equipages, toutes au-dessus de sa Fortune, qu'il ne se procuroit qu'en faisant des Dettes, & en allant finir sa Carriere dans une Prison; *Hélas!* aije dit, *il a payé trop pour son Sifflet.* —Quand j'ai vu une trèsbelle Fille, d'un Naturel bon & doux, mariée à un Homme féroce & brutal, qui la maltraite continuellement, *C'est grande Pitié*, ai-je dit, *qu'elle ait tant payé pour un Sifflet!* —Enfin, j'ai conçu, que la plus grande Partie des Malheurs de l'Espece humaine viennent des Estimations fausses qu'on fait de la Valeur des choses, & de ce *qu'on donne trop pour les Sifflets.*

Néamoins je sens que je dois avoir de la Charité pour ces Gens malheureux, quand je considere qu'avec toute la Sagesse dont je me vante, il y a certaines Choses dans ce bas Monde si tentantes; par Exemple, les Pommes du Roi Jean, lesquelles heureusement ne sont pas à acheter; car si elles étoient mises à l'Enchere, je pourrois être très-facilement porté à me ruiner par leur Achat, & trouver que j'aurois encore une fois *donné trop pour le Sifflet.*

Adieu, ma très-chere Amie, croyez-moi toujours le vôtre, bien sincerement, & avec une Affection inaltérable.

Dialogue entre La Goute et M. F.

22 October, 1780

M. F.

Eh! Oh! Eh! Mon Dieu! qu'ai-je fait pour mériter ces Soufrances cruelles?

La Goute.

Beaucoup de choses. Vous avez trop mangé, trop bu, & trop indulgé vos jambes en leur Indolence.

M. F.

Qui est-ce qui me parle?

La G.

C'est moi-même, la Goute.

M. F.

Mon Ennemie en Personne!

La G.

Pas votre Ennemie.

M. F.

Oui mon Enemie; car non seulement vous voulez me tuer le Corps par vos Tourmens, mais vous tâchez aussi de detruire ma bonne Réputation. Vous me representez comme un Gourmand et un Ivrogne. Et tout le monde qui me connoit, sçait qu'on ne m'a jamais accusé auparavant d'être un homme qui mangeoit trop, ou buvoit trop.

La G.

Le Monde peut juger comme il lui plait; il a toujours beaucoup de Complaisance pour lui même, et quelquefois pour ses Amis. Mais je sçais bien, moi, que ce qui n'est pas trop boire, ni trop manger pour un homme qui fait raisonablement d'Exercice, est trop pour un homme qui n'en fait *point*.

M. F.

Je prends—Eh! Eh!—autant d'Exercice—Eh!—que je puis, Madame la Goute. Vous connoissez mon Etat Sedentaire; et il me semble, qu'en conséquence vous pourriez, Madame la Goute, m'épargner un peu, considerant que ce n'est pas tout à fait ma faute.

La G.

Point du tout. Votre Rhétorique & votre Politesse sont également perdues. Votre Excuse ne vaut rien. Si votre Etat est sedentaire, vos Amusements, vos Recréations doivent être acti*fs*. Vous devez *vous* promener à Pied ou à Cheval, ou si le Tems *vous en* empêche, jouer au Billard. Mais examinons votre Cours de vie. Quand les Matinées sont longues et que vous avez assez de tems pour *vous* promener, qu'est ce que vous faites? Au lieu de gagner de l'Appetit pour votre dejeuner par un éxercice salutaire, Vous vous amusez *à lire des* Livres, *des* Brochures, ou Gazettes dont la pluspart *n'en valent* pas la peine. Vous dejeunez neanmoins largement; Quatre Tasses de Thé à la Crême avec une ou deux grandes Tartines de Pain et de Beurre couvertes de Tranches de Beuf fumé, qui je crois ne sont pas les choses du monde les plus faciles à digérer. Tout de suite vous vous placez à votre Bureau, vous y écrivez, ou vous parlez aux gens qui viennent vous chercher pour affaires. Cela dure jusqu'à une Heure après midi sans le moindre Exercice de Corps. Mais tout cela je vous *le* pardonne, parce*que cela tient* comme vous dites, à votre *Etat Sedentaire*. Mais après diner, que faites vous? Au lieu de *vous*promener dans les beaux Jardins de vos Amis *chez lesquels* vous avez diné, comme font les Gens sensés Vous voilà établi à l'Echiquier jouant aux Echecs, où on peut vous trouver deux ou trois Heures. C'est là votre Recréation éternelle. La Recréation qui de toutes est la moins propre à* un homme Sedentaire; parce qu'au lieu d'accelerer le mouvement des fluides, il demande une Attention si forte et si fixe, que la Circulation est retardée & les Secretions internes empechées. Enveloppé dans les Speculations de ce miserable jeu, vous detruisez votre

Constitution. Que *peut-on attendre d'une* telle façon de vivre, sinon un Corps plein d'humeurs Stagnantes prêtes à se corrompre, un Corps prêt à tomber en toutes sortes de maladies dangereuses, Si moi la Goute, je ne viens pas de tems en tems à votre Secours pour agiter ces humeurs et les purifier ou dissiper? Si c'étoit dans quelque petite Rue ou Coin de Paris, depourvu de promenades, que vous pass*iez* quelque tems aux Echecs après diner, vous pourriez dire cela en Excuse: Mais c'est la même chose à Passy, à Auteuil, à Montmartre, à Epinay, à Sanoy, où il y a les plus beaux Jardins & Promenades & belles Dames, l'Air le plus pur, *les* Conversations les plus agréables, les plus instructives, que vous pouvez avoir tou*t* en *vous* promenant, mais tous sont negligés, pour cet abominable jeu d'Echecs. Fi donc, M. Franklin! Mais en continuant mes Instructions, J'oubliois de vos donner vos Corrections. Tenez cet Elancement; & celui

M. F.

Oh! Eh! Oh! Ohhh! — Autant que vous *voudrez* de vos Instructions, Me. La Goute, même de vos Reproches, mais de grace plus de *vos* Corrections.

La G.

Tout au contraire, je ne vous rabattrois pas *le quart d'une*. Elles sont pour votre bien. Tenez.

M. F.

Oh! Ehhh! Ce n'est pas juste de dire que je ne prends aucun Exercice. J'en *fais* souvent dans *ma* voiture, en sortant pour aller à diner, & en revenant.

La G.

C'est de tous les Exercices imaginables le plus léger et le plus insignifiant, *que* celui *qui est*donné par le Mouvement d'une voiture suspendue *sur* des Ressorts. En observant la Quantité de chaleur obtenue des differentes Especes de mouvement, on peut former quelque Jugement de la quantité d'Exercice qui est donnée par chacun. Si, par Exemple, vous sortez à pied en hiver, avec les Pieds froids, en marchant une Heure, vous aurez vos Pieds et tout votre Corps bien échauffés. Si vous montez à Cheval, il faut troter quatre heures avant de trouver le même Effet. Mais si vous vous placez dans une telle Voiture, vous pouvez voyager toute une Journée et entrer votre derniere Auberge avec vos Pieds encore froids.— Ne vous flattez donc pas qu'en passant une demi*e*-heure dans votre Voiture vous preniez de l'Exercice. Dieu n'a pas donné de*s* Voitures à Roues à tout le Monde, mais il a donné à chacun deux Jambes qui sont des Machines infiniment plus commodes et plus Serviables; soyez en reconnoissant, et faites usage des votres. Voulez vous savoir comment elles font circuler vos fluides en même tems qu' *elles* vous transportent d'un lieu à un autre, pensez que quand vous marchez, tout le poids de votre Corps est jetté alternativement sur l'une et l'autre Jambe; cela presse avec grande force sur les Vaisseaux du Pied & *refoule ce qu'ils contiennent*. Pendant que le Poids est *ôté* de ce Pied et jetté Sur l'autre, les Vaisseaux ont le tems de se remplir, et par le Retour du Poids *ce refoulement* est repeté, ainsi la Circulation du sang est accélerée en marchant. La Chaleur produite en un certain Espace de tems est en raison de l'Accélération, les Fluides sont battus les Humeurs attenuées, les Secretions facilitées, et tout va bien. Les joues prennent *du* Vermeil, et la Santé est établie. Regardez votre Amie d'Auteuil, une Femme qui a reçu de la Nature plus de Sience vraiment utile, qu'une demi-douzaine ensemble de vo*us* Philosophes pretendus n'en n'ont tiré de tous vos Livres. Quand elle voulut vous faire l'honneur de sa Visite, elle vint à Pied; elle *se* promene du matin jusqu'au soir, & elle laisse toutes les maladies d'Indolence en *partage* à ses Chevaux. Voilà comme elle conserve Sa Santé, même sa Beauté. Mais vous, quand vous allez à Auteuil c'est dans la Voiture. Cependant il n'y a pas plus loin de Passy à Auteuil, que d'Auteuil à Passy

M. F.

Vous m'ennuiez avec tant de Raisonnements.

La G.

Je le crois bien. Je me tais, et je continue mon office. Tenez cet Elancement et *celui-ci*.

M. F.

Oh! Ohh! — Continuez de parler je vous prie.

La G.

Non. J'ai un nombre d'Elancements à vous donner cette Nuit, et vous aurez le reste demain.

M. F.

Mon Dieu, La Fievre! Je me perds. Eh Eh! N'y at'il Personne qui puisse prendre cette peine pour moi.

La G.

Demandez cela à vos Chevaux. Ils ont pris la peine de marcher pour vous.

M. F.

Comment pouvez vous être si cruelle, de me tourmenter tant pour Rien.

La G.

Pas pour Rien. J'ai ici une Liste de tous vos Pechés, contre votre Sante bien distinctement écrite, & je peux vous rendre Raison de tous les Coups que je vous donne.

M. F.

Lisez la, donc.

La G.

C'est trop long à lire. Je vous en donnerai le Montant.

M. F.

Faitez le. Je suis tout Attention.

La G.

Souvenez vous combien *de fois* vous vous étez proposé de *vous* promener le matin *suivant*dans le Bois de Boulogne, dans le Jardin de La Muette ou dans le votre, et que vous avez manqué de parole; alleguant quelquefois que le tems étoit trop froid, d'autres fois qu'il étoit trop chaud, trop venteux, trop humide, ou trop quelqu'autre chose, quand en verité, il n'y avoit rien de trop qui empechoit, excepte votre trop de Paresse.

M. F.

Je confesse que cela peut arriver quelquefois, peutêtre pendant un An dix fois.

La G.

Votre Confession est bien imparfaite, le vrai Montant est cent quatrevingt dix neuf.

M. F.

Est'il possible?

La G.

Oui, c'est possible parceque c'est un fait. Vous pouvez rester assuré de la justesse de mon Compte.— Vous connoissez les Jardins de M. Brillon, comme ils sont bons a promener. Vous connoissez le bel Escalier de 150. Dégrés, qui méne de la Terrasse en haut, jusqu'à la Plaine en bas. Vous avez visité deux fois par Semaine dans les après midi, cette aimable Famille. C'est une Maxime de votre Invention, qu'on peut avoir autant d'Excercice en montant et descendant un Mile en Escalier; qu'en marchant dix sur une plaine. Quelle belle Occasion vous avez eue de prendre tous les deux Excercices ensemble. En avez vous Profité? et combien de fois?

M. F.

Je ne peux pas bien repondre à cette Question.

La G.

Je repondrai donc pour vous. Pas une fois.

M. F.

Pas une fois!

La G.

Pas une fois. Pendant tout le bel Eté passé, vous y etez arrivé à six heures. Vous y avez trouvé cette charmante Femme et ses beaux Enfans, & ses amis prêts à vous accompagner dans ces Promenades, & de vous amuser avec leurs agréables Conversations. Et qu'avez vous fait? Vous vous étez assis sur la Terrasse, *vous avez* loué la belle Vue, regardé la Beauté des Jardins en bas; mais vous n'avez pas bougé un Pas pour descendre *vous* y promener. Au contraire vous avez demandé du Thé et l'Echiquier. Et vous voila collé à votre Siege jusqu'à neuf Heures. Et cela après avoir joué peutêtre deux Heures où vous avez diné. Alors au lieu de retourner chez vous à Pied *ce qui pourrait* vous remuer un peu, vous prenez votre Voiture. Quelle Sottise de croire qu'avec tout ce déreglement, on peut se conserver en Santé, sans moi.

M. F.

A cette heure je suis convaincu de la Justesse de cette Remarque du Bon Homme Richard, que nos Dettes et nos péchés sont toujours plus *grands* qu'on ne pense.

La G.

C'est comme *cela* que vous autres Philosophes, avez toujours les Maximes d*es* Sage*s* dans votre Bouche, pendant que votre Conduite est comme celle des Ignorans.

M. F.

Mais faites vous un de mes Crimes *de ce* que je retourne en Voiture de chez Me. Brillon.

La G.

Oui assûrement, car vous qui avez été assis toute la journée, Vous ne pouvez pas dire que vous étez fatigué du travail du Jour. Vous n'avez pas besoin donc d'étre soulagé par une Voiture.

M.F.

Que voulez vous donc que je fasse de ma Voiture?

La G.

Brulez la, si vous voulez. Alors vous en tirerez au moins pour une fois de la chaleur. Ou si cette Proposition ne vous plait pas, je vous en donnerai une Autre. Regardez les Pauvres Paysans qui travaillent la terre dans les Vignes et les Champs autour des Villages de Passy, Auteuil, Chaillot, &c. Vous pouvez tous les jours, parmi ces bonnes Creatures, trouver quatre ou cinq vieilles Femmes et vieux Hommes, courbés et peutêtre estropiés sous le poids des Années et par un travail *trop* fort et continuel, qui après une longue Journée de Fatigue ont à marcher peutêtre un ou deux Miles pour trouver leur*s* Chaumiere*s*. Ordonnez à votre Cocher de les prendre et de les placer chèz eux. Voilà une bonne Oeuvre! qui fera du bien *à* votre Ame; et si en même tems vous retournez de votre Visite chèz les Brillons à Pied, cela sera bon pour votre Corps.

M. F.

Ah! comme vous étez ennuyeuse!

La G.

Allons donc à notre Metier, il faut souvenir que je suis vôtre Medecin. Tenez.

M. F.

Ohhh!— Quel Diable de Medecin!

La G.

Vous étez un Ingrat de me dire cela. N'est-ce pas moi qui en qualité de Votre Medecin vous *ai*sauvé de la Paralysie, de l'Hydropisie et de l'Apoplexie dont l'une ou l'autre vous auroient tué il y a long tems si je ne le*s* *en* avoi*s* empeché*es*.

M. F.

Je le confesse. Et je vous remercie pour *ce* qui est passé. Mais de Grace quittez-moi, pour jamais. Car il me semble qu'on aimeroit mieux mourir que d'être gueri si doloureusement. Souvenez vous que j'ai aussi été votre ami. Je n'ai jamais loué de combattre contre vous, ni les Medecins, ni les Charlatans d'aucune Espece, Si donc vous ne me quittez pas, vous Serez aussi accusable d'Ingratitude.

La G.

Je ne pense pas que je vous doive grande obligation de cela. Je me moque des Charlatans, ils peuvent vous tuer, mais ils ne peuvent pas me nuire. Et quant aux vrais Médecins, ils sont enfin convaincu de cette verité, que la Goute n'est pas une Maladie, mais un Veritable Remede, & qu'il ne faut pas guerir un Remede. Revenons à notre Affaire. Tenez.

M. F.

Oh de grace quittez moi, et je vous promets fidelement, que desormais je ne jouerai plus aux Echecs *que je ferai de l'exercice* journellement, et *que* je vivrai sobrement.

La G.

Je vous connois bien; vous étez un beau Prometteur. Mais après quelques mois de bonne Santé, vous commencerez à aller votre ancien train. Vos belles Promesses seront oubliées comme on oublie les formes des Nuages de la derniere année. Allons donc, finissons notre Compte. Après cela je vous quiterai; mais soyez assuré que je vous revisiterai en *tems & lieu*. Car c'est pour votre bien, et je suis, vous sçavez, votre bonne Amie.

Dialogue between Gout and Monsieur Franklin

22 October, 1780

M. F.

Oh! Oh! Oh! My God! What have I done to deserve these cruel sufferings?

Gout.

Many things. You have eaten too much, drunk too much, & indulged your legs too much in their idleness.

M. F.

Who is speaking to me?

Gout.

It is myself, Gout.

M. F.

My enemy in person!

Gout.

Not your enemy.

M. F.

Yes my enemy; for not only do you want to kill my body with your torments, but you also try to destroy my good reputation. You portray me as a glutton and a drunkard. And everyone who knows me knows that I have never been accused before of being a man who eats too much, or drinks too much.

Gout.

The world may judge as it pleases; it always has much complacency for itself, and sometimes for its friends. But I know well that what is not too much drinking, nor too much eating for a man who reasonably exercises, is too much for a man who does not.

M. F.

I take—Eh! Eh!—as much exercise—Eh!—as I can, Madame Gout. You know my sedentary state; and it seems to me, Madame Gout, that you might, in consequence, spare me a little, considering that it is not entirely my fault.

Gout.

Not at all. Your rhetoric & politeness are equally lost. Your excuse is worth nothing. If your state is sedentary, your amusements, your recreations should be active. You should walk on foot or on horseback, or if the weather prevents it, play billiards. But let's examine your course of life. When the mornings are long and you have plenty of time to walk, what do you do? Instead of earning an appetite for your breakfast through healthy exercise, you amuse yourself by reading Books, Pamphlets, or Newspapers, most of which are not worth the trouble. You have a hearty breakfast nonetheless; Four cups of Cream Tea with one or two large slices of Bread and Butter covered with Slices of Smoked Beef, which I believe are not the easiest things in the world to digest. Immediately you sit at your Desk, writing, or talking to people who come to see you on business. This lasts until one hour after noon without the slightest bodily exercise. But I forgive you all this, because as you say, it pertains to your *Sedentary State*. But after dinner, what do you do? Instead of walking in the beautiful Gardens of your friends where you have dined, as sensible people do, there you are settled at the Chessboard playing Chess, where you can be found for two or three hours. That is your eternal Recreation. The Recreation least suited for a sedentary man; because instead of accelerating the movement of fluids, it requires such strong and fixed Attention that the Circulation is slowed & the internal Secretions are hindered. Wrapped in the speculations of this miserable game, you destroy your Constitution. What can one expect from such a way of living, if not a Body full of stagnant humours ready to corrupt, a Body ready to fall into all sorts of dangerous diseases, If I,

Gout, do not come from time to time to your Aid to agitate these humours and purify or disperse them? If this were in some small street or corner of Paris, deprived of walks, where you spend some time at Chess after dinner, you might say that in excuse: But it's the same at Passy, Auteuil, Montmartre, Epinay, Sanoy, where there are the most beautiful Gardens & Walks & beautiful Ladies, the purest Air, the most agreeable and instructive Conversations, that you can have all while walking, but all are neglected, for this abominable game of Chess. Shame on you, Mr. Franklin! But by continuing my Instructions, I forgot to give you your Corrections. Here's this Twinge; & that one.

M. F.

Oh! Eh! Oh! Ohhh! — As many of your Instructions as you like, Madame Gout, even your Reproaches, but for mercy's sake, no more of your Corrections.

Gout.

Quite the contrary, I will not abate them by a quarter. They are for your own good. Here.

M. F.

Oh! Ehhh! It's not fair to say that I take no exercise. I often do so in my carriage, going out to dine, and coming back.

Gout.

Of all the conceivable exercises, the lightest and most insignificant is that given by the motion of a carriage suspended on springs. By observing the amount of heat obtained from different kinds of movement, one can form some judgment of the amount of exercise given by each. For example, if you go out on foot in winter with cold feet, walking for an hour, you will have your feet and your whole body nicely warmed. If you ride on horseback, you must trot for four hours before feeling the same effect. But if you take such a carriage, you can travel all day and still enter your last inn with cold feet.—So do not flatter yourself that by spending half an hour in your carriage you are taking exercise. God has not given wheeled carriages to everyone, but He has given each person two legs which are infinitely more convenient and useful machines; be grateful for them, and use yours. Do you want to know how they circulate your fluids at the same time as they transport you from one place to another? Think that when you walk, the full weight of your body is alternately thrown on one leg and then the other; this presses with great force on the vessels of the foot & drives out what they contain. While the weight is removed from that foot and thrown onto the other, the vessels have time to refill, and with the return of the weight, this expulsion is repeated, so the circulation of the blood is accelerated by walking. The warmth produced in a certain space of time is proportional to the acceleration, the fluids are agitated, the humors attenuated, the secretions facilitated, and all goes well. The cheeks take on a rosy hue, and health is established. Look at your friend from Auteuil, a woman who has received from Nature more truly useful knowledge than half a dozen of you so-called philosophers have derived from all your books. When she wanted to honor you with her visit, she came on foot; she walks from morning till night, and she leaves all the diseases of indolence to her horses. That's how she preserves her health, even her beauty. But you, when you go to Auteuil, it's in the carriage. Yet it's no further from Passy to Auteuil than from Auteuil to Passy.

M. F.

You bore me with so much reasoning.

Gout.

I believe it. I will be silent, and continue my office. Here's this Twinge and this one.

M. F.

Oh! Ohh! — Please continue speaking.

Gout.

No. I have a number of Twinges to give you tonight, and you will have the rest tomorrow.

M. F.

My God, Fever! I am lost. Eh Eh! Isn't there anyone who can take this pain for me?

Gout.

Ask your Horses. They have taken the trouble to walk for you.

M. F.

How can you be so cruel, tormenting me so much for nothing.

Gout.

Not for nothing. I have here a List of all your Sins against your Health distinctly written, & I can account for all the Strokes I give you.

M. F.

Read it then.

Gout.

It's too long to read. I will give you the Sum.

M. F.

Do it. I am all ears.

Gout.

Remember how many times you have resolved to take a walk the next morning in the Bois de Boulogne, in the Garden of La Muette, or in your own, and how you broke your word; sometimes alleging the weather was too cold, other times too hot, too windy, too damp, or too something else, when in truth, there was nothing too extreme that prevented it, except your too much Laziness.

M. F.

I confess that may happen sometimes, perhaps ten times in a year.

Gout.

Your confession is very imperfect, the true sum is one hundred ninety-nine.

M. F.

Is it possible?

Gout.

Yes, it's possible because it's a fact. You can rest assured of the accuracy of my account.— You know the gardens of Mr. Brillon, how good they are for walking. You know the beautiful Staircase of 150 Steps, which leads from the Terrace above, down to the Plain below. You have visited this charming family twice a week in the afternoons. It's a maxim of your own invention, that one can have as much exercise in going up and down a Mile of stairs; as in walking ten on a plain. What a beautiful opportunity you had to take both exercises together. Did you take advantage of it? And how many times?

M. F.

I cannot answer that question well.

Gout.

Then I will answer for you. Not once.

M. F.

Not once!

Gout.

Not once. Throughout all the beautiful summer past, you arrived there at six o'clock. You found this charming woman and her beautiful children, & her friends ready to accompany you in these walks, & to entertain you with their pleasant conversations. And what did you do? You sat on the Terrace, praised the beautiful View, looked at the Beauty of the Gardens below; but you did not move a step to go down and walk there. On the contrary, you asked for Tea and the Chessboard. And there you were, glued to your Seat until nine o'clock. And that after perhaps having played two hours where you dined. Then instead of returning home on foot which might stir you a little, you take your Carriage. What folly to think that with all this irregularity, one can maintain health without me.

M. F.

Now I am convinced of the accuracy of that remark by Good Man Richard, that our debts and sins are always greater than we think.

Gout.

That's how you philosophers always have the maxims of the wise on your lips, while your conduct is like that of the ignorant.

M. F.

But do you make it one of my crimes that I return in a carriage from Mrs. Brillon's?

Gout.

Yes, indeed, for you who have been sitting all day, you cannot say that you are tired from the day's work. You do not need, therefore, to be relieved by a carriage.

M. F.

What do you want me to do with my carriage?

Gout.

Burn it, if you wish. Then you will at least get some heat from it once. Or if that proposition does not please you, I will give you another. Look at the poor peasants who work the land in the vineyards and fields around the villages of Passy, Auteuil, Chaillot, etc. You can daily find among these good creatures four or five old women and old men, bent and perhaps crippled under the weight of years and by too hard and continuous labor, who after a long day of fatigue have to walk perhaps one or two miles to find their cottages. Order your coachman to take them and place them at their homes. That's a good deed! which will do good to your soul; and if at the same time you return from your visit to the Brillons on foot, it will be good for your body.

M. F.

Ah! how tedious you are!

Gout.

Let us proceed with our business, remember I am your physician. Here.

M. F.

Ohhh!— What a devil of a physician!

Gout.

You are ungrateful to say that. Is it not I who, in the capacity of your physician, have saved you from paralysis, dropsy, and apoplexy, one or the other of which would have killed you long ago if I had not prevented them.

M. F.

I confess it. And I thank you for what is past. But for mercy's sake, leave me forever. For it seems to me one would rather die than be cured so painfully. Remember I have also been your friend. I have never praised fighting against you, neither the physicians, nor the quacks of any kind, so if you do not leave me, you will also be accused of ingratitude.

Gout.

I do not think I owe you much obligation for that. I laugh at the quacks, they might kill you, but they cannot harm me. And as for the true physicians, they are at last convinced of this truth, that gout is not a disease, but a true remedy, & that one must not cure a remedy. Let's get back to our business. Here.

M. F.

Oh, for mercy's sake leave me, and I faithfully promise you that henceforth I will no longer play chess, that I will exercise daily, and that I will live soberly.

Gout.

I know you well; you are a fine promiser. But after a few months of good health, you will start to go back to your old ways. Your fine promises will be forgotten like the shapes of last year's clouds. Come on then, let's finish our account. After that, I will leave you; but be assured that I will revisit you in time & place. For it is for your own good, and I am, you know, your good friend.

The Deformed and Handsome Leg

23 November, 1780

There are two Sorts of People in the World, who with equal Degrees of Health & Wealth and the other Comforts of Life, become, the one happy, the other unhappy. This arises very much from the different Views in which they consider Things, Persons and Events; and the Effect of those different Views upon their own Minds.

In whatever Situation Men can be plac'd, they may find Conveniencies and Inconveniencies: In whatever Company, they may find Persons & Conversations more or less pleasing: At whatever Table they may meet with Meats and Drinks of better and worse Taste, Dishes better and worse dress'd: In whatever Climate they will find good and bad Weather: Under whatever Government, they may find good and bad Laws, and good and bad Administration of those Laws: In every Poem or Work of Genius, they may see Faults and Beauties: In almost every Face & every Person, they may discover fine Features and Defects, good & bad Qualities. Under these Circumstances, the two Sorts of People above-mention'd fix their Attention, those who are to be happy, on the Conveniencies of Things the pleasant Parts of Conversation, the well-dress'd & well-tasted Dishes, the Goodness of the Wines, the Fine Weather, &c. &c. &c. and enjoy all with Chearfulness. Those who are to be unhappy think and speak only of the contraries. Hence they are continually discontented themselves, and by their Remarks sour the Pleasures of Society, offend personally many People, and make themselves every where disagreeable.

If this Turn of Mind was founded in Nature, such unhappy Persons would be the more to be pitied. But as the Disposition to criticise and be disgusted is perhaps taken up originally by Imitation, and unawares grown into a Habit, which tho' at present strong, may nevertheless be cured, when those who have it are convinc'd of its bad Effects on their Felicity, I hope this little Admonition may be of Service to them, and put them on changing a Habit, which tho' in the Exercise is chiefly an Act of Imagination, yet it has serious Consequences in Life, as it brings on real Griefs and Misfortunes. For, as many are offended by, and nobody well loves this sort of People, no one shows them more than the most common Civility & Respect, and scarcely that; and this frequently puts them out of humour, and draws them into Disputes and Contentions. If they aim at obtaining some Advantage in Rank or Fortune, nobody wishes them Success, or will stir a Step, or speak a Word to favour their Pretensions. If they incur public Censure or Disgrace, no one will defend or excuse, and many join to aggravate their Misconduct, and render them compleatly odious.

If these People will not change this bad Habit, and condescend to be pleas'd with what is pleasing, without fretting themselves and others about the Contraries, it is good for others to avoid an Acquaintance with them, which is always disagreeable, and sometimes very inconvenient, particularly when one finds one's self entangled in their Quarrels. An old philosophical Friend of mine was grown from Experience very cautious in this particular and carefully shun'd any Intimacy with such People. He had, like other Philosophers, a Thermometer to show the Heat of the Weather, & a Barometer to mark when it was likely to prove good or bad; but there being no Instrument yet invented to discover at first Sight this unpleasing Disposition in a Person, he for that purpose made use of his Legs; one of which was remarkably handsome, the other by some Accident crooked and deform'd. If a Stranger at the first Interview, regarded his ugly Leg more than his handsome one, he doubted him. If he spoke of it, and took no Notice of the handsome Leg, that was sufficient to determine my Philosopher to have no farther Acquaintance with him.

Everybody has not this two-legged Instrument, but everyone with a little Attention may observe Signs of that carping fault-finding Disposition, and take the same Resolution of avoiding the Acquaintance of those infected with it.

I therefore advise these critical, querulous, discontented unhappy People, that if they wish to be loved & respected by others and happy in themselves, they should *leave off looking at the ugly Leg*.

La Belle et la Mauvaise Jambe.

Il y a dans le monde deux sortes de gens, qui avec un égal partage de santé, de richesses et de tous les autres biens de la vie, sont les uns heureux et les autres malheureux: cela vient sur-tout de la maniere différente dont ils considerent les choses, et de l'effet que produit sur leur ame cette maniere différente de voir.

Dans quelque position qu'on place les hommes, ils y trouveront des biens et des maux; dans quelque compagnie qu'ils soient admis, ils y trouveront des personnes et des conversations plus ou moins agréables; à quelque table qu'ils soient assis, ils y trouveront des mets et des boissons du meilleur et du plus mauvais goût, des plats le mieux et le plus mal préparés. Dans quelque climat qu'ils soient transportés, ils y trouveront du beau et du mauvais temps; sous quelque gouvernement qu'ils vivent, ils y trouveront de bonnes et de mauvaises loix, une bonne et une mauvaise administration de ces loix. Dans quelque poëme ou ouvrage de génie que ce soit, ils trouveront des défauts et des beautés; sur presque toutes les figures, dans presque toutes les personnes, ils découvriront des traits agréables et des défectuosités, des bonnes et des mauvaises qualités. D'après cet état des choses de ce monde, les gens dont il est parlé ci-dessus, fixent leur attention; ceux qui sont destinés à être heureux, sur le côté satisfaisant des choses, sur ce qu'il y a d'intéressant dans la conversation, sur la table bien servie, sur les mets bien préparés, sur la bonté des vins, sur le beau temps, &c.

&c. et ils en jouissent avec une pleine satisfaction. Ceux qui sont destinés à être malheureux, ne jettent les yeux que sur le mauvais côté de tout, et ne parlent que des inconvéniens: de-là ils sont toujours mécontens, et par leurs remarques aigres sur les plaisirs de la société, ils blessent personnellement beaucoup de gens et se rendent désagréables par-tout.

Si cette tournure d'esprit étoit naturelle, ces malheureux seroient plus dignes de pitié; mais comme la disposition à critiquer et à être dégoûté de tout se contracte peut-être originellement par l'imitation, et se change, sans qu'on y pense, en habitude, qui, quoique déja fortifiée, est pourtant susceptible de guérison, quand ceux qui l'ont prise sont convaincus de ses mauvais effets sur leur bonheur; j'espere que ce petit avertissement leur sera de quelque utilité, et les engagera à quitter cette habitude, qui, bien qu'elle ne soit dans la pratique qu'un acte d'imagination, a pourtant de sérieuses conséquences dans la vie, attendu qu'elle cause des chagrins réels et même des malheurs; car comme elle blesse tout le monde, et que personne n'aime ceux qui l'ont contractée, personne ne leur montre que la politesse et le respect le plus ordinaire, et même encore avec la plus grande économie: cet accueil excite leur humeur et les pousse dans toutes sortes de disputes et de constestations. S'ils ambitionnent ou des honneurs ou de la fortune, personne ne leur souhaite du succès, et ne fait un pas ou ne dit un mot pour favoriser leurs prétentions. S'ils encourent la censure publique ou le déshonneur, personne ne les défend, ne les excuse, et beaucoup de gens joignent leur voix pour aggraver leur mauvaise conduite et les rendre complettement odieux.

Si cette sorte d'hommes ne veut point changer une si mauvaise habitude, et ne peut se résoudre à trouver agréable ce qui l'est effectivement, sans chagriner les autres, et eux-mêmes, par les contraires affligeans, il est bon pour les autres d'éviter de former avec eux une liaison, à coup sûr, désagréable, et qui peut devenir dangereuse, sur-tout lorsqu'on se trouve mêlé dans leurs quérelles. Un Philosophe de mes anciens amis étoit devenu par expérience très-attentif sur cela en particulier, et évitoit avec le plus grand soin toute liaison avec ces personnes. Il avoit comme les autres Philosophes, un thermometre pour lui marquer le chaud et le froid, et un barometre pour lui indiquer les probabilités du beau et du mauvais temps: mais comme il n'y a point d'instrument pour découvrir à la premiere vue dans les personnes la disposition désapprobatrice; il faisoit pour cela usage de ses deux jambes, dont l'une étoit fort belle, et dont l'autre étoit devenue, par quelque accident, tortue et difforme. Si un étranger à la premiere entrevue jettoit plus souvent les yeux sur la mauvaise jambe que sur la belle, il entroit en soupçon; s'il lui en parloit sans faire mention de la belle, cela suffisoit pour déterminer mon Philosophe à n'avoir plus aucune relation avec lui.

Chacun n'a pas cet instrument à deux jambes; mais chacun peut, avec un peu d'attention, observer les signes de cette disposition pointilleuse, qui ne trouve que les défauts, et prendre la résolution d'éviter ceux qui en sont infectés.

J'avertis donc ces gens désapprobateurs, quérelleurs, mécontens et malheureux, que s'ils désirent se voir aimés et respectés et vivre paisiblement avec eux-mêmes, ils doivent cesser de *regarder toujours la mauvaise jambe*.

Letter to the Royal Academy of Brussels

1781

*To the Royal Academy of ******[1]

—

GENTLEMEN,

I Have perused your late mathematical Prize Question, proposed in lieu of one in Natural Philosophy, for the ensuing year, viz. "*Une figure quelconque donnée, on demande d'y inscrire le plus grand nombre de fois possible une autre figure plus petite quelconque, qui est aussi donnée.*"[2] I was glad to find by these following Words, "*l'Académie a jugé que cette découverte, en étendant les bornes de nos connoissances, ne seroit pas sans UTILITÉ*"[3] , that you esteem *Utility* an essential Point in your Enquiries,

---

1. The Royal Academy of Brussels was a short-lived academy founded in 1772(-1794) in an attempt to lift what had been a negligible literary society from a state of "frivolity." Despite the regal aura of the academy, its intellectual output was embarrassingly little. In response to a particularly arbitrary 1779 Prize Question of the Year, Franklin couldn't help but submit his own sarcastic response.

2. *"Given any figure, the task is to inscribe within it the largest possible number of times another, smaller given figure."*

3. *"The Academy has judged that this discovery, by extending the boundaries of our knowledge, would not be without UTILITY."*

which has not always been the case with all Academies; and I conclude therefore that you have given this Question instead of a philosophical, or as the Learned express it, a physical one, because you could not at the time think of a physical one that promis'd greater *Utility*.

Permit me then humbly to propose one of that sort for your consideration, and through you, if you approve it, for the serious Enquiry of learned Physicians, Chemists, &c. of this enlightened Age.

It is universally well known, That in digesting our common Food, there is created or produced in the Bowels of human Créatures, a great Quantity of Wind.

That the permitting this Air to escape and mix with the Atmosphere, is usually offensive to the Company, from the fetid Smell that accompanies it.

That all well-bred People therefore, to avoid giving such Offence, forcibly restrain the Efforts of Nature to discharge that Wind.

That so retain'd contrary to Nature, it not only gives frequently great present Pain, but occasions future Diseases, such as habitual Cholics, Ruptures, Tympanies, &c. often destructive of the Constitution, & sometimes of Life itself.

Were it not for the odiously offensive Smell accompanying such Escapes, polite People would probably be under no more Restraint in discharging such Wind in Company, than they are in spitting, or in blowing their Noses.

My Prize Question therefore should be, *To discover some Drug wholesome & not disagreable, to be mix'd with our common Food, or Sauces, that shall render the natural Discharges of Wind from our Bodies, not only inoffensive, but agreable as Perfumes.*

That this is not a chimerical Project, and altogether impossible, may appear from these Considerations. That we already have some Knowledge of Means capable of *Varying* that Smell. He that dines on stale Flesh, especially with much Addition of Onions, shall be able to afford a Stink that no Company can tolerate; while he that has lived for some Time on Vegetables only, shall have that Breath so pure as to be insensible to the most delicate Noses; and if he can manage so as to avoid the Report, he may any where give Vent to his Griefs, unnoticed. But as there are many to whom an entire Vegetable Diet would be inconvenient, and as a little Quick-Lime thrown into a Jakes will correct the amazing Quantity of fetid Air arising from the vast Mass of putrid Matter contain'd in such Places, and render it rather pleasing to the Smell, who knows but that a little Powder of Lime (or some other thing equivalent) taken in our Food, or perhaps a Glass of Limewater drank at Dinner, may have the same Effect on the Air produc'd in and issuing from our Bowels? This is worth the Experiment. Certain it is also that we have the Power of changing by slight Means the Smell of another Discharge, that of our Water. A few Stems of Asparagus eaten, shall give our Urine a disagreable Odour; and a Pill of Turpentine no bigger than a Pea, shall bestow on it the pleasing Smell of Violets. And why should it be thought more impossible in Nature, to find Means of making a Perfume of our *Wind* than of our *Water?*

For the Encouragement of this Enquiry, (from the immortal Honour to be reasonably expected by the Inventor) let it be considered of how small Importance to Mankind, or to how small a Part of Mankind have been useful those Discoveries in Science that have heretofore made Philosophers famous. Are there twenty Men in Europe at this Day, the happier, or even the easier, for any Knowledge they have pick'd out of Aristotle? What Comfort can the Vortices of Descartes give to a Man who has Whirlwinds in his Bowels! The Knowledge of Newton's mutual *Attraction* of the Particles of Matter, can it afford Ease to him who is rack'd by their mutual *Repulsion*, and the cruel Distensions it occasions? The Pleasure arising to a few Philosophers, from seeing, a few Times in their Life, the Threads of Light untwisted, and separated by the Newtonian Prism into seven Colours, can it be compared with the Ease and Comfort every Man living might feel seven times a Day, by discharging freely the Wind from his Bowels? Especially if it be converted into a Perfume: For the Pleasures of one Sense being little inferior to those of another, instead of pleasing the *Sight* he might delight the *Smell* of those about him, & make Numbers happy, which to a benevolent Mind must afford infinite Satisfaction. The generous Soul, who now endeavours to find out whether the Friends he entertains like best Claret or Burgundy, Champagne or Madeira, would then enquire also whether they chose Musk or Lilly, Rose or Bergamot, and provide accordingly. And surely such a Liberty of *Ex-pressing* one's *Scent-iments*, and *pleasing one another*, is of infinitely more Importance to human Happiness than that Liberty of the *Press*, or *abusing one another*, which the English are so ready to fight & die for. —In short, this Invention, if compleated, would be, as *Bacon* expresses it, *bringing Philosophy home to Mens Business and Bosoms*. And I cannot but conclude, that in Comparison therewith, for *universal* and *continual UTILITY*, the Science of the Philosophers above mentioned, even with the Addition, Gentlemen, of your "*Figure quelconque*" and the Figures inscrib'd in it, are, all together, scarcely worth a

FART-HING.

Letter to Sarah Bache

26 January, 1784

Passy Jany.

My dear Child.

Your care in sending me the news-papers is very agreeable to me. I received by Captn. Barney those relating to the *Cincinnati.* My opinion of the institution cannot be of much importance. I only wonder that when the united wisdom of our nation had, in the Articles of Confederation, manifested their dislike of establishing ranks of nobility, by authority either of the Congress or of any particular state, a number of private persons should think proper to distinguish themselves and their posterity, from their fellow citizens, and form an order of hereditary Knights, in direct opposition to the solemnly declared sense of their country. I imagine it must be likewise contrary to the good sense of most of those drawn into it, by the persuasion of its projectors, who have been too much struck with the ribbands and crosses they have seen hanging, to the button holes of foreign officers. And I suppose those who disapprove of it have not hitherto given it much opposition, from a principle somewhat like that of your good mother, relating to punctilious persons who are always exacting little observances of respect, that "*if People can be pleased with small matters, it is pity but they should have them*". In this view, perhaps I should not myself, if my advice had been asked, have objected to their wearing their ribband and badge themselves according to their fancy, though I certainly should to the entailing it as an honour on their posterity. For, honour worthily obtained, as that for example of our officers, is in its nature a personal thing, and incommunicable to any but those who had some share in obtaining it. Thus among the Chinese, the most antient, and from long experience the wisest of nations, honour does not *descend,* but *ascends.* If a man from his learning, his wisdom, or his valour, is promoted by the emperor to the rank of Mandarin, his parents are immediately entitled to all the same ceremonies of respect from the people, that are established as due to the Mandarin himself; on the supposition, that it must have been owing to the education, instruction and good example afforded him by his parents that he was rendered capable of serving the public. This *ascending* honour is therefore useful to the state, as it encourages parents to give their children a good and virtuous education. But the *descending honour,* to a posterity who could have no share in obtaining it, is not only groundless and absurd, but often hurtful to that posterity, since it is apt to make them proud, disdaining to be employed in useful arts, and thence falling into poverty, and all the meannesses, servility and wretchedness attending it; which is the present case with much of what is called the *Noblesse* in Europe. Or if, to keep up the dignity of the family, estates are entailed entire on the eldest male heir, another pest to industry and improvement of the country is introduced, which will be followed by all the odious mixture of pride, and beggary, and idleness that have half depopulated and decultivated Spain; occasioning continual extinction of families by the discouragements of marriage, and neglect in the improvement of estates. I wish therefore that the Cincinnati if they must go on with their project, would direct the badges of their order to be worn by their fathers and mothers, instead of handing them down to their children. It would be a good precident and might have good effects. It would also be a kind of obedience to the fourth commandment, in which God enjoins us to *honour* our father and mother, but has no where directed us to honour our children. And certainly no mode of honouring those immediate authors of our being can be more effectual, than that of doing praise worthy actions, which reflect honour on those who gave us our education; or more becoming than that of manifesting by some public expression or token, that it is to their instruction and example we ascribe the merit of those actions.

But the absurdity of descending honours is not a mere matter of philosophical opinion, it is capable of mathematical demonstration. A man's son, for instance, is but half of his family, the other half belonging to the family of his wife. His son too, marrying into another family, his share in the Grand son is but a fourth; in the great grandson by the same process it is but an eighth. In the next generation a sixteenth; the next a thirty second; the next a sixty fourth; the next an hundred and twenty eighth; the next a two hundred and fifty sixth; and the next a five hundred and twelfth. Thus in nine generations which will not require more than 300 years, (no very great antiquity for a family) our present Chevalier of the Order of Cincinnatus's share in the then existing knight will be but a 512th part; which, allowing the present certain fidelity of American wives to be insured down through all those nine generations, is so small a consideration, that methinks no reasonable man would hazard, for the sake of it, the disagreeable consequences of the jealousy, envy, and ill will of his countrymen.

Let us go back with our calculation from this young noble, the 512th. part of the present Knight, through his nine generations till we return to the year of the institution. He must have had a father and mother, they are two; each of them had a father and mother, they are four. Those of the next preceeding generation will be eight; the next sixteen, the next thirty two; the next sixty four; the next One hundred and twenty eight; the next two hundred and fifty six; and the ninth in this retrocession five hundred and twelve, who must be now existing and all contribute their proportion of this future Chevalier de Cincinnatus. These, with the rest, make together as follows.

2
4
8
16
32

64

128

256

512

—

Total 1022

—

One thousand and twenty two men and women contributors to the formation of one knight. And if we are to have a thousand of these future knights there must be now and hereafter existing one million and twenty two thousand fathers and mothers who are to contribute to their production, unless a part of the number are employed in making more knights than one. Let us strike off then the 22000 on the supposition of this double employ and then consider whether after a reasonable estimation of the number of rogues and fools, and Royalists and scoundrels, and prostitutes, that are mixed with and help to make up necessarily their million of predecessors, posterity will have much reason to boast of the noble blood of the then existing set of chevaliers of Cincinnatus. The future genealogists too of these Chevaliers in proving the lineal descent of their honour through so many generations, (even supposing honour capable in its nature of descending,) will only prove the small share of this honour which can be justly claimed by any one of them, since the above simple procession arithmetic makes it quite plain and clear, that in proportion as the antiquity of the family shall augment, the right to the honour of the ancestor will diminish; and a few generations more would reduce it to something so small as to be very near an absolute nullity. I hope therefore that the order will drop this part of their project, and content themselves as the Knights of the Garter, Bath, Thistle, St Louis, and other orders of Europe do, with a life enjoyment of their little badge and ribband, and let the distinction die with those who have merited it. This I imagine will give no offence. For my own part, I shall think it a convenience when I go into a company where there may be faces unknown to me, if I discover, by this badge, the persons who merit some particular expression of my respect; and it will save modest virtue the trouble of calling for our regard, by awkward round about intimations of having been heretofore employed as officers in the continental service.

The gentleman who made the voyage to France to provide the ribbands and medals; has executed his commission. To me they seem tolerably done; but all such things are criticised. Some find fault with the Latin, as wanting classical elegance and correctness; and since our nine universities were not able to furnish better Latin, it was pity, they say, that the mottos had not been in English. Others object to the Title, as not properly assumable by any but General Washington, and a few others who served without pay. Others object to the bald eagle, as looking too much like a *Dindon* or turkey. For my own part I wish the bald eagle had not been chosen as the representative of our country. He is a bird of bad moral character. He does not get his living honestly. You may have seen him perched on some dead tree, where, too lazy to fish for himself, he watches the labour of the fishing hawk; and when that diligent bird has at length taken a fish, and is bearing it to his nest for the support of his mate and young ones, the bald eagle pursues him, and takes it from him. With all this injustice, he is never in good case, but like those among men who live by sharping and robbing he is generally poor and often very lousy. Besides he is a rank coward: the little *king bird* not bigger than a sparrow attacks him boldly and drives him out of the district. He is therefore by no means a proper emblem for the brave and honest Cincinnati of America, who have driven all the *king birds* from our country, though exactly fit for that order of knights which the French call *Chevaliers d'Industrie.* I am on this account not displeased that the figure is not known as a bald eagle, but looks more like a turkey. For in truth, the turkey is in comparison a much more respectable bird, and withal a true original native of America. Eagles have been found in all countries, but the turkey was peculiar to ours, the first of the species seen in Europe being brought to France by the Jesuits from Canada, and served up at the wedding table of Charles the ninth. He is besides, (though a little vain and silly tis true, but not the worse emblem for that) a bird of courage, and would not hesitate to attack a grenadier of the British guards who should presume to invade his farm yard with a red coat on.

I shall not enter into the criticisms made upon their Latin. The gallant officers of America may not have the merit of being great scholars, but they undoubtedly merit much as brave soldiers from their country, which should therefore not leave them merely to *fame* for their *virtutis premium,* which is one of their Latin mottos. Their *esto perpetua,* another, is an excellent wish, if they meant it for their country; bad, if intended for their order. The states should not only restore to them the *omnia* of their first motto, which many of them have left and lost, but pay them justly, and reward them generously. They should not be suffered to remain with all their new created chivalry *entirely* in the situation of the gentleman in the story, which their *omnia reliquit* reminds me of. You know every thing makes me recollect some story. He had built a very fine house and thereby much impaired his fortune. He had a pride however in showing it to his acquaintance. One of them after viewing it all, remarked a motto over the door, ŌIA VANITAS. What says he is the meaning of this ŌIA? 'tis a word I don't understand. I will tell you said the gentleman: I had a mind to have the motto cut on a piece of smooth marble, but there was not room for it between the ornaments, to be put in characters large enough to be read. I therefore made use of a contraction antiently very common in Latin manuscripts whereby the *m*'s and *n*'s in words are omitted, and the omission noted by a little dash above, which you may see there, so that this word is OMNIA, OMNIA VANITAS. O. says his friend, I now comprehend the meaning of your motto, it relates to your edifice; and signifies, that if you have abridged your *omnia* you have nevertheless left your VANITAS legible at full length.

I am as ever Your affectionate father

BF

Letter to Samuel Mather

12 May, 1784

Revd. Sir,

I received your kind Letter with your excellent Advice to the People of the United States, which I read with great Pleasure, and hope it will be duly regarded.— Such Writings tho' they may be lightly pass'd over by many Readers, yet if they make a deep Impression on one active Mind in an hundred, the Effects may be considerable. Permit me to mention one little Instance, which tho' it relates to my self, will not be quite uninteresting to you. When I was a Boy, I met with a Book intitled *Essays to do Good,* which I think was written by your Father. It had been so little regarded by a former Possessor, that several Leaves of it were torn out: But the Remainder gave me such a Turn of Thinking as to have an Influence on my Conduct thro' Life; for I have always set a greater Value on the Character of a *Doer of Good,* than on any other kind of Reputation; and if I have been, as you seem to think, a useful Citizen, the Publick owes the Advantage of it to that Book.— You mention your being in your 78th Year. I am in my 79th. We are grown old together. It is now more than 60 Years since I left Boston, but I remember well both your Father and Grandfather having heard them both in the Pulpit, and seen them in their Houses. The last Time I saw your Father was in the Beginning of 1724, when I visited him after my first Trip to Pennsylvania. He receiv'd me in his Library, and on my taking Leave show'd me a shorter way out of the House thro' a narrow Passage which was cross'd by a Beam overhead. We were still talking as I withdrew, he accompanying me behind, and I turning partly towards him, when he said hastily Stoop, Stoop! I did not understand him till I felt my Head hit against the Beam. He was a Man that never miss'd any Occasion of giving Instruction, and upon this he said to me, *You are young and have the World before you;* STOOP *as you go through it, and you will miss many hard Thumps.* This Advice, thus beat into my head has frequently been of use to me, and I often think of it when I see Pride mortified, & Misfortunes brought upon People by their carrying their Heads too high.—

I long much to see again my native Place, and once hoped to lay my Bones there. I left it in 1723; I visited it in 1733, 1743, 1753, & 1763. In 1773 I was in England; in 1775 I had a Sight of it, but could not enter, it being in Possession of the Enemy. I did hope to have been there in 1783, but could not obtain my Dismission from this Employment here. And now I fear I shall never have that Happiness. My best Wishes however attend my dear Country. *Esto perpetua*: It is now blest with an excellent Constitution. May it last forever.—

This powerful Monarchy continues its Friendship for the United States. It is a Friendship of the utmost Importance to our Security, & should be carefully cultivated. Britain has not yet well digested the Loss of its Dominion over us, and has still at times some flattering Hopes of recovering it. Accidents may encrease those Hopes, and encourage dangerous Attempts. A Breach between us and France would infallibly bring the English again upon our Backs. And yet we have some wild Heads among our Country-men, who are endeavouring to weaken that Connection!— Let us preserve our Reputation by performing our Engagements, our Credit by fulfilling our Contracts, and our Friends by Gratitude & Kindness; for we know not how soon we may again have occasion for all of them.

With great and sincere Esteem, I have the honour to be, Reverend Sir, Your most obedient & most humble Servant

B FRANKLIN

The Levée

6 November, 1784

In the first chapter of Job we have an account of a transaction said to have arisen in the court, or at the levée, of the best of all possible princes, or of governments by a single person, viz. that of God himself.

At this *levée,* in which the sons of God were assembled, Satan also appeared.

It is probable the writer of that ancient book took his idea of this *levée* from those of the eastern monarchs of the age he lived in.

It is to this day usual at the *levées* of princes, to have persons assembled who are enemies to each other, who seek to obtain favor by whispering calumny and detraction, and thereby ruining those that distinguish themselves by their virtue and merit. And kings frequently ask a familiar question or two, of every one in the circle, merely to show their benignity. These circumstances are particularly exemplified in this relation.

If a modern king, for instance, finds a person in the circle who has not lately been there, he naturally asks him how he has passed his time since he last had the pleasure of seeing him? the gentleman perhaps replies that he has been in the country to view his estates, and visit some friends. Thus Satan being asked whence he cometh? answers, "From going to and fro in the earth, and walking up and down in it." And being further asked, whether he had considered the uprightness and fidelity of the prince's servant Job, he immediately displays all the malignance of the designing courtier, by answering with another question: "Doth Job serve God for nought? Hast thou not given him immense wealth, and protected him in the possession of it? Deprive him of that, and he will curse thee to thy face." In modern phrase, Take away his places and his pensions, and your Majesty will soon find him in the opposition.

This whisper against Job had its effect. He was delivered into the power of his adversary, who deprived him of his fortune, destroyed his family, and completely ruined him.

The book of Job is called by divines a sacred poem, and with the rest of the Holy Scriptures, is understood to be written for our instruction.

What then is the instruction to be gathered from this supposed transaction?

Trust not a single person with the government of your state. For if the Deity himself, being the monarch, may for a time give way to calumny, and suffer it to operate the destruction of the best of subjects; what mischief may you not expect from such power in a mere man, though the best of men, from whom the truth is often industriously hidden, and to whom falsehood is often presented in its place, by artful, interested, and malicious courtiers?

And be cautious in trusting him even with limited powers, lest sooner or later he sap and destroy those limits, and render himself absolute.

For by the disposal of places, he attaches to himself all the placeholders, with their numerous connexions, and also all the expecters and hopers of places, which will form a strong party in promoting his views. By various political engagements for the interest of neigboring states or princes, he procures their aid in establishing his own personal power. So that, through the hopes of emolument in one part of his subjects, and the fear of his resentment in the other, all opposition falls before him.

A Petition of the Left Hand

1785

To Those Who Have the Superintendency of Education

I address myself to all the friends of youth, and conjure them to direct their compassionate regards to my unhappy fate, in order to remove the prejudices of which I am the victim. There are twin sisters of us; and the two eyes of man do not more resemble, nor are capable of being upon better terms with each other, than my sister and myself, were it not for the partiality of our parents, who make the most injurious distinctions between us. From my infancy, I have been led to consider my sister as a being of a more elevated rank. I was suffered to grow up without the least instruction, while nothing was spared in her education. She had masters to teach her writing, drawing, music, and other accomplishments; but if by chance I touched a pencil, a pen, or a needle, I was bitterly rebuked; and more than once I have been beaten for being awkward, and wanting a graceful manner. It is true, my sister associated me with her upon some occasions; but she always made a point of taking the lead, calling upon me only from necessity, or to figure by her side.

But conceive not, Sirs, that my complaints are instigated merely by vanity. No; my uneasiness is occasioned by an object much more serious. It is the practice in our family, that the whole business of providing for its subsistence falls upon my sister and myself. If any indisposition should attack my sister,—and I mention it in confidence upon this occasion, that she is subject to the gout, the rheumatism, and cramp, without making mention of other accidents,—what would be the fate of our poor family?

Must not the regret of our parents be excessive, at having placed so great a difference between sisters who are so perfectly equal? Alas! we must perish from distress; for it would not be in my power even to scrawl a suppliant petition for relief, having been obliged to employ the hand of another in transcribing the request which I have now the honour to prefer to you.

Condescend, Sirs, to make my parents sensible of the injustice of an exclusive tenderness, and of the necessity of distributing their care and affection among all their children equally.

I am, with a profound respect, Sirs, your most obedient servant,

The Left Hand

The Morals of Chess

December, 1786

Sir,

Playing at Chess, is the most ancient and the most universal game known among men; for its original is beyond the memory of history, and it has, for numberless ages, been the amusement of all the civilized nations of Asia, the Persians, the Indians, and the Chinese. Europe has had it above 1000 years; the Spaniards have spread it over their part of America, and it begins lately to make its appearance in these northern states. It is so interesting in itself, as not to need the view of gain to induce engaging in it; and thence it is never played for money. Those, therefore, who have leisure for such diversions, cannot find one that is more *innocent;* and the following piece, written with a view to correct (among a few young friends) some little improprieties in the practice of it, shows at the same time, that it may, in its effects on the mind, be not merely *innocent*, but *advantageous*, to the vanquished as well as to the victor.

The MORALS of CHESS.

The game of Chess is not merely an idle amusement. Several very valuable qualities of the mind, useful in the course of human life, are to be acquired or strengthened by it, so as to become habits, ready on all occasions. For life is a kind of chess, in which we have often points to gain, and competitors or adversaries to contend with, and in which there is a vast variety of good and ill events, that are, in some degree, the effects of prudence or the want of it. By playing at chess, then, we may learn:

1. *Foresight*, which looks a little into futurity, and considers the consequences that may attend an action: for it is continually occurring to the player, "If I move this piece, what will be the advantages[9] of my new situation? What use can my adversary make of it to annoy me? What other moves can I make to support it, and to defend myself from his attacks?

2. *Circumspection*, which surveys the whole chess-board, or scene of action, the relations of the several pieces and situations, the dangers they are respectively exposed to, the several possibilities of their aiding each other; the probabilities that the adversary may make this or that move, and attack this or the other piece; and what different means can be used to avoid his stroke, or turn its consequences against him.

3. *Caution*, not to make our moves too hastily. This habit is best acquired by observing strictly the laws of the game, such as, *if you touch a piece, you must move it somewhere; if you set it down, you must let it stand*. And it is therefore best that these rules should be observed, as the game thereby becomes more the image of human life, and particularly of war; in which, if you have incautiously put yourself into a bad and dangerous position, you cannot obtain your enemy's leave to withdraw your troops, and place them more securely; but you must abide all the consequences of your rashness.

And, *lastly*, we learn by chess the habit of *not being discouraged* by *present* bad appearences in the state of our affairs, the habit of *hoping for a favourable change*, and that of *persevering in the search of resources*. The game is so full of events, there is such a variety of turns in it, the fortune of it is so subject to sudden vicissitudes, and one so frequently, after long contemplation, discovers the means of extricating one's self from a supposed insurmountable difficulty, that one is encouraged to continue the contest to the last, in hopes of victory by our own skill, or, at least, of giving a *stale mate*, by the negligence of our adversary. And whoever considers, what in chess he often sees instances of, that particular pieces of success are apt to produce *presumption*, and its consequent, inattention, by which more is afterwards lost than was gained by the preceding advantage; while misfortunes produce more care and attention, by which the loss may be recovered, will learn not to be too much discouraged by the present success of his adversary, nor to despair of final good fortune, upon every little check he receives in the pursuit of it.

That we may, therefore, be induced more frequently to chuse this beneficial amusement, in preference to others which are not attended with the same advantages, every circumstance, that may increase the pleasure of it, should be regarded; and every action or word that is unfair, disrespectful, or that in any way may give uneasiness, should be avoided, as contrary to the immediate intention of both the players, which is to pass the time agreeably.

Therefore, 1*st*. If it is agreed to play according to the strict rules, then those rules are to be exactly observed by both parties; and should not be insisted on for one side, while deviated from by the other: for this is not equitable.

2. If it is agreed not to observe the rules exactly, but one party demands indulgencies, he should then be as willing to allow them to the other.

3. No false move should ever be made to extricate yourself out of a difficulty, or to gain an advantage. There can be no pleasure in playing with a person once detected in such unfair practice.

4. If your adversary is long in playing, you ought not to hurry him, or express any uneasiness at his delay. You should not sing, nor whistle, nor look at your watch, nor take up a book to read, nor make a tapping with your feet on the floor, or with your fingers on the table, nor do anything that may disturb his attention. For all these things displease. And they do not show your skill in playing, but your craftiness or your rudeness.

5. You ought not to endeavour to amuse and deceive your adversary, by pretending to have made bad moves, and saying you have now lost the game, in order to make him secure and careless, and inattentive to your schemes; for this is fraud, and deceit, not skill in the game.

6. You must not, when you have gained a victory, use any triumphing or insulting expression, nor show too much pleasure; but endeavour to console your adversary, and make him less dissatisfied with himself by

every kind and civil expression, that may be used with truth, such as, You understand the game better than I, but you are a little inattentive; or, You play too fast; or, You had the best of the game but something happened to divert your thoughts, and that turned it in my favour.

7. If you are a spectator, while others play, observe the most perfect silence. For if you give advice, you offend both parties; him, against whom you give it, because it may cause the loss of his game; him, in whose favour you give it, because, though it be good, and he follows it, he loses the pleasure he might have had, if you had permitted him to think till it occurred to himself. Even after a move or moves, you must not, by replacing the pieces, shew how it might have been played better: for that displeases, and may occasion disputes or doubts about their true situation. All talking to the players, lessens or diverts their attention, and is therefore unpleasing; nor should you give the least hint to either party, by any kind of noise or motion.— If you do, you are unworthy to be a spectator.— If you have a mind to exercise or show your judgments, do it in playing your own game when you have an opportunity, not in criticising or meddling with, or counselling, the play of others.

Lastly. If the game is not to be played rigorously, according to the rules above mentioned, then moderate your desire of victory over your adversary, and be pleased with one over yourself. Snatch not eagerly at every advantage offered by his unskilfulness or inattention; but point out to him kindly that by such a move he places or leaves a piece in danger and unsupported; that by another he will put his king in a dangerous situation, &c. By this generous civility (so opposite to the unfairness above forbidden) you may indeed happen to lose the game to your opponent, but you will win what is better, his esteem, his respect, and his affection; together with the silent approbation and good will of impartial spectators.

Epitaph

1728

17 JANUARY, 1706 – 17 APRIL, 1790

The Body of
B. Franklin,
Printer;
Like the Cover of an old Book,
Its Contents torn out,
And stript of its Lettering and Gilding,
Lies here, Food for Worms.
But the Work shall not be wholly lost:
For it will, as he believ'd, appear once more,
In a new & more perfect Edition,
Corrected and amended
By the Author.

BAUER
WORLD PRESS

Paperback ISBN: 979-8-9920278-0-8
Hardcover ISBN: 979-8-9920278-2-2

www.ingramcontent.com/pod-product-compliance
Lightning Source LLC
Chambersburg PA
CBHW020528110726
47899CB00004B/1300
9798992027808